LIVING WITH FEAR

Isaac M. Marks, M.D.

LIVING WITH FEAR

Understanding and Coping with Anxiety

McGraw-Hill, Inc.

New York San Francisco Washington, D.C. Auckland Bogotá
Caracas Lisbon London Madrid Mexico City Milan
Montreal New Delhi San Juan Singapore
Sydney Tokyo Toronto

First Paperback edition, 1980

pbk   16   17   18   19   20   21   22   23   24   FGR/FGR   9   9   8   7   6   5

Library of Congress Cataloging-in-Publication Data

Marks, Isaac Meyer.
    Living with fear.

    Bibliography: p. 285
    Includes index.
    1. Fear.   2. Anxiety.   3. Peace of mind.
  1. Title. (DNLM: 1. Anxiety—Popular works.
WM172 M346L)
BF575.F2M37   616.8′322   77-17085
ISBN 0-07-040396-1 (Paperback)
ISBN 0-07-15776-X (Hardbound)

The editors for this book were Thomas Quinn, Cheryl Hanks, and Michael Hennelly. Marcy J. Katz was the designer and Thomas Kowalczyk supervised the production. This book was set in Souvenir with display lines in Optima by University Graphics, Inc.
NS
3811

Contents

Contents

Contents

Preface

This book aims to help you understand the nature of fear and how to overcome it. Worry is an everyday trouble for us all. There is no clear dividing line between normal fear, which we all have and can cope with by ourselves, and intense phobias, which need professional help. The chief difference is one of degree, and trained helpers are usually needed only when our fears begin to restrict our lives in some way. Guides are needed to explain the origins of nervous tension, its various manifestations, and what to do about worry when it gets on top of us. It helps to know what troubles other people have and what they do about them.

Many people feel that they are the only ones to have their problems. This book contains vignettes of problems you may have that have also troubled others. It describes the main patterns of anxiety which are found in normal life and in the clinic, be they fears of dying, of injury, of contamination, or of going mad. Many problems are more common than they are generally thought to be. If you recognize some of these problems in yourself, you will find that you are not alone in having them. Just as important, this book enables you to learn what can be done about such difficulties. It outlines the professional methods now available for the relief of nervous suffering.

The treatment of anxiety has advanced impressively in recent years, and many sufferers can now be helped for the first time. The behavioral revolution has led to a radical change in thinking about treatment, which has led to effective new methods for helping selected problems. No longer is it necessary to look back at one's childhood to get over these worries. That approach often made people feel helpless, because we can't reconstruct our life histories, and blaming parents achieves little beyond inducing burdensome guilt. Therapists used to believe in the need to uncover something in order to help. Along with this went the myth of symptom substitution, the belief that if one reduced the fear without dealing with the supposed "underlying" problem, some other trouble would pop up in its place. Research has shown time and again that this notion is largely groundless. People who lose their phobias or rituals, far from developing fresh symptoms, usually improve also in other areas of their life as a result of being freed from the constraints formerly imposed by their fears.

There is now abundant evidence that behavioral treatments work for many, and could for you if you have one of the problems described in this book. Phobias, obsessions, and sexual difficulties can all respond well, and improvement usually continues in the years after active treatment. However, not everybody can be helped. For success you must be clear about what you want help with, and you must feel that you will be better off without rather than with your problem. You need to be prepared to tolerate some discomfort and actively cooperate in the treatment plan, including doing a fair amount of "homework" on the problem. Sometimes your relatives will also need to lend a hand. Obsessions can implicate the family, who then have to be enlisted as aides to the therapist; and for most sexual difficulties your partner will need to be involved in some way.

This volume explains the principles of treatment and tries to take the mystery out of it. Severe problems are best handled by professional therapists, but you can help them help you if you understand your difficulty a bit better and get some idea of how to cope with it. If professional aid is not available, some self-help may be possible. Skilled behavioral therapists are still thin on the ground, and you may live far away from one. Or your problem may be fairly recent or mild and so need only a bit of self-management.

More and more self-help is becoming possible as the principles of treatment are worked out and simplified. This is a recurring theme in health. Malnutrition was common in the past before doctors worked out the balanced diet we need for normal development and function. Now that nutritional principles are common knowledge by virtue of being taught in school, covered in the media, and disseminated in popular books, most people can keep themselves in a state of normal nutrition. Severe diarrhea from whatever cause used to kill innumerable infants until it was discovered how important it is to maintain the body's fluids and salts in proper balance. Until recently this was done by the giving of intravenous fluids, which needs medical or nursing help. But then it was found that babies with gastroenteritis can take certain special liquids by mouth without vomiting, thus doing away with the need to give fluids intravenously. So when there are epidemics of gastroenteritis in babies, their mothers can give them the correct fluid by mouth. This the child will not vomit, and so its stomach can absorb the liquid and its life is saved. As doctors worked out the principles of treatment and simplified the management of the problem, they could fade themselves out of treatment and let the mothers themselves do much of the management.

A process rather like this is beginning to happen with behavioral treatments for various types of anxiety. The cry is "power to the people," and research on self-help is leading to the scientific approach to willpower which is necessary for success. Emphasis is shifting toward patients carrying out much of their own treatment, with the therapist merely setting the course and giving a touch to the rudder at intervals. The last chapter in this book gives some guidance on self-help, so that those who are so inclined can see to what extent they can treat themselves without the need to consult a therapist. This is not a detailed manual for treatment but is intended as a rough guide to self-help and to the professional methods now available for the relief of nervous suffering.

The book is dedicated to the many sufferers and their therapists whose penetrating observations have made this work possible. Their cooperation has steadily increased our knowledge and pointed the way to ever more effective techniques of easing nervous tension. Although this book is primarily written for the layperson, it might be of some interest to many health care students and professionals, including doctors, psychiatrists, psychologists, nurses, social workers, and probation officers.

Readers may wish to know a bit about the author. I am a clinical psychiatrist with a special interest in anxiety and its management and a background of fifteen years of research into the causes of tension and the ways in which it can be treated effectively. This work resulted in the publication of four books and 120 scientific articles, and rather more lectures. Much was learned on four continents from patients, colleagues, and students, including nurses, psychologists, and psychiatrists. During my experience with over a thousand sufferers from anxiety, the need became evident for a popular guide to modern ideas on the subject. I hope this book may fill that need to a small extent. It is designed to help you help yourself.

THANKS AND ACKNOWLEDGMENTS

The author is deeply indebted to the legion of authors quoted in this book. They include:

Dr. Douglas Bond (*The Love and Fear of Flying,* International Universities Press, Inc., New York, 1952), Dr. Leonard Cammer (*Freedom from Compulsion,* Simon and Schuster, New York, 1976), Joyce Emerson (*Phobias,* National Association of Mental Health, London, 1971), the late Professor Carney Landis (*Varieties of Psychopathological Experience,* ed. F. A. Mettler, Holt, Rinehart and Winston, Inc., New York, 1964), Mary McArdle

Preface

(*"Treatment of a Phobia,"* Nursing Times, 1974, pp. 637–639), Dr. Don Meichenbaum (*Cognitive Behavior Modification,* Plenum Press, Plenum Publishing Corporation, New York, 1977), Dr. Colin Parkes (*"The First Year of Grief,"* Psychiatry, vol. 33, pp. 444–467, 1970), Dr. John Price (unpublished paper on aversions), Dr. S. Rachman (*The Meaning of Fear,* Penguin Books, Inc., 1974), Dr. Gerald Rosen (*Don't Be Afraid,* Prentice-Hall, Inc., 1976), Dr. Claire Weekes (*Peace from Nervous Suffering: Self-Help for Your Nerves,* Angus and Robertson, 1972). Special thanks are due to Dr. John Greist for helpful comments on the final manuscript.

Extensive citations in this book are also culled from among the thousands of sufferers on four continents in whose treatment the author has been involved over the past fifteen years, and from the author's previous three books on the subject published by Heinemann Medical Press (*Fears and Phobias,* 1969; *Clinical Anxiety,* 1971, coauthor M. H. Lader) and by the Royal College of Nursing (*Nursing in Behavioral Psychotherapy,* coauthors R. H. Hallam, J. Connolly, and R. Philpott, 1977).

Sometimes English colloquialisms and spellings in quotations have been amended to make them understandable to American readers; for example, "nappies" has been changed to "diapers," "pyjamas" to "pajamas," "rubbish bin" to "garbage can," and so forth.

Really, I consider total absence of fear, in situations such as mine, to be the mark not of a valiant fellow but of a dolt.

—Erasmus, in the fifteenth century, on fleeing from the Plague

1

The Nature of Fear and Anxiety

1

Recognizing Normal and Abnormal Fear

ANXIETY AFFECTS EVERYBODY

Like all of us, you get worried sometimes. You'd be abnormal if you didn't. Anxiety has always been part of the human condition and is destined to remain with us for the foreseeable future. The caveman worried where his next meal was coming from, the Roman Emperor brooded on the next attempt to be made on his life, today's airline pilot bites his nails when his landing system is faulty, and you live with plenty of worries—your threatened job, your children's health or education, your faltering marriage, or simply things that go bump in the night. Though the things we worry about change as our styles of living alter, the tensions continue.

Anxiety is normal in that it is widespread and affects almost everyone. The triggers of anxiety may vary from one person to the next, but certain activities regularly evoke tension in most people. Anxiety is thus part of the fabric of everyday life. It can be brought on by our daily routine, which commonly involves some danger. On crowded highways we must be constantly alert—near misses are quite common and the unexpected is always happening. The insecure assistant worries over his job, the top executive dithers over decisions, and the telephone operator is harassed by frantic callers. Skyrocketing prices make the house-wife struggle to stretch her tight budget to feed her family. Husband and wife bicker, parents and children get at logger-heads—it is almost impossible to live without some kind of anxiety.

Because anxiety is an inevitable part of life, we have to learn to live with it. Much of this book will describe the anxieties which occur normally or exceptionally. Understanding the main patterns which anxiety assumes will help people be better judges of what they experience and when they need help. Whenever possible the words of actual sufferers will be used to depict their feelings and problems. The last part of this book will deal with the many different ways in which anxiety can be treated, both by therapists and by sufferers themselves.

WHAT IS ANXIETY?

Anxiety is the emotion which we feel when we find ourselves in a tight corner. We then feel threatened, although the source of the threat may not always be obvious to us. The feeling of anxiety is related to that of fear and similar emotions. The English language is rich in terms which describe anxiety and related emotions. Think of the following list: *apprehension, uneasiness, nervous-ness, worry, disquiet, solicitude, concern, misgiving, qualm, edgi-ness, jitteriness, sensitivity, dis-ease; being pent up, troubled, wary, unnerved, unsettled, upset, aghast, distraught, or threat-ened; defensiveness, disturbance, distress, perturbation, conster-nation, trepidation, scare, fright, dread, terror, horror, alarm, panic, anguish, agitation.* All these words tell us about subtle nuances of emotions similar to anxiety. When society develops a rich vocabulary for certain feelings, we can be sure that the area of experience is common and important.

In general, anxiety and fear are very similar. When the cause of the worry is readily apparent, we tend to call the emotion *fear*. Somebody who is facing a charging lion tends to be called *frightened*. One worried about a minor examination months ahead is called *anxious*. The word fear comes from the old English *faer* for sudden calamity or danger. Anxious comes from the Latin *anxius*, meaning troubled in mind about some uncertain event, and is related to a Greek root meaning to press tight or to strangle.

Most children and adults have minor fears of one kind or another. Children are afraid of their parents leaving them, of strangers, animals, and unusual noises and situations. Adults can be frightened by heights, elevators, darkness, airplanes, spiders, mice, taking examinations, and of superstitions such as being haunted by ghosts, passing under ladders in the streets, and so on. These minor fears do not lead to total avoidance of the situations concerned and can often be overcome by explanation. They do not require treatment.

Fear is a normal response to an active or imagined threat. The emotion produces disturbances in one's actions and bodily changes which are both felt by the person and visible to others. What a person who is afraid will experience as a pounding heart will be felt as a racing pulse by someone holding his wrist. An onlooker might notice a sweaty brow. Other changes may be more subtle and measurable only by delicate instruments, for example by increase in the electrical conductance of the skin.

Two of the most obvious changes in behavior during fear can be in striking contrast. One is the tendency to freeze and remain motionless and mute. This can reach an extreme form in animals in the shape of death-feigning or playing possum. The opposite tendency is to become startled and to scream while running away. Both these patterns of behavior can occur during fear, and the animal (and human) may change rapidly from one to the other, as when a frightened animal freezes and then suddenly scurries for shelter.

Strong fear and anxiety cause unpleasant feelings of terror; paleness of the skin; sweating; hair standing on end; dilation of the pupils; rapid pounding of the heart; rise in blood pressure; tension in the muscles and increased blood flow through them; trembling; a readiness to be startled; dryness and tightness of the throat and mouth; constriction of the chest and rapid breathing; a sinking feeling in the stomach; nausea; desperation; contractions of the bladder and rectum leading to urges to pass urine and feces; irritability and a tendency to lash out; a strong desire to cry, run, or hide; difficulty in breathing; tingling in the hands and feet; feelings of being unreal or far away; paralyzing weakness of the limbs; and a sensation of faintness and falling. If fear or anxiety goes on for a long time, even healthy people become tired, depressed, slowed down, restless, and lose their desire to eat. They are unable to sleep, have bad dreams, and avoid further frightening situations.

Bodily changes during anxiety

Our emotions are largely felt in our bodies. The English language is full of references to show this relationship, though we are so used to these expressions that we often forget the bodily experiences. My colleague, Dr. Julian Leff, illustrated this connection with the following passage:

> My heart was in my mouth as I strode up the driveway. Although I hated his guts, my stomach turned over as I approached his house. I knocked on the door and my heart leapt as I heard his footsteps inside. Shivers went down my back as he fumbled with the catch; then as he flung open the door my skin crawled at the sight of him.
>
> "I speak from the heart when I say I can't stomach you," I blurted out. He laughed sneeringly and I felt my gorge rise.
>
> "You're a pain in the neck," he growled. His retort stuck in my throat.
>
> "I am here because of the woman whose heart you have broken," I asserted, and the thought of Amanda brought a lump to my throat. He turned his back on me so suddenly that I almost jumped out of my skin. My brain reeled as I reached for my. . . .[1]

You could extend this series of experiences in your body which you feel when scared. The body chemistry also changes: substances such as epinephrine are secreted by the adrenal glands and norepinephrine at the tiny nerve endings around the body, to mention just two of many changes. Many of these occur not only in fear and anxiety but also during other emotions.

Darwin, to whom we owe the theory of evolution, drew a vivid picture of fear.

> The frightened man first stands like a statue motionless and breathless. . . . the heart beats quickly and violently. . . . the skin instantly becomes pale. . . . perspiration immediately exudes from the skin and as the surface is then cold [we have what is termed] a cold sweat. . . . the hairs also on the skin stand erect and superficial muscles shiver. . . . in connection with the disturbed action of the heart, the breathing is hurried. . . . the mouth becomes dry. . . . one of the best marked symptoms is trembling of all the muscles of the body and this is often first seen in the lips[2]

As fear becomes more intense, we begin to call it terror. Darwin goes on:

> The heart beats wildly or may fail to act and faintness ensues; there is a death-like pallor; the breathing is laboured; the wings of the nostrils are widely dilated . . . there is a gulping of the throat, protruding eyeballs . . . dilated pupils, rigid muscles. [In the final stages] as fear rises to an extreme pitch, the dreadful scream of terror is heard. Great beads of sweat stand on the skin. All the muscles of the body are relaxed, utter prostration soon follows, and the mental powers fail. The intestines are affected. The sphincter muscles cease to act, and no longer retain the contents of the body.[3]

Can the onlooker recognize anxiety?

It might seem obvious to us that we recognize easily when people feel frightened rather than happy or surprised. In fact there are cultural differences, and Westerners find it difficult to read the emotions experienced by Japanese, and vice versa. Orientals and Occidentals can be inscrutable to each other, especially with more minor degrees of feeling. With very intense emotions, differentiation might be easier. If a series of photographs is prepared of people who are happy, sad, envious, disgusted, or frightened and we ask other people to say what feelings are portrayed in the photographs, we do not always get agreement among observers. Perhaps it is not surprising that the emotions of babies are more difficult to judge than those of adults, who show a wider and more finely differentiated range of emotions. While it may be simple to tell contentment from terror, fear is less easy to disentangle from surprise, anger, or disgust. Similarly the cries and tears of great joy on a photograph can be mistaken for those of anguish and grief.

Tension can be pleasurable

Although anxiety is usually thought of as an unpleasant feeling, people do not always try to avoid it. On the contrary, some persons actively seek anxiety and get great pleasure from their mastery of dangerous situations. Race car drivers, bullfighters, and mountaineers willingly expose themselves to awful hazards. Furthermore, thousands of spectators throng to experience at second hand the tensions which are produced by dangerous sports. Thriller films and books are multimillion-dollar forms of entertainment. Demolition derbies in which drivers deliberately crash one another's cars to destruction, again show how some people enjoy being anxious at times.

The game of peekaboo that babies so love to play is another form of pleasure from mild anxiety. Toddlers enjoy seeing their parents disappear for a few moments behind the corner of a room, only to emerge again a few seconds later. While Mom and Dad are hidden, the youngster may look tense until they reappear and upon their reappearance give a squeal of joy. If the parents take too long to reappear, this tension mounts to fear, and the child may cry with apprehension.

WHEN IS ANXIETY HELPFUL AND WHEN IS IT NOT?

Extreme fear can paralyze us, and severe anxiety hinders performance. In contrast, mild anxiety and fear can actually be quite useful. They lead to rapid action in the face of threat and help us to be alert in difficult situations. Actors and politicians often report mild anxiety before their performance and say that this helps them keep on their toes. Fear normally accompanies activities like writing examinations or parachuting. Fighter pilots report that feeling afraid makes them better fighters.

There seems to be an optimum amount of fear for good performance—too little and we risk being careless, too much and we may become clumsy or paralyzed through fear. Among parachute jumpers, an experimenter found that veterans had only mild fear whereas novices were more frightened, especially before the jump, although this fear subsided fairly quickly after landing. Experience of dangerous situations can lead people to develop a healthy respect for danger that helps to preserve them. In a study of American soldiers, it was found that inexperienced troops displayed little fear and carelessly disregarded safety measures. After exposure to battle, they became more watchful, began to express fear, and made fewer careless errors.

A little fear seems to help people deal with problem situations. In people undergoing major surgery, one research worker found that patients who were apparently fearless preoperatively suffered excessive postoperative discomfort and pain, and they also showed more anger and resentment than did patients who had been moderately fearful before the operation. The latter group coped better and showed little fear after the operation and less pain. In contrast, patients who had been highly anxious preoperatively showed a lot of fear after their operation and complained of much pain and discomfort. Thus, although lesser amounts of fear and anxiety may be useful, extreme degrees are not beneficial and can in fact be very destructive. Trainee parachutists tend to do badly if they are too frightened, and even trained paratroopers may become so afraid that they lose their nerve and become unable to jump.[4]

In the acute panic provided by fire or an earthquake, people might flee blindly in any possible direction and may disregard their usual social responsibilities; for example, a mother running out of a burning house may forget to take her baby with her. Soldiers under bombardment may vomit, pass feces, and become paralyzed with fear so that they fail to take shelter or to move others for whom they are responsible into shelter. Actors or public speakers may become so terrified that they forget their lines and become speechless.

Less intense anxiety can also be resistant to any attempt to reduce it. Patients in states of anxiety often report episodes of panic which come repeatedly out of the blue, last for a variable length of time, and then disappear without regard to what the patient does. There is usually no obvious trigger for such anxiety. Sometimes upsurges in anxiety are attributed to the behavior which a person happens to be engaged in at that time. He may thereafter avoid that situation in the belief that it helps his anxiety; for example, a patient who has just started a new drug may attribute his panic to it and cease taking the drug forthwith even though identical symptoms occurred repeatedly before he ever took the drug. This reaction is a form of superstition.

ANXIETY THAT FOLLOWS WHEN THE EMERGENCY IS OVER

In a sudden crisis when we have to act quickly without thinking to avoid disaster, we may feel anxiety only after the worst danger has passed. After a near miss while driving an automobile one driver reported:

> I was driving up a hill and noticed a 6-year-old boy standing next to the road a few yards away. He looked as though he'd

Recognizing Normal and Abnormal Fear

seen me and was waiting for me to go by. Just before I reached him he made a sudden dash across the road right in front of my car. Automatically I jammed on the brake and came to an abrupt stop with a screech of tires and a smell of burning rubber. I missed the lad by a fraction of an inch. It all seemed as though it was happening to someone else in a film, until a few seconds later, when I resumed driving on, my heart began to thump rapidly, I broke out in a sweat, felt shaky and my fingers and toes began to tingle with fear as I realized the calamity which had just been averted. This lasted for about 15 minutes and only died down slowly after that.[5]

This delay before we feel anxiety can take several hours. In war combat it is common. One bomber pilot in World War II was on his sixth mission. At the start of the bomb run, the copilot's face was shot off by flak, killing him instantly. The pilot did not realize this and kept trying to replace the oxygen mask. The mission was very tricky and required three separate runs on the target and several 360-degree turns directly over it. The pilot completed his mission very coolly and successfully and was complimented for his performance on returning to base. On the ground, while changing his clothes he began to tremble, went to a sympathetic doctor, and broke into a sobbing panic.

People who have many duties in an emergency often cope well at the time and only later feel any emotion. Another pilot, a nineteen-year-old whose plane and crew were badly damaged in World War II, gave his doctor a dramatic picture of events in the plane:

Then the gunner came up and said "Terry's dead." I said "Are you sure? Maybe I can do something for him." I went back there and looked at the back of his head—it was completely blown off. The plane was covered with blood. I opened his heated clothing—couldn't hear his heart. [Were you scared?] Hell, I wasn't scared of nothing yet! If I'd been scared I'd have just jumped out. I lifted up his eyelid—nothing there! If he is still alive he must be breathing. Looked at the diaphragm on the oxygen system—not moving! Poor guy, he must be dead. "You're dead, you've had it." So I went up front. How could I be scared when I have to get my navigator back? I didn't feel scared until I got on the ground. Then I began to shake like a leaf.[6]

After this assignment the pilot became so nervous he could not fly planes again for a year.

"AM I NORMAL? DO I NEED HELP?"

These questions bother many people. In fact normal troubles which don't require treatment and abnormal worries which do are opposite ends of a continuum, and shade into one another at some point. In threatening situations it is abnormal *not* to feel fear. This was captured beautifully by Erasmus in the fifteenth century. He fled from the plague as people died from it in swarms and wrote to a fellow fugitive: "Really, I consider total absence of fear, in situations such as mine, to be the mark not of a valiant fellow but of a dolt."[6] We're all a bit wary at the top of a cliff, or when meeting a lot of strangers in a new country. Far from being a sign that professional help is needed, this anxiety is protective, common, and normal. However, very few of us have to stay away from work because we're so afraid of the bus ride to get there. This is uncommon, handicapping, and abnormal. You have a *phobia* if automatically you become so upset and afraid in relatively harmless situations that you feel you must avoid or run out of them.

Though we all get tense and frightened at times, this can reach the point where we wonder, "Am I going crazy?" Anxiety does not drive one mad, and usually we can deal with our own troubles successfully, perhaps with help from our relatives and friends. But a thorough examination from a doctor may fail to convince us that we haven't got cancer, or rabies, and we may get plagued by doubt. When our worries get so bad that commonsense ways of dealing with them don't work, it can be useful to call in specialist help.

Anxieties which are so intense that they need help are often called *clinical* or *abnormal,* but they differ from normal fear and tension only in degree, not in kind. Scared patients often ask: "Am I normal, Doctor? Am I going round the bend?" The answer is that *they* are normal even if their fears are not. Certain worries can be so unusually intense or handicapping that they may be "abnormal" in a statistical sense, but the people who happen to have these worries are perfectly "normal" in all other respects. Someone developing agoraphobia is not on the first step to going insane but is simply a normal person getting a common fear to such unusual intensity that it handicaps his daily activities.

Other questions many anxious people ask are, "Will I ever be free? Can I pass it on to my family? What happens if I can't hug my kids or prepare their meals? Will I injure my family if I have these obsessive thoughts?"

With the right treatment given by a therapist or undertaken yourself, most phobias can be overcome fairly readily; the last two chapters of this book describe what you need to do. Sometimes fears do rub off on other relatives, but with effective treatment this needn't happen. If family members already share some of your fears, they can be treated in the same way as yourself. Certainly if your fears prevent you from acting lovingly like a normal parent, your children could become deprived, but they might get all the love they need from your spouse or another relative. In any case, with correct treatment you can get over your hang-ups and resume being a warm, affectionate parent; most people who worry endlessly about harming others have very little chance of succumbing to their impulses (see page 160).

Many quirks are adaptive, and far from their being bothersome, you may be proud of them. If you are precise, orderly, and perfectionist, you may approve of your conscientious discipline and attention to detail, which probably aids you in your work. It is quite a different story when these habits get out of hand so that you spend most of your day plagued by indecision and self-doubt, resisting intrusive thoughts, endlessly checking the locks on your doors and windows, and driving everybody around you crazy with your odd ways. At that point, pride is likely to be replaced by loathing of your obsessions and rituals, which have become burdensome, time-wasting, and unpleasant.

Minor fears and tension do not need treatment, though professional advice might be reassuring. There is comfort in learning to understand one's troubles and knowing that other people have similar worries. We can usually overcome everyday anxieties on our own, perhaps using some of the methods described in this book and with the aid of friends and relatives. However, professional help is worth seeking when our lives begin to be constricted by our fears. When fear of sex prevents us from establishing a normal marital relationship or when we are so worried about dirt that we spend six hours a day washing our hands till they are raw and bleeding, then treatment by a trained professional is indicated and can be of great value.

Most nervous tension can be treated without admission to a hospital. This book will describe many of the ways in which sufferers can learn to overcome their problems. Often people can deal with their tensions by themselves; to this end the principles of self-help will be outlined. Self-help is especially feasible when the problem is in its early stages. Nevertheless, even long-standing worries can be eased surprisingly quickly if one follows a few basic principles. When the difficulties are widespread, you may be unable to apply these principles without professional help, and we will see later what forms this help can take.

THE SPECTRUM OF FEAR

Some definitions

To avoid misunderstandings later in this book, let us define anxiety and some related terms.

Anxiety is the unpleasant emotion associated with a feeling of impending danger that is not obvious to the observer. *Fear* is a very similar feeling that arises as a normal response to realistic danger or threat. *Timidity* indicates a lasting tendency to show fear easily. *Panic* denotes a sudden upsurge of acute terror. *Phobic anxiety* is the anxiety which occurs only in contact with a particular situation or object.

Though the distinction between fear, anxiety, and phobia must be arbitrary at some point, the three terms are best kept separate, because they usually describe rather different things. A *phobia* is a special kind of fear which is out of proportion to demands of the situation, can't be explained or reasoned away, is beyond voluntary control, and leads to avoidance of the feared situation. Phobic patients usually recognize that their fear is unrealistic and that other people would not be unduly afraid of the same things. Because they are unable to quell their phobia, it is considered irrational, although rationalizations may be offered for the fear.

The disproportion between a phobia and its stimulus

The disparity between a phobic object and the reaction to it is obvious in phobias of things like feathers or moths, but such disproportion is also found in more complex phobias like those of leaving one's home or of cancer.

An example of this disproportion is the case of a woman who was terrified by moths and butterflies. She had to keep her windows tightly shut at home in summer and several times had to leave buses and trains when she discovered moths or butterflies on them. Several accidents were caused directly by her phobia. When she was riding a bicycle and saw a butterfly, she fell off and brought down her friends who were riding behind her. Twice she fell backward into a stream when avoiding large butterflies which had flown across her path. On another occasion she stood on a chair to clean a wardrobe, by mistake picked up a large dead brown moth, fell off the chair in her surprised fear, and sprained her ankle. She could never enter a room containing moths or butterflies and always checked for their absence before entering.

Interestingly this fear did not extend to "creepy-crawlies" like spiders, earwigs, stag beetles, or furry caterpillers. "I'd rather deal with a boxful of black widow spiders than one large English moth," she insisted.[7]

In their extreme form, fears cripple people's lives. "To go outside to me was fear," said one woman.

> If I went outside I couldn't breathe, I had trembly legs. So I stayed in—I stayed in for four years, and never went out. It was very gradual at first. I noticed that in crowds I couldn't breathe or I got panicky and if I went shopping for food and the shop was full I used to walk out. On a bus, I used to want to get there quicker than what a bus generally takes to get there. All these things were gradual at first, you see, but they got worse. I was always crying, crying because I wanted to go out and I missed it when my husband took my son out for the day, but I kept the tears, of course, until my son had left the house and then I cried. I was so lonely that I used to crawl to bed sometimes; take a drug and crawl to bed and sleep.[8]

Patients experience overwhelming anxiety when confronted with their phobic situation. They also rehearse their frightening experiences in their mind until they are in an agony of fearful anticipation about the next time they will meet their phobic object. This fear of fear becomes a fresh source of threat.

Phobics avoid the triggers of their fears

To escape their anxiety, patients avoid their phobic situations and restrict their activities and daily functions. They are always on the lookout and become very sensitive to the presence around them of anything connected with their phobia. A spider phobic will glance round any room she enters for signs of spiders before she will sit down happily. A bird phobic will avoid those streets in the town where she might be likely to encounter pigeons and confine her walks to areas where birds are less frequent. In order to avoid the phobic object, the patient is continually seeking it out, finds it in obscure places, and sees it with her peripheral vision. One sign of improvement during treatment is decreased awareness of the phobic object in the surroundings.

Many phobic situations are common and cannot be easily avoided. The life of a patient with phobias of cats, crossing streets or bridges, being in a crowd, or traveling in a bus or train can be seriously disturbed. Even uncommon events like thunderstorms in cool countries cause much misery to sufferers. One woman aged forty-eight had had this phobia for twenty-eight years.

> I just can't carry on with my housework during a thunderstorm. I sit and wait for it to happen. When and if it does I sit in a darkened cupboard until it's over—all night if necessary. I also clamp right up as regards talking and get aggressive. I listen to every weather forecast, which I know is silly. I wish to God I could cure myself. I know I make my husband and daughter fed up with me.[9]

Thunderstorms phobics may phone the weather bureau endlessly for forecasts and if storms are predicted will not leave their home that day. One man became so frightened when he heard a forecast of storms that he took the train 200 miles from London to Manchester to escape the weather.

LAY PEOPLE FIND PHOBIAS HARD TO UNDERSTAND

The more common and familiar the phobic object, the greater the incomprehension and lack of sympathy which the phobic encounters in normal people. Most people cannot understand how anybody can be scared of a playful puppy, a fluttering bird, or going outside his home. It is often thought that the patient pretends or exaggerates and should pull himself together or be forced to do so.

The average man in the street does not realize the intensity of feeling and handicap caused by phobias. One phobic said, "I do find that people generally tend to brush these phobias aside. The attitude seems to be: 'Don't be silly, they can't hurt you.' What people don't realize is the difference between being afraid of—or not liking—something, and having a phobia which is absolute cold fear and stark terror of the object concerned."[10]

It would be easier for lay people to sympathize if they knew more about the deep fear of everyday objects which phobias cause. One woman had such a dread of wigs and false hair that she could only visit her hairdresser after he had hidden all wigs away. She could not go near anybody wearing a wig in a store and would rush past false hair and be unable to have a meal opposite anybody wearing one. As an adult she nearly rushed through a glass window when somebody who did not know of her fear walked into a room wearing a wig. She felt ashamed and embarrassed by her fear.

Lay people may wonder how on earth such strange fears get generated. While we often don't know why such fears start in the first place, we can understand how they spread thereafter. Each time we run away from a fear, it becomes more likely that we will want to escape next time as well. If one takes no steps to deal with fear, but instead spends all one's energy running away from it and rearranges life to avoid contact with any possible trigger for the fear, the chances are that it will spread. This is all the more likely if we keep our worries secret so that we don't find out from friends how they deal with similar problems.

Shame and concealment of phobias

The lack of understanding on the part of some people makes many phobic patients sensitive and ashamed of their fears. They are afraid of being ridiculed by others for having these fears and so suffer in silence and hide their anxieties as long as they can. Even when the fears can no longer be hidden, phobics may not outrightly confess what they are frightened of but complain instead of headaches, palpitations, diarrhea, or tiredness. They may also have the secret fear that they are going insane. Because of this secrecy, their phobias may not be obvious to the casual observer. Housewives who are agoraphobic (afraid of going out) can be housebound for years without acquaintances or relatives realizing that there is any problem. For example, many new cases of agoraphobia were discovered by accident in the course of a rehousing scheme in New York. Poor families who had been living in single rooms were rehoused, and their cases were followed up by welfare workers. It soon became apparent that many of the women had been agoraphobic and still were phobic in their new environment. Some mothers who could not sleep without close contact with their children or another adult tried to restore this sleeping arrangement; such a woman might invite a sister or friend to come and stay with her. Although the new apartments had several rooms, only a single room would be used. It soon became obvious that many of these women were afraid of traveling or doing anything alone.

Phobias cannot be shed as easily as normal superstitions, but in times of extreme hardship phobics might have to conceal their phobias for a while. The alternative might be death. In one concentration camp in Nazi-occupied Europe in which 120,000 people died or were sent east to extermination camps, people did not complain of phobias, or hid them so that they would be allowed to work rather than be shot or gassed. No new case of phobia was obvious, though other mental disorders did develop in some people. Several months after liberation and return home, some of the former neurotics who did not complain during their stay in camp again manifested their former symptoms.[11]

PROBLEMS WHICH CAN BE CONFUSED WITH PHOBIAS

Certain phenomena resemble phobias, yet it is possible and important to separate them. *Superstitious fears* and *taboos* are an example. These are the collective beliefs about bad and good luck which are shared by other members of the cultural group, for example, the idea that harm will come to someone walking under a ladder, or that good luck comes from placing the middle finger over the ring finger, crossing the heart, or muttering "God willing." A cynic tartly said that "superstition is the other guy's religion."

Obsessions are the insistent recurrence of unwanted thoughts despite active resistance against their intrusion; for example, a mother may be plagued by unsought urges to strangle her baby in its sleep. The origin of obsession is the Latin *obsidere,* "to besiege," and the sufferer is indeed besieged by unwanted thoughts. Commonly he is also plagued by *compulsive rituals* he feels compelled to carry out repeatedly against his will, for example, to wash his hands ninety times a day because he feels dirty, despite all evidence to the contrary.

Preoccupations are the repetitive rumination of ideas without the subject feeling any resistance against them, for example, the incessant worry of an adolescent that he is sexually inadequate. *Sensitive ideas of reference* are the fears that actions and words of other people refer to oneself when in fact they don't, for example, the repeated idea that a roomful of people are talking about oneself as one enters. *Paranoid delusions* can include the fear that somebody is against one for no good reason.

Counterphobias

Counterphobic behavior is the attraction which some people have to the phobic situation or object so that they seek it out repeatedly. This might happen when a phobia is relatively mild or when the phobic is attempting to master the problem. A woman who was originally so afraid of heights that she would not ride an elevator mastered her fear by becoming an airline stewardess. Counterphobic behavior can be useful in helping the phobic overcome his fear by gradually allowing him to become familiar with the phobic situation until it loses its frightening aspect. Delight in mastery of the problem may then lead the patient with a phobia of the sea to turn into an enthusiastic swimmer and sailor, or a person with a form of stage fright may seize every opportunity for public speaking.

Counterphobic behavior is similar to that observed in children who enjoy playing frightening games, or in some adults who carry out risky pursuits such as high-speed racing or dangerous mountaineering. Not all such activities are counterphobic, however. Many persons engage in these recreations without at any point experiencing fear, only excitement, challenge, or pleasure.

Aversion

Quite a few people are not actually afraid of certain situations but have a strong dislike of touching, tasting, or hearing things which most people are indifferent to, or may even enjoy. The horrible feeling one gets with aversions is a bit different from that of fear. Aversions set one's teeth on edge, send shivers down the spine, make one suck one's teeth, go cold and pale, and take a deep breath. One's hair stands on end, and one feels unpleasant and sometimes nauseated, but not frightened. Sometimes there is a desire to wet one's fingers, to wash them, or to cover them with cream. Some aversions are made worse when the skin is rough or the nails are unevenly clipped, so that there is a sensation of the fingertips catching as they pass over a surface.

A prominent man who had an intense dislike of fuzzy textures such as those of the skins of peaches, new tennis balls, or certain carpets could not enter a room containing a new carpet with that particular texture. When playing tennis, he would have to wear a glove to handle the ball until the fuzz wore off. Other people find it difficult to handle old pearly buttons, cotton wool, velvet, and similar articles. Some people may like the *sight* of velvet in the shops even though they dislike its touch. Similar discomfort can be produced by the squeak of chalk on a blackboard or the scrape of a knife on a plate.

These aversions may sound trivial but they can be disabling. One woman disliked the sound of chalk scraping on a blackboard so much that she gave up a cherished ambition to be a teacher. Another woman found velvet so unbearable that she couldn't bring herself to go to children's parties. A third said, "All kinds of buttons make me squeamish. I've been like this since I was a young baby and my uncle had the same thing. I can only wear clothes with zip fasteners and hooks, not buttons."[12]

We could make an endless list of different kinds of aversions. In a British radio broadcast, Dr. John Price and his coworkers invited listeners to write in about any aversions they might have. The letters poured in, and they help us understand how unpleasant aversions can be. Most of the letters described more than one touch aversion, and several people were fascinated by the surface they could not touch, especially those who could not touch shiny buttons.

The commonest revulsion was of touching cotton wool, wire or steel wool, or velvet. Also common were taste or smell aversions which caused people to avoid certain foods—onions were a frequent example. Many of of the letters expressed the agony of children who were made to wear velvet party clothes and whose mothers could not understand why their children did not appreciate them.

Ever since I have been able to remember, I have been quite unable to touch velvet. My mother tells me it was all the rage to have a velvet party frock (age about 3 years) with a white lace collar and cuffs that she had made for me in a very pretty blue. When the time for the party arrived I was duly dressed in this creation, and to her horror, I just stood with my arms six inches from my sides, with fists clenched, and would only say "it's nasty" and my opinion has never altered (I am in my late forties now).

Last summer, when shopping for some dress material, I made my way to the velvet display (I have always liked the look of it), telling myself "this is ridiculous; you are a big girl now; be brave; handle it—it won't bite." I think I stood there for quite two minutes, persuading myself that it really was lovely stuff. I stretched out my hands and grabbed a handful—but the effect was the same! teeth all on edge! sheer horror! Isn't it just ridiculous?

I have now given up hope that I shall ever be able to sail into a party or theater in a lovely jewel-colored velvet dress! Of course, if I visit anyone with velvet scatter cushions, I make sure it comes nowhere near my bare hand or arm![13]

An adolescent not only disliked velvet but also suede, cotton wool, and fluffy ties.

Immediately I come in contact with any of these fibers my body from top to bottom tingles. I am only 15 and when I was a young child my mother had no idea what I felt like when she put me in ghastly velvet dresses or gave me fluffy ties. Also a thing which has stopped me smoking is the fact that the tip of a cigarette is sort of velvety and I cannot bear it.[14]

Some of the letters indicated that aversions can run in families:

My father would not allow my mother to wear velvet as he could not bear to touch it (when dancing). This applied to anything like velvet—plush, brushed nylon, etc. I have inherited this phobia now. Also my daughter (age 27) follows with this dislike, even as a baby, of plush type toys with furry sides, so that it is a case of three generations (I am 54) hating the same materials, for no reason.[15]

Interestingly enough, the sensation of one's teeth being set on edge seems not to depend upon our actually having teeth.

Most of my family were "sufferers" from this kind of torture. My mother hated saucepans being scraped by a spoon and referred to her "teeth going on edge" when, in fact, she was *completely toothless and wore dentures top and bottom.* A brother hated those blocks of cooking salt being cut up, also fingernails scraping down a wall. My dislike is children making balloons squeak with fingers, or squeaking and polished floors—the thought makes me feel horrible as I write. I cannot bear to touch cotton wool, which sort of makes a scroopy feeling in my fingers. Neither can I bear the feel of wire wool or Brillo pads. My eldest daughter cannot stand me filing my fingernails for one thing, and the youngest daughter hates touching velvet.[16]

Dry cotton wool

Another woman felt so shivery when touching cotton wool that she decided not to study nursing because of it. Then, "as modern methods use forceps for most dressings, I applied to do nursing. I found at first the irritation was quite severe but as the cotton wool was placed in a cold solution such as methylated spirits or cleaning solution this awkwardness of touching the wool disappeared. Today, although I do not like touching it, it does not send the shiver up me quite so much."[17]

This dislike seemed to run in one family. "My husband cannot stand cotton wool anywhere near him, our son is the same, our daughter likewise when small. For her I left pieces of it around the house and so cured her but the other day she told me that the fear is returning. She is 27 years old; isn't that odd!"[18]

Suede

A man wrote, "I have had an aversion all my life to touching suede, or items of a similar texture. If I accidentally brush against a suede coat I instantly become covered in goosepimples, my hair tingles, cold shivers run up my spine and I recoil as if I have been burnt! Even the thought of it causes a skin prickling! I have never enjoyed tennis as much as I would have liked because of the texture of the ball. Card tables mean brushing the tips of my fingers over the nap of the cloth—I do not play cards as a result. Having to clean a carpet with shampoo is an exercise that makes me grit my teeth and sweat, not from effort but physical abhorrence of the feel of the wet rug tufts. I cannot wipe a wet wooden spoon—a standing joke to my wife, over twenty years of marriage!"[19]

Wet wool

"I cannot bear the feel of wet wool or synthetic woolens such as Acrilan or Orlon, and after handling them in the wash cannot even stand the touch of my own fingers against each other until my hands are thoroughly dry. I have the sensation of my teeth being 'on edge' and have to put my tongue between my teeth to cushion the feeling."[20]

Peach skin

Aversions to peach skin can prevent people from peeling peaches; those who love the fruit report that they get others to do the job. The aversion can become extreme. "I have a very acute and pronounced aversion to the skin of peaches, and to a lesser degree apricots. To see anyone bite the skin of a peach produces immediate revulsion and even after several hours the recollection of such an act can make me shudder violently."[21]

Rubber

"As a child I used to dread having to play games with balloons at birthday parties, and how often I tearfully tried to convince my mother not to make me put on Wellington boots. I did not mind wearing them as long as somebody else put them on for me. . . .

"The reason for the antipathy is that at the touch of these two objects I get goosepimples and shivers down my back, my teeth begin to chatter and I get short of breath . . . as if I had been plummeted into cold water.

"Admittedly I *can* bear to touch these things when it is necessary for my own children, and my reaction is not quite so violent as when I was a child, but I still have to take a deep breath in order to overcome the shivery feeling."[22]

As Dr. Price pointed out, these aversions are more the pinpricks than the burdens of life, but they may in a few cases affect choice of career, for example, nursing or teaching, and work in the home. People who complain that they cannot wash dishes because of the touch of pots and pans are not necessarily malingering. Only rarely, however, do aversions reach the extreme described in this final letter.

> We have a son, James, aged 8, who has a vast and ever-increasing list of aversions, both tactile and oral. . . . this only started at about the age of six and grows all the time. It would be almost easier to list the things that don't give him "the shivers." . . . he is averse to all synthetic materials, many kinds of wool, and brushes, paper tissues, the sound of skipping, floor scrubbing, oh! yes, sand—the beach! I am bewildered at this ever-growing list and never know when purchasing a garment whether it can be worn or not. He manifests his aversion by going pale, sucking in his lips, shivering and in extreme cases his hair stands up. . . . if it increases much more he will be going to school stark naked! He is the elder child of two [the second being a girl showing no such aversions]. My husband and I, like most people, have one or two aversions to a minor degree. He is still very attached to a soft toy, a smelly, tattered dog, who gives him enormous pleasure both to touch and smell.[23]

Linus's blanket: soterias

The tattered toy dog introduces us to Linus's blanket. Do you remember Linus, that adorable prodigy child in the *Peanuts* cartoon strip? He often carries round with him an old blanket that is his greatest solace. Linus's blanket is one form of *soteria*. Soterias are objects to which one gets attached, the opposite of aversions and phobias. They are those personal objects which give special comfort to certain people, even though most of us would not really enjoy those objects. Examples are toys and stuffed animals which young children carry around with them and talismans and charms which many adults wear. Many children take with them, wherever they go, their beloved blanket or stuffed toy animal until it gets so worn that it is no more than a dirty old rag trailing behind them. But so attached are they to their rag that mother tries to remove it at her peril. Its loss may well provoke a paroxysm of grief. Phobic patients might develop a soterial attachment to an object which reduces their fear. Some persons get comfort from carrying around a bottle of smelling salts in case they feel faint, while others are comforted by the knowledge that they have a supply of sedative drugs in their pockets, the presence of which reassures them without their actually taking the tablets.

HISTORICAL ASPECTS OF FEAR

Fears have not changed much over the ages. Nearly two thousand years ago Hippocrates described a man who was phobic of flutes. If he were eating at a banquet at night, as soon as he heard the first note of the flute he would be terrified, although by day he did not mind hearing the instrument. Another description is given by Hippocrates of a height-phobic man who could not go near a precipice or over a bridge or even stand beside a shallow ditch. Many references to phobias appear in subsequent historical writings, and a detailed description of a phobic reaction appeared in 1621 when Robert Burton published his famous *Anatomy of Melancholy*. "Many lamentable effects this causeth in men, as to be red, pale, tremble, sweat. . . . They that live in fear are never free, resolute, secure, never merry, but in continual pain . . . no greater misery, no rack, no torture, like unto it."[24] In his book Burton pointed out the difference between the emotions of depression and of fear and mentioned several historical figures who had fears, such as Tully and Demosthenes, both of whom had stagefright, and Augustus Caesar, who could not bear to sit in the dark.

Burton wrote of a patient who would

> not walk alone from home, for fear he should swoon, or die. A second fears every man he meets will rob him, quarrel with

him, or kill him. A third dare not venture to walk alone, for fear he should meet the devil, a thief, be sick. . . . another dares not go over a bridge, come near a pool, brook, steep hill, lye in a chamber where cross-beams are, for fear he be tempted to hang, drown or precipitate himself. If he be in a silent auditory, as at a sermon, he is afraid he shall speak aloud, at unawares, something indecent, unfit to be said. If he be locked in a close room, he is afraid of being stifled for want of air, and still carried bisket, aquavitae, or some strong waters about him, for fear of deliquiums [fainting], or being sick; or if he be in a throng, middle of a church, multitude, where he may not well get out, though he sit at ease, he is so misaffected.[25]

From this time onward phobias were increasingly described in history and literature. King James I of England was terrified at the sight of an unsheathed sword to the point where a contemporary witness commented that "Elizabeth was King, James I was Queen."[26] Another king, Germanicus, couldn't stand the sight or sound of cocks. When syphilis became part of the European scene, a phobia of this condition also became recognized. One physician gave a clear description of syphilophobia in 1721:

If but a pimple appears or any slight ache is felt, they distract themselves with terrible apprehensions: by which means they make life uneasy to themselves and run for help. . . . And so strongly are they for the most part possessed with this notion that an honest practitioner generally finds it more difficult to cure the imaginary evil than the real one.[27]

Other phobias in historical figures are those of cats by Henry III of France and the Duke of Schonberg, and a famous Russian general who was so frightened of mirrors that the Empress Catherine always took care to give him audience in a room without any. The Italian writer Manzoni was afraid of leaving home alone and had fears of fainting while out of his house, and so he would carry a small bottle of concentrated vinegar wherever he went. Feydeau, the French playwright, practically never went out during the day because of a morbid fear of daylight. Even Sigmund Freud had anxiety symptoms, including fears of travel, for some years in his thirties.

2
Normal Anxieties
and Fears

Like other species, human beings are preprogrammed to respond to certain situations with anxiety and fear. The capacity to experience these emotions is built in and has survival value. Somebody who is completely fearless is much more likely to enter dangerous situations, and survival depends on a judicious blend of courage and caution. We need to steer a path between cowardice on the one hand and foolhardiness on the other.

In general, fear and anxiety develop through the interaction of three influences—those which are largely innate and present from birth, those which are dependent on later maturation of the nervous system, and those which have developed through learning in the course of individual and social experience. The human infant takes a long time to mature ,and his limited range of innate responses is soon greatly altered as he matures and learns by his own experience and by modeling on the experience of other people.

The enduring tendency to react in a frightened way is called *timidity.* This is partly genetically determined, especially in lower animals, with experience playing an increasingly important part as one ascends the phylogenetic scale to men. Some animal species are very timid, and this might increase the chances of their survival. Rabbits are more timid than tigers. In addition, however, some rabbits are more timid than other rabbits. The same applies to human beings. Identical-twin infants tend to resemble each other in the amount of fear they show with strangers over the first year of life. Adult twins are also similar to each other in the number of neurotic symptoms which they show.

FEARS WHICH HUMANS ARE NATURALLY "PREPARED" TO DEVELOP

Although animals and humans may show fear of any situation at some time or another, in general certain stimuli are much more feared than others. Furthermore, these fears may follow little or no experience of such situations. Many of these situations have special evolutionary significance for us as a species.

Though occasionally people develop a fear of an object immediately after some trauma, some stimuli seem to trigger phobias much more readily than others. The point is made by the experience of one little girl of seven who heard a rustling of grass in a park, thought it was a snake, and ran away down the hill, not telling anybody what she had seen. An hour later she caught her hand in the door of her parents' car and it had to be bandaged. Later she told her parents of the snake, and she became steadily more frightened of snakes. To protect her, her parents then mistakenly avoided mentioning them and would switch off television programs and remove newspaper articles concerning snakes so that she could avoid all contact with the object of her fear. Her phobia of snakes increased and continued until she was at least twenty.

We can see that this girl in fact suffered far more pain from the car door on her hand than from any snake, yet she became phobic not of car doors but of snakes. This may be because as a species we humans have our brains programmed to show fear easily to wiggly things but not to artificial objects like car doors. Given a painful experience with cars, bricks, grass, animals, and bicycles, we are more likely to fix our fear on the animals than on the other items. Certain stimuli seem to be lightning conductors toward which our fears are directed.

Another example of the way an aversion is attached more easily onto some stimuli rather than others comes from the experience of an adult. An Israeli Arab drove his truck by mistake onto the Lebanese side of the border and was immediately seized by Lebanese border guards, interrogated, and tortured. He was tied to a chair, beaten about the head, and had his teeth knocked out. This continued for three days, during which time he refused to eat any food for fear of being poisoned and accepted only water to drink. After three days he was allowed to return to his family in Israel. He found he was now unable to eat solid food without gagging and retching, so that he had to confine himself to a liquid diet. When false teeth were fitted, these too provoked vomiting and had to be discarded even after they had been fitted under anesthesia. His inability to eat solids continued for a year, and he lost much weight. The interesting point is that this man did not develop fears of driving trucks or of sitting in chairs. These are not natural things to fear. Rather his painful gums and abstinence from solid food over a few days led to a gross exaggeration of the natural gag reflex, which we all have if we touch the back of our throats, into an intense aversion for swallowing solid food.

COMMON FEARS IN CHILDREN: NOVELTY, STRANGERS, AND MOVEMENTS

At birth human infants already startle readily to *noise* or to any other *intense, sudden,* or *novel* stimulus which is unexpected. Between the ages of six and twelve months the majority of normal infants begin to develop a fear of strangers. This fear develops after the baby has learned to tell the difference between strangers and members of its own family.

The fear of strangers is a special example of the well-known fact that the novel, strange, and unfamiliar is apt to provoke fear in many species. The Canadian psychologist Hebb documented how chimpanzees were extremely frightened of coming near a plaster death mask which was taken from one of their number who had died. Young children are often afraid of strange masks or other unfamiliar objects whose unfamiliarity consists of a slight departure from what they are already used to. The elder sister of a three-year-old girl brought home a wig from her school play to show her parents for their approval. The sister put it away in a cupboard in which the toys were kept. The little girl went to get some toys out of the cupboard and accidentally touched the wig. Terrified that it might be an animal of some kind, she screamed endlessly. A fear of wigs started which lasted for many years, although fears of this sort in children are usually short-lived.

Though novelty may provoke fear, those same novel stimuli can on other occasions cause pleasure and be eagerly sought out. Novel stimulus patterns can attract and repel in turn, and so cause a conflict between approach and avoidance responses. Konrad Lorenz gave a good description of this in the raven:

A young raven, confronted with a new object, which may be a camera, an old bottle, a stuffed polecat, or anything else, first reacts with escape responses. He will fly up to an elevated perch and from this point of vantage stare at the object . . . maintaining all the while a maximum of caution and the expressive attitude of intense fear. He will cover the last distance from the object hopping sideways with half-raised wings, in the utmost readiness to flee. At last, he will deliver a single blow with his powerful beak at the object and forthwith fly back to his safe perch. If nothing happens he will repeat the same procedure in much quicker sequence and with more confidence. If the object is an animal that flees, the raven loses all fear in the fraction of a second and will start in pursuit instantly. If it is an animal that charges, he will either try to get behind it or, if the charge is sufficiently unimpressive, lose interest in a very short time. With an inanimate object, the raven will proceed to apply a number of further instinctive movements. He will grab it with one foot, peck at it, try to tear off pieces, insert his bill into any existing cleft and then pry apart his mandibles with considerable force. Finally, if the object is not too big the raven will carry it away, push it into a convenient hole and cover it with some inconspicuous material.[1]

The terror which unfamiliar things inspire in young children, especially if they move in writhing fashion, was dramatically seen in my son when he was a toddler aged 2½ years. At that time he had never seen snakes and did not know the word for them. I had carried him over rocky terrain from a car to a beach at low tide. The sand had dried, exposing thousands of residual skeins of brown-black seaweed up to a foot long. They looked like myriads of eels or tiny snakes lying dead still. There were similar fronds of green seaweed waving in the shallow seawater nearby. As soon as the boy saw the dried seaweed on the sand, he screamed in terror and clutched me tightly, trying to stop me from sitting in the sand. When I touched the seaweed he shrieked and refused to do the same. His panic increased when gentle waves rolled the seaweed nearby or when I held him over the water to show him the moving fronds. Slowly I tried to get him used to the dried seaweed on the sand by playing with it myself and encouraging him to do the same. Only after one-half hour of this was he prepared even to sit on the sand without any seaweed. Then he became able to grab the seaweed gingerly and quickly fling it away. He would not go near the water. The next day he touched the seaweed a bit more readily but was still obviously afraid. A week later he was able to throw the fronds away, but he was still unhappy to leave them in his hand. His continued exposure to the frightening situation led to its gradually losing its terrors. We will see later that this principle of exposure is central to the treatment of fear.

That writhing or jerky movements frighten monkeys and men is well known. This might be the basis for their fear of snakes which is particularly pronounced from the age of two through four. Fears of spiders fall into the same category. Fears of animals tend to occur at about the same ages of two through four, and animals are also much more frightening to children if they are moving rapidly toward the child in a jerky way or if they loom above the child.

Young toddlers may handle live animals fearlessly until they see the animals stalking or rushing toward them—this is likely to frighten them immediately. Their fear goes away as soon as the same animal changes into another position. The fear is thus triggered by a particular kind of movement rather than by the animal itself.

MODELING OF FEAR

Some children's fears are modeled on those of their parents. When a parent has a phobia, a child is more likely to develop the same phobia. In a frightening situation children tend to look at any adult who happens to be with them at the time. If the adult shows fear, then the child may pick it up quite easily. By way of illustration, a mother was spooning supper to her eighteen-month-old toddler sitting in her high chair when suddenly a bat flew in. The mother became panic-stricken, pulled her little girl by her ankles from the high chair, and ran screaming from the room clutching her daughter upside down. The chair was upset and the dishes were broken. After this, the little girl also developed a fear of flying things that persisted into her adult life as a fear of moths and butterflies. Though such modeling of fear can start a phobia, this is frequently not the case, and only about one-sixth of adults with phobias have close relatives with a similar phobia.

CHILDREN'S FEARS ARE VOLATILE AND CHANGE AS THEY GROW

Fears occur in children for little or no apparent reason and die down as mysteriously without further contact with the phobic situations. When children become more babyish during illness, forgotten fears may reappear. When the child is well again, the fears disappear once more. The common fears change as the child grows. Fears of animals are more common from the age of two through four, but by age four to six fears of the dark and imaginary creatures like ghosts are more common. After the age of six, people seem resistant to acquiring new phobias of animals. Fears of animals diminish very rapidly in boys and girls between the ages of nine and eleven. Other widespread fears in childhood are of winds, storms, thunder and lightning, cars and trains. The rather constant ages at which some fears come and go have varying explanations. Where the objects are encountered frequently by most children of all ages, for example, animals and birds, fears of such objects may partly reflect changes within the child due to maturation. Experiments with the infants of rhesus monkeys show that they are specially liable to show fear to the threat display of another monkey from the ages of two through four months.

Some fears start at a given age simply because that is the age at which the child is first exposed to a particular situation. School phobias are a case in point. When children are exposed to a totally new situation, they generally show anxiety but adapt rapidly. Some fear of school is the rule during the first term or when the child changes to another school, but complete refusal to go to school because of fear is uncommon.

Most children show fears at some time or another, though really incapacitating phobias are uncommon. In general girls tend to have more fears than boys. Fears tend to be less common after puberty.

FIVE CHILDREN'S FEARS IN A FAMILY

It is interesting to record the observations made by a British psychologist, C. W. Valentine, on the fears shown by his own five young children, who were carefully observed for more than ten years. Valentine found that loud sounds startled his infants from the age of two weeks to a few months. This was especially true for new sounds. Fears of strange objects began after the age of one year, and between age one and three several of the children had fears of the sea. These fears could not have been learned or suggested as he was with four of his five children the first time they saw the ocean. The children were encouraged to like and go into the sea. Their only previous experience of water had been in their baths, which had always been a delight to them. Also, after the age of one year, several of the children showed fear of animals despite previous familiarity and ease with animals at a younger age, and the absence of any unpleasant experiences to account for the fear. Fear of the dark appeared in only two of the children at the age of five years.

The children varied greatly in their tendencies to show fear. One of them was almost fearless from birth onward, whereas the other children showed frequent fear. When the children had a trusted companion, their fear would greatly diminish. None of the fears occurred every single time a particular stimulus was presented. The degree of fear varied with the overall timidity of the child, the presence of a companion, the details of the stimulus, and the condition of the child at the time.[2]

FEARS WHICH ARE COMMON IN BOTH CHILDREN AND ADULTS

Staring and stage fright

Staring readily evokes fear in children and even in adults. We can see how this fear develops out of our sensitivity as a species to the gaze of others. From our earliest months onward, we pay great attention to two eyes moving together. The suckling infant fixes his gaze on his mother's eyes. By the age of two months he will smile readily at a mask waved in front of him with two "eyes" painted on it. Young children's drawings emphasize eyes from an early age. Staring eyes can arouse intense emotion in adults sensitive to the gaze of others, so that being looked at is an important trigger of social phobias and of stage fright. *Stage fright* is frequent in actors, public speakers, and sometimes even in experienced politicians.

Heights

Adults continue to have the same dislike of heights which is apparent in young infants as soon as they can crawl. Most of us have been aware of the urge to throw ourselves off a precipice and have drawn back in a protective reflex. Fears of heights commonly inconvenience people who live in high-rise buildings. Many inhabitants feel uncomfortable in such buildings, particularly if the exterior walls of glass run from floor to ceiling. This is partly because they feel they lack privacy, partly because they feel dizzy looking down outside through windows which extend from the floor to the ceiling, and partly because they feel their apartments are too brightly lit. These discomforts are eased a bit by curtaining the window, which darkens the room and makes it feel smaller. At daytime parties in apartments of this kind, many guests retreat from the well-lit side of the room to throng the darker interior in preference.

A woman who lived in an apartment twenty-two floors above London described the discomfort produced by a sense of space and light:

> When my husband first saw the view, he was lyrical. He said at night it was like fairyland. When we've company, they often spend the first half-hour looking out of the window. Some get dizzy though. We'd a fellow here, like a wrestler he is, short but muscular, and he wouldn't go near the windows at all. Just stood by the stove all evening. I felt like that at first. Now I only notice it when I'm cleaning the windows. The windows run right over for cleaning, but I have to get my husband to do it. My stomach just leaves me.
>
> To begin with, we put the children's bunks in the little bedroom. It's such a tiny room we had to put them up against the window, and my eldest daughter just refused to go to bed in the top bunk; she got in with the little one down below. I didn't know what was wrong, so one day I got up myself to see what put her off. It was terrifying! Like lying on the edge of a cliff, just the glass between you and all that space.[3]

Another high-living tenant commented: "There's something about it which makes it feel unlike home. If you draw the curtains, you're cozy, but you're cut off from the world till next morning."[4]

FEARS WHICH ARE COMMON IN ADULTS

In adult life many situations produce anxiety. *Examinations* and other tests often make young people tense; this tension can become so severe that they do badly and fail their examinations despite high ability. Fear and anxiety regularly accompany stressful situations such as *combat* or *parachuting.* Most people have some kind of *dental or medical treatment* each year. Before an operation it is perfectly normal to feel anxious as the hour for surgery approaches. This anxiety reaches its peak in the operating room. Anxiety tends to decrease rapidly shortly after dental treatment and less quickly after surgery. Many people are so anxious about their visits to the dentist that they do not go as regularly as necessary. Worry about doctors or dentists can become so marked that people become afraid even of seeing ambulances or hospitals and avoid the sight of these like the plague, even switching off television programs on the subject.

Anxiety during driving

Driving motor vehicles is a common source of stress. The heart rate can increase from 80 beats per minute at rest to 150 when overtaking another car. In a study of London transport workers, bus drivers were compared with bus conductors and were found to have higher blood pressure, nearly twice as many heart attacks, and a higher blood cholesterol. Accidents are especially likely to happen when drivers are experiencing problems such as marital conflicts, work troubles, or worries about money. At such times they are also more likely to take alcohol, which in turn greatly increases the chances of error.

Such influences affect various people differently. Despite many beliefs to the contrary, women and elderly drivers are less often involved in serious traffic accidents, presumably because they take fewer risks than daring young men, whose fast reaction times may not be enough to compensate for excess bravado.

Stress during driving is increased at night and in the early hours of the morning. Especially stressful are prolonged periods of driving, particularly in older people. The practical consequence of this finding is that very long runs—beyond nine hours, including rest breaks—should be discouraged, particularly after the age of forty-five. Drivers should not be permitted to drive more than three hours without a reasonable break.

Separation anxiety

Separation anxiety is another normal response to stress of a different kind, namely the threat of loss of a loved object. *Grief* is a special form of separation reaction to the actual loss of a loved object. Most young mammals show separation anxiety when removed from a familiar figure.

In mammals the first bond is usually that between mother and young. They tend to remain near each other and if separated try to come close together again. Separation of the bonded pair by a third party is resisted, and the stronger of the partners attacks the intruder while the weaker flees or clings to the stronger partner. If bonded partners are separated and cannot find each other, they become *distressed,* that is, they show separation anxiety. Once a young creature has become attached to a mother figure, his behavior in her presence is different from that in her absence. With her present he is relaxed and adventurous, while in her absence he becomes tense and inert. In man, bonding is often accompanied by the feeling of love or dependency.

A primate or human toddler separated from his mother is likely to curl up on the floor and cry. The stranger the surroundings in which a separated child finds himself, the more anxious he becomes. When children are admitted to a hospital, they are comforted by having their familiar toys around them despite the strange environment. After the child returns home, people and events which recall the hospitalization often start up his anxiety again.

As children grow older, they gradually learn to separate from their parents without much trouble. The first few times they go away with their friends on vacation they might feel a bit homesick and shed a few tears, but the distress soon clears and they steadily become more independent. Leaving home for periods seems to be a necessary part of growing up, in preparation for living away from home. Absence of trial periods like this can lead to separation anxiety in adult life. An extreme form of this particular anxiety was shown by one married woman of twenty who had been separated from her mother for more than a day at a time only once—when her mother went abroad for two weeks, and then the patient tried to phone her several times. She had had severe fear of separation from her mother from childhood, always insisted on remaining near her mother whenever possible, and on being phoned frequently when separation was unavoidable. Even when seen in the hospital outpatient department, she wanted to know where her mother would be at the end of the hour's appointment. When she had been twelve years old, she had gone on vacation with a friend a hundred miles away from home, but phoned home in distress several times daily; after a few days she could stand it no longer and returned home. She disliked being left completely alone at home and even avoided elevators. After marrying, she, her husband, and their two children lived with her mother. Fortunately, such an extreme degree of separation anxiety is rare.

3

Normal Reactions
to Death
and Disaster

DEATH AND DYING

A horror of death is present in most cultures. The dread is not necessarily about the process of dying itself but about the end of all opportunity for people to achieve their goals and pursue their pleasures.

Children on the whole speak quite freely of death. Adolescents tend to be more circumspect, and for adults in Western countries death is often a taboo subject. It is customary not to speak of another's death in his presence. In speaking of dying we employ euphemisms like "passing on," "departing this life," "going to heaven," or "kicking the bucket." The mourning ceremonies of many religions soften the loss by emphasizing continuing contact with the dead person in heaven or in the spirit world. The American way of death to a large extent denies the finality of bereavement. This denial serves to lessen the anxiety caused by death.

Toward old age more people become resigned to the inevitable, and fear of death is less common over the age of sixty than one might suppose. In studying dying patients, one research worker found that less than a third of those over sixty were very anxious compared with two-thirds of the people under fifty who were anxious. This is understandable, as death in early life disrupts more hopes and expectations. Young mothers and fathers with dependent children were more uneasy about their impending deaths.[1]

Some of the greater anxiety found in dying patients who were younger might be caused by the way in which they were dying. Persistent pain, nausea, vomiting, and breathlessness can be most distressing to the dying, and these symptoms tend to be more common in younger adults, who frequently have longer-lasting illnesses and more physical distress than do older patients.

Nevertheless the process of dying is often perfectly comfortable. A famous physician, William Hunter, said when he was dying, "If I had strength enough to hold a pen, I would write how easy and pleasant a thing it is to die."[2] Another renowned doctor, William Osler, commented that "most people go out of life as they came into it, oblivious."[3] Onlookers can easily think the dying person is in more pain than he really is. Many dying people are only semiconscious and not aware of what is happening. Dying is commonly more distressing to observers who are about to be bereaved than to the one who is departing.

Once someone has died, the body is liable to become the focus of a new fear. Quite a few cultures have strong taboos which prohibit anyone from touching a corpse, from which evil powers are said to emanate. Ghosts and evil spirits are believed to hover around the corpse and later the grave. Many plays make use of these beliefs in their plots. In Shakespeare's *Macbeth,* Banquo's ghost haunts his murderer, Macbeth, while the ghost of Hamlet's father plays a key role in the beginning of that play.

Some anxiety about dead bodies centers over their altered state at death and during decomposition. Where there is belief in a future life, disfigurement at death threatens this promise. Elaborate steps are taken in different cultures to ensure there is no handicap to resurrection. The body is embalmed to preserve its shape; food, valuables, and retainers are buried with it; easy exits are built into the grave. The Great Pyramids of Egypt testify to the Pharaoh's beliefs in the afterlife. Precautions like these emphasize that much anxiety concerning death relates to the way in which it ends ongoing activity. Views are valued which suggest that we continue existing in some way after death.

Religious belief can modify the amount of anxiety people feel about dying. However, more important than one's actual beliefs is whether one is confident in them, whatever they are. People who are firmly agnostic are less anxious than lukewarm churchgoers.

Anxiety is increased by uncertainty about what is going to happen. Dying patients may suspect their fate and feel apprehensive until they are told the truth. Anxiety might then abate and be replaced for a while by depression, which gradually passes off. This gloom is like a grief reaction in which the patient comes to terms with the loss of his own future.

Some people are so afraid of dying, however, that they avoid learning about their progress at all costs. Even when they are told the truth they forget it immediately, or deny it. Denial may not be effective for long, and the patient may then break down in acute distress. There can therefore be no golden rule about concealing or telling the truth about dying. One has to decide in the light of the dying person's past responses to other stress, the stability of his personality, and whether he genuinely wants to know or strives to avoid learning about his true position.

GRIEF

Grief is a special kind of separation anxiety. Generally it takes some time for people to accept the death of a loved one, and until they do, separation anxiety is marked. They feel yearning for the deceased person, the so-called pangs of grief. Pining is accompanied by crying and searching for the lost one. The bereaved move restlessly about, think a lot about the lost person, attend to stimuli which suggest that person, and ignore other things. Sometimes they find themselves calling for the dead person. After repeated failure to find the dead person, the intensity of searching gradually dies down until the attachment to the lost person is finally broken.

The pain of grief is partly the result of disrupted role functions between the bereaved and the deceased. The housewife particularly mourns her dead husband in the evening at the time when he used to return home from work. During early mourning the bereaved rehearse over and over in their minds what they used to do with the dead person. These rehearsals are painful. After a while the bereaved cease these abortive attempts to interact with the deceased and develop new ties with other people instead.

Although nearly every adult eventually loses a close relative or friend through death, relatively little systematic study has been made of grief reactions. One of the best studies was made by a London psychiatrist, Dr. Colin Parkes, and his findings are well worth reading in detail. He interviewed twenty-two widows, all under the age of sixty-five, at least five times in the thirteen months after their husbands died.

Numbness and disbelief

Most of the women had been unable to accept warnings of the impending demise of their husbands. When their husbands actually died, the most frequent reaction was numbness, although this was sometimes preceded by great distress. In one widow's words, "I suddenly burst. I was aware of a horrible wailing and knew it was me. I was saying I loved him and all that. I knew he'd gone but I kept on talking to him."[3] She went to the bathroom and vomited, and then the feeling of numbness set in. "I felt numb and solid for a week. It's a blessing. . . . everything goes hard inside you like a heavy weight."[4] Another widow felt "in a dream . . . I just couldn't take it all in . . . I couldn't believe it."[5]

At first, sixteen of the women had trouble accepting that their husbands were really dead. Among their comments were the following: "There was so much to do but I didn't feel like I was doing it, for anyone—not for him, if you see. I couldn't take it in." "There must be a mistake." "I wouldn't believe it until I see him [dead] on the Monday [4 days later]". "I didn't register at all . . . it didn't seem real."[6] Although the sense of being numb or stunned was usually short-lived, even a year later thirteen widows still went through times when they couldn't believe that their husband was really dead.

In the early phase of grief the women often cried but sometimes were angry or even elated. One widow was quite calm at first. "I looked into his eyes, and as he stared at me, something happened to us. As if something had gone into me. I felt all warm inside, I'm not interested in this world any longer. It's a sort of religious feeling. . . . I feel as big as a house. I fill the room."[7] Later she cried several times and once tried to kill herself halfheartedly. Another woman reacted in anger, saying, "Why did he do this to me?" The next few days she kept herself very busy. Then four days later, at dawn, "Something suddenly moved in on me—invaded me—a presence almost pushed me out of bed. It was my husband—terribly overwhelming. This was followed by a series of pictures like photographic plates, of faces."[8] At the time she was uncertain that she might have been dreaming. A sense of numbness lasted for two weeks.

Panic and distress

During the first month of bereavement and later as well, panic attacks were common. Several times in the first month, Mrs. Jones ran out of her flat and took refuge with friends next door. She felt so fragile that "if somebody gave me a good tap I'd shatter into a thousand pieces." She avoided thinking of her husband as dead. "If I let myself think Bob's dead I'll be overcome. I couldn't look at it and stay sane." When events made it impossible for her to forget her husband's death, she felt desperate. These panics slowly diminished as the year passed by, although even at the end of the year she still felt panicky "from time to time."[9] Individuals varied tremendously in the ways they reacted to death of a loved one. Periods of distress alternated with others of numbness or restless "business." The widows tried to thrust aside the pain or the sense of loss, and when it broke through it seemed overwhelming. Usually the numbness came to an end after about a week. At this point distress became more severe.[10]

Many experts believe that grief cannot be permanently postponed and that keeping it in increases the distress which will eventually break through. As Shakespeare wrote in *Macbeth,* act iv, scene 3, line 208: "Give sorrow words: the grief that does not speak whispers the o'erfraught heart, and bids it break." Among the widows interviewed by Parkes, this was true up to a point.

Pining and preoccupation

When the numbness ceased, pangs of intense pining for the dead person began. The widows became preoccupied with thoughts of the deceased, kept on looking toward places and things around them associated with their dead husbands, and attended to sights and sounds suggesting his presence. They would also cry out for him and become restless. An American psychiatrist, Eric Lindemann, reported in Boston about this phase of grief. "There is a rush of speech, especially when talking about the deceased. There is restlessness, inability to sit still, moving about in aimless fashion, continually searching for something to do. There is, however, at the same time, a painful lack of capacity to initiate and maintain normal patterns of activity."[11]

The typical widow in London constantly thought of her husband and imagined him in his accustomed place in the room at home. "I can almost feel his skin or touch his hands." At night or when relaxed during the day she would go over and over in her mind the events in the past in which her husband took part. This occurred especially during the early months and again as the anniversary of the death approached. The husband's final illness would haunt the woman: "I find myself going through it all over again."[12]

Sometimes happy memories of the past would be recalled. "A

year ago today was [the royal] wedding day. I said to him, don't forget the wedding. When I got in I said did you watch the wedding? He said no, I forgot. We watched it together in the evening except he had his eyes shut. He wrote a card to his sister and I can see him so vividly I could tell you every mortal thing that was done on all those days. I said you haven't watched or anything. He said no, I haven't."[13]

Nearly half the widows felt drawn toward places which reminded them of their husbands. They visited old haunts or went to the cemetery or the hospital "to be near him." Most of the women treasured possessions which had previously belonged to their husbands, although often they also avoided items like articles of clothing or photographs which evoked too intense a pining. As the year passed, this tendency to avoid reminders grew less marked. Some familiar things and places which had seemed comforting during the early period gradually lost their hold so that a room which had strongly reminded a woman of her husband could be redecorated and the furniture changed. At the same time things which had been put away shortly after death because they evoked such painful pangs of grief were gradually brought out again—for example, photographs were rehung on the wall.

Frequently the widows "saw," "heard," or "felt" their husbands nearby, especially during the first month after death. They would interpret small sounds about the house as indicating their husbands' presence or momentarily misidentify people in the street and then realize their mistake. One woman "saw" her husband coming home through the door in the fence; another was upset by her hallucination of her husband sitting in a chair on Christmas Day. We can easily see how the belief in ghosts arises on the basis of such experiences.

Crying, irritability, and anger

Crying is such an expected feature of grief that it is likely to be taken for granted. Sixteen of the widows cried during the first interview a month after bereavement. In later interviews they cried much less frequently. Although crying is associated with the "pangs" of grief, a widow may find it hard to say why she is crying.

A less well known feature of grief is irritability and anger. Thirteen of the widows showed some of this anger and felt that the world had become more insecure and dangerous. Sometimes anger was directed at the dead husband: "Why did he do this to me?" At other times it might be aimed at the medical attendants. "I still go over in my mind the way those doctors behaved," said one woman, and another expressed great bitterness toward a nurse who had hurt her husband by ripping off an adhesive dressing.[14] As time passed irrational anger subsided. One widow had been very angry with the hospital staff at the time of her bereavement, but when asked at the end of the year if she still felt angry, denied it, though admitting, "I wish there was something I could blame." A few women blamed themselves for the way they behaved after their husbands died. Referring to her irritability, one woman said, "I get furious with myself."[16]

Guilt and self-reproach

Feelings of guilt and self-reproach are common during mourning. The women typically commented, "I think, what could I have done?" "I think to myself, did I do right?"[15] Self-reproach might be about minor matters. A year after her husband died one widow noted that she felt guilty because she had never made her husband a bread pudding. More often the matter was more serious, but it was dubious whether the widow had been to blame; for example, one widow had supported her husband in his refusal to undergo a palliative operation, while another blamed herself for failing to encourage her husband's literary talents during his lifetime and tried to make amends by getting his poems published after his death.

Several women felt that they had failed their husbands during the last phase of illness. "I seemed to go away from him. He wasn't the person I'd been married to. When I tried to share his pain, it was so terrible I couldn't stop. I wish I could have done more. I don't think I could have done enough because he was so helpless."

Restlessness and overactivity

Another feature of grief reactions is restlessness and overactivity. The widows complained of feeling "strung up" or "jumpy" or "all in a turmoil inside." "I am always on the go," "I am at the end of my tether," "I can't pin myself down to anything," "Stupid little things upset me," were other complaints. When the women became very tense, they would also be trembly and sometimes stammer. When restless the women were likely to flare up from time to time or to fill their lives with activities. "I think if I didn't work all the time I'd have a nervous breakdown," said one widow. Interviews with her were carried out on the trot as she passed from one household chore to another; she appeared distraught, irritable, and tense. At the end of the year she could see "nothing to live for, it all seems so pointless."[17]

Fluctuation of grief

The distress caused by bereavement is not continuous and lets up occasionally; at these times the bereaved might feel relatively calm, even after very intense pangs of grief. To some extent the pain might be controlled by avoidance of people and places associated with the dead person, by disbelief in what has happened, by trying to distract oneself. As an example, Mrs. Smith had lost her husband suddenly from a cerebral hemorrhage. She found it hard to believe that he was dead and cried a great deal during the first week. She managed to stop the crying by keeping her mind occupied by other things. She avoided going into her husband's room and persuaded her son to get rid of most of her husband's possessions. At the interview a month after her husband's death, she broke off several times for fear she might cry. A year later she was much calmer but still avoided possessions which reminded her of her husband, and she disliked visiting his grave. She insisted, "If he comes in my mind I try to think of something else."[18]

It is common to *idealize* the dead. Mrs. White was a woman of fifty-nine who had quarreled frequently with her alcoholic husband. She had left him several times during their married life and during the first interview remarked, "I shouldn't really say so but it's more peaceful now that he's gone."[19] During her first year as a widow, her two youngest daughters married and left home, leaving her alone in her apartment. She became very lonely and depressed and spoke nostalgically of the old days. By the final interview she had forgotten her marital problems and said she wished to marry again to "someone kind, like my husband."[20]

Identification with the deceased

After bereavement, quite a few people identify with the deceased more than they did when he was alive. "I enjoy the things my husband used to do. . . . it's like a thought in my head—what he would say or do," said Mrs. Black, who cited watching the soccer Cup Final and racing on television as activities deriving from him.

> I quite enjoy it because he liked it. It's a most queer feeling. . . . My young sister said, "You're getting like Fred in all your ways." . . . She said something about food—I said, "I couldn't touch that," and she said, "Don't be stupid, you're getting just like Fred." . . . There are lots of things I do that I wouldn't think of doing. . . . I suppose he's guiding me the whole of the time.[21]

Less often, people might develop symptoms resembling those the deceased had during his last illness. Mrs. Brown's husband had died from a coronary thrombosis, which had caused chest pain and breathlessness for a week. Afterward his wife had fainting attacks, palpitations, and panics in which she gasped for breath and felt that her heart was bursting, "just like my husband's." Later in the year she developed uncontrollable spasms and pain in her left face and leg which her doctor diagnosed as mimicry of the stroke her husband had suffered five years earlier.

Uncommonly, widows felt as if their dead husbands were actually inside them.

> My husband's in me, right through and through. I've got like him. . . . I can feel him in me doing everything. He used to say, "You'll do this when I'm gone, won't you?" He is just guiding my life. I can feel his presence within me because of his talking and doing things. It is not a sense of his presence, he is *here* inside me. That's why I am happy all the time. As if two people were one. . . . although I am alone we are, sort of, together if you see what I mean. . . . I don't think I have the willpower to carry on on my own, so he must be.[22]

Sometimes the dead husband was located within the children. One widow said of her daughter: "Sometimes I feel as if Diane is my husband. . . . she has his hands—it used to give me the creeps."[23]

Dreams of the dead husband were present in half the widows. These were vivid and realistic and often ended with the dreamer awakening with surprise and disappointment to find that her husband was not present after all. "He was trying to comfort me and put his arms around me. I kept turning away and crying. Even in the dream I knew he was dead. . . . but I felt so happy and I cried and he couldn't do anything about it. . . . When I touched his face it was as if he was really there—quite real and vivid."[24] Another typical dream was, "He was in the coffin with the lid off and all of a sudden he came to life and got out. . . . I looked at him and he opened his mouth—I said, 'he's alive, he's alive.' I thought 'Thank God, I'll have him to talk to.'"[25]

Physical and other problems

During the painful period of grieving, people pay little attention to less urgent matters like sleeping and eating. Insomnia is the rule in the beginning; half the widows took a sedative drug in the first month of bereavement. Many could not get to sleep, or woke during the night, or woke early. At night they were at their most lonely. Several were unable to sleep in the bed which they had shared with their husband, and several lay awake thinking of him during much of the night. Commonly they ate poorly and lost weight in the first couple of months. Some even lost their affection for surviving children, cut themselves off from friends, and shut themselves up at home. Those seven who had jobs stayed away from work for nearly two weeks on the average but eventually found fresh interests and new friends again, sooner than those widows who had no jobs to take them out of their homes.

Recovery from grief

Fortunately most people get over their bereavement in time. As an example, Mrs. Green had had a close relationship with her husband. After his death she felt numb for several days, became anxious and depressed, was preoccupied with her husband's memory, and felt his presence strongly. Her family supported her, and her grief began to diminish during the third and fourth months after her husband's death. During the seventh month she visited her sister in the United States. She felt wanted and returned confident and refreshed, prepared to care for an ailing relative and to be the center of a united family.

The time it takes for grief to subside varies, and it is not always gone even after a year. In some senses grief never ends, and longstanding widows may say that "you never get over it." During anniversaries or when an old friend comes to call unexpectedly or when a forgotten photograph gets discovered in a drawer, all the feelings of acute pining and sadness return, and the bereaved person goes through another bereavement in miniature. However, as time goes on grief becomes less frequently aroused and less intense than before, and the interests and appetite which were lost after the death gradually return.

When we grieve the loss of a loved person or a missed

opportunity, we need to "work through" our feelings triggered by the loss. We should be able to talk about the meaning to us of the person we have lost, of things we used to do with him or her, and be able to cry unashamedly. In many cultures it is well recognized that people need to mourn when their relatives have died, and there is a ritual period of grieving which helps the bereaved to get over their loss. In some cultures the bereaved are expected to wail and express their grief openly. In working through our grief, however, it is important not only to mourn the past but also to explore new ways of living in the future and of replacing the loss we have suffered by new relationships and activities.

Perhaps the most anxiety-provoking event most of us will need to come to terms with one day is that of our own dying. We tend to associate successful treatment with getting well, but care for the dying assumes the inevitable will happen and tries to smooth the path toward death as much as possible. It is now recognized in many medical centers that dying people need special care to reduce their worries. Dying people can be helped to accept their own impending demise calmly, even when this takes a long time. An elderly lady in a ward for the terminally ill watched six of her roommates die over several months. When asked whether she had found any meaning and purpose in these many days of suffering, she thought for a while and said, "Yes, I feel I have honestly had a helpful relationship with the other patients in my room who have died."[26] It is possible to die in peace and dignity despite pain, provided preparation for the event has occurred.

SUDDEN CALAMITY

Disasters like fire, airplane crashes, and tornadoes produce complicated reactions. During a brief period while danger is approaching, people become acutely afraid and try to escape.

Normal Reactions to Death and Disaster

Long after the danger has subsided, many of them continue to be frightened, jittery, and alert to minor threats that would ordinarily be disregarded. During and immediately after the disaster strikes, there is often stunned immobility and acute freezing of movement, which is usually brief. Some people, however, might wander about for hours in a dazed, distracted state. Shortly after the obvious danger has disappeared, people frequently become depressed and apathetic, lack energy, initiative, and interest, but they do not generally feel suicidal. They might cling passively to authority and show automatic obedience to anybody providing leadership. During the recovery period, once the most urgent rescue and relief operations are over, people often become aggressive and irritable.

In extreme stress, anxiety and panic are not the major problems in saving the community involved. Rather, the problem is lack of coordination among many people, all acting on their own different personal definitions of the situation at the time. Emotional reactions to disaster might be increased by separation from family and by intimate contact with dead or injured people.

It is surprising that panic is not a more common reaction to disaster. Sociologists define panic as an acute fear reaction marked by loss of self-control which is followed by nonsocial and irrational flight. Panic occurs when a person feels immediately threatened and believes escape is possible at the moment but will shortly become impossible. Panic tends to disrupt organized group activity and during it ordinary social relations are disregarded. Panic is thus different from controlled withdrawal, where the conventional patterns of response are still maintained, despite some confusion. Panic occurs when possibilities for escape still seem available, not when a person feels completely trapped. Panic is accompanied by a sense of helplessness, impotence, and aloneness and is more likely to arise when there is contact with other agitated individuals who feel in similar danger. During panic there is blind flight from the threat with no attempt to deal directly with the danger itself.

DANGEROUS COMBAT

Soldiers in battle face extreme hazards. This could be an unexpected sharp exchange of fire for a few seconds in a week, or constant bombardment for days on end. It would be unnatural not to feel anxious under such circumstances, and it is surprising that combat neurosis is relatively uncommon, tending to occur more during continuing and severe danger.

In American airmen during World War II, the main factor responsible for emotional breakdown during air combat was danger itself. The greater the number of aircraft lost, the greater the number of emotional casualties among the bomber crews. Anxiety increased sharply when losses were high, thus increasing the chances of witnessing a disaster. Chance factors played a very large part in determining whether a particular trauma would lead to breakdown. The position of a pilot in a flying formation influenced what he could see of harrowing events. It mattered much whether the parachute of an escaped friend opened safely or caught fire or blew into another aircraft. It made a difference whether the flak burst directly in the bomb bay so that all pieces of the ship and its occupants were blown beyond the field of vision, or whether the expression on a wounded or a parachuting man's face could be seen. The physical appearance of the man in danger, how well he was known to the observer, or how well liked by him, all played a part in deciding whether the surviving crewman might subsequently break down.

Extreme danger can induce fear in the bravest of men, who are perplexed and disbelieving at the phobias they develop. A nineteen-year-old American flying cadet said when he developed a flying phobia in World War II, "I have a yellow streak up my back a yard wide and I don't know where I got it. I never used to be yellow."[27]

When airmen became anxious, they complained of airsickness and dizziness and became overcautious in their flying. Phobias of flying often developed when something happened to remind the man of his dangerous situation. This might be a trivial accident, an unexpected gust of wind, a momentary sticking of the controls. Fear often began at the beginning of an advanced step in training—the first night flight, the first flight on instruments or in formation, the first flight in a more complicated or new type of aircraft.

After three to six weeks of rest, almost all casualties were fit for noncombatant duty again, although many of those returning to duty had persistent nightmares. A few casualties were able to return to combat flying. One man's reaction had developed on a mission during which his plane was twice damaged badly and two men aboard were killed. At a rest home this man spent the first two weeks lying on the grass with his face down, deeply depressed, speaking to no one, preoccupied with guilt and whether or not he was alive. At first he was unable to eat, sleep, or mingle with others. He was unable to talk about flying or to listen to others talk about it and was extremely sensitive to noise of any kind. He had an intense phobia for his air base. He improved slowly at first and then suddenly quite rapidly. At the end of six weeks he was able to do ground duty.

PROLONGED EXTREME STRESS

The longer that severe stress continues, the more widespread and lasting the disturbance it causes. This happens all too often as a result of a man's inhumanity to man, for example, the torture of political prisoners or concentration camp experiences. Former inmates of Nazi concentration camps were studied twelve to twenty-five years after they were liberated.[28] Even after this long interval anxiety was still troublesome in nearly half the survivors, while the remainder had other problems. Anxiety was associated with nightmares and other sleep disturbances. Horrible memories of past events would be stirred up repeatedly and could not be discussed with closest friends or relatives. These memories would be triggered by the most harmless events; for example, seeing a person stretching his arms would revive memories of fellow prisoners hung up by their arms during torture; seeing an avenue of trees would be associated with rows of gallows with swinging corpses, a commonplace sight in the camps; children playing peacefully might suddenly call to mind other children, who had been emaciated, tortured, and murdered.

Two-thirds of the survivors reported psychological disturbances while they had been in the camps—severe chronic anxiety, tension, inner restlessness, despair, and severe depression. Anxiety was particularly experienced by those who had been in death cells for long periods or who had taken part in illegal organizations which had been exposed, resulting in execution of other participants. The more serious the cause of arrest, the greater was the likelihood of anxiety. Bombing attacks were terrifying for those locked in their cells while the bombs and buildings fell around them.

Anxiety which developed in prison or camp was associated with continued anxiety after release. The more severe the psychological or physical torture in the camp, the greater the subsequent disturbance. Symptoms of anxiety were actively disturbing in people up to a quarter of a century after the traumatic experiences.

SUMMING UP PART 1

Let us briefly review the ground we have covered so far, and then look ahead. We have seen that anxiety and fear, being normal responses to everyday worries, affect everybody. Mild anxiety can help us to be especially alert in carrying out tasks, and tension becomes troublesome only when it is extreme. In the extreme, tension may lead to many forms of handicap, and at that point it requires treatment in the shape of self-help or professional aid. Though people with severe fears or worries may need help, this does not mean they are crazy, just that they have a particular problem. Phobics go to great lengths to avoid the situations they fear, and there may be gross disproportion between the apparently trivial nature of the phobic stimulus and the extreme emotional reaction it produces. This disparity makes it hard for laymen to understand or sympathize with the sufferer. The result is that many phobics are ashamed of and conceal their fear, making it all the harder for them to learn how to overcome their difficulties.

Like other species, humans are preprogrammed to develop certain fears very readily, even without any traumatic experiences of them. At certain stages young children usually develop fears of sudden noise, movement, strangers, and animals. Most of us dislike being stared at, or being near the edge of a cliff, or being pricked or cut by a dentist or doctor. No one likes being separated from his or her loved ones, and their death is a pain we all have to bear eventually. Many people also have to endure calamities like fires, tornadoes, or floods. Fortunately the human spirit shows considerable resilience in the face of such adversity.

Up to this point we have dealt with worries which afflict most people. In the next section we will turn to more severe anxieties which bother only a minority and which often need treatment. Phobics have nothing to be ashamed of. Because you are afraid of dirt or the dark does *not* mean you are guilty about dirty thoughts or dark secrets which have to be uncovered before you can get well. There is no need to delve into the past to help somebody lose his worries. Usually, successful treatment requires the person to allow himself to approach those dreaded situations he has hitherto avoided and to remain exposed to them until he gets used to them; slowly but surely his anxiety will then reduce. To carry out this approach may require some ingenuity. We will use cases illustratively as we go along, and conclude with principles of self-help.

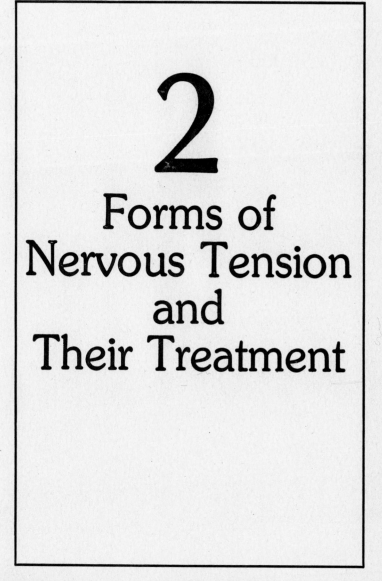

2
Forms of Nervous Tension and Their Treatment

4

Depressive Disorders and Anxiety States

The rest of this book will outline the different forms which severe worries can take and modern approaches to the treatment of anxiety. Some readers may have experience of one or another of the problems to be described. None of the problems need professional help unless they interfere with your life and you can't cope with them unaided. It can be helpful to know that you are not alone in your burden and that treatment is available. Many of the examples you will read about come from people who have been treated successfully by my colleagues or myself. Description of each type of problem will be followed by a glimpse of how it can be treated. In the final chapter, I will bring together the different strands into a general explanation of treatments which are used today and which you can learn to apply in coping with your own fears.

As we have seen, anxiety and fear are considered abnormal only when they are greater than the usual response to stress in a given culture and a handicap to a person in everyday life. When these problems become so bad, sufferers usually decide to ask for treatment. By then their problems are more marked, frequent, or persistent than is usual for them or for their peers. Anxiety and phobias occur in many psychiatric problems. Several of these problems have distinctive features that we call *syndromes.* A syndrome is simply a pattern of disturbances which tend to occur together over a period of time. Each pattern has special implications regarding cause and course of treatment, and so the labels are useful, although a cynic once quipped:

A group of symptoms unexplained you label a neurosis.
And this is rather clever, for you've made a diagnosis.[1]

The various syndromes differ with respect to their sex incidence, frequency, and age of onset. In psychiatric clinics more women than men complain of serious depression, yet anxiety states, social phobias, and obsessive-compulsive problems are found equally in both sexes. Depression is probably the most common psychiatric disorder, and anxiety states the next most common, while severe phobias and obsessions occur less often. Anxiety states were found in about 3 percent of people in America and Europe, while in Vermont disabling phobias were found in only 0.2 percent of people, though nearly 8 percent of those interviewed had milder phobias.[2] A sobering thought is that depressive disorders are more likely to commence and to increase in frequency as we get older. In contrast, anxiety states, phobias, and obsessions start more often in young adult life.

CAUSES OF NERVOUS TENSION

Depression has several well-known causes which may act together in varying combinations. There is a clear genetic contribution to severe depression, especially that of the manic-depressive type. Loss of a loved person, status, or ideal is a normal cause for gloom, which eventually clears up in most people, but in a few can go on to become a depressive illness. Those who lost parents when young or had childhoods which were emotionally deprived are especially vulnerable to such loss. Other factors making people susceptible to depression are severe life stresses, isolation, poverty, illness, and the unaided rearing of many small children.

This book concentrates on those types of anxiety not associated with severe depression, for example, anxiety states, phobic and obsessive-compulsive troubles, social and sexual disorders. In these conditions the genetic contribution is less clear than it is in depression, with research on twins finding that the genes play some role, though not a large one. Several of the various phobias tend to appear much more often at certain ages than at others, and the range of stimuli which can become the targets of phobias tends to be limited, presumably because of the biological boundaries of learning. As we have seen, many phobias are gross exaggerations of normal fears that we seem to be programmed as a species to experience.

What causes normal mild fears to become exaggerated into phobias is often a mystery. Sometimes depression can act as a trigger which starts phobias or obsessions. Occasionally trauma can begin the process. An overprotected childhood may increase the chances that phobias will develop, or rather that normal fears will not be extinguished naturally as time goes on. Parents and other relatives with phobias and obsessions can by their example pass them on to other members of the family, though the passing on of phobias from one person to another is less common than one might have supposed. Certain subcultures pass on particular taboos and fears, as we know all too well from the sexual anxieties of various religious and ethnic groups.

One important point has emerged from recent research. There is no need to look for hidden origins to phobias and obsessions. They do not point to dark, unconscious secrets which have to be uncovered for treatment to succeed. The anxieties can be cleared by working on the assumption that the sufferer needs to get used to the situation which troubles him, without any need to reconstruct his personality.

Let us look now at the various patterns of disorder in which anxiety can be a troublesome feature in adults.

DEPRESSIVE DISORDERS

Anxiety commonly occurs in depressive states and rises and falls with other features characteristic of depression. Depression can vary from brief spells of moodiness, which nearly everyone has at some time, to serious illness, which can lead to suicide. There is a genetic contribution to severe depression. In one form of the disorder sufferers can fluctuate from periods of mania, when they feel euphoric, on top of the world, able to do anything, to the opposite world of despair and utter dejection. More commonly there are only depressive spells, of varying durations and degrees of gloom. One optimistic feature of depressive disorders is their natural tendency to improve without any treatment, although there is the chance that there will be other depressive periods some time in the future, but with long periods of normality in between. Another positive feature is that though depression is common, it is also fortunately one of the most treatable conditions in psychiatry. We will deal with this treatment in Chapter 11.

People with depression tend to be gloomy, cry often, have difficulty sleeping, lose their appetite, feel guilty about things they may have done, reproach themselves unnecessarily, feel suicidal, and lose all enjoyment or pleasure in previously satisfying activities. Depressed people often imagine that they have cancer, heart trouble, or many other diseases. They may show great agitation and pace up and down, wringing their hands in trembling apprehension.

ANXIETY STATES

Anxiety state , or anxiety neurosis, is the next common syndrome in which anxiety is found in psychiatric patients. This syndrome is a cluster of symptoms based on anxiety, the source of which is not recognized by the patient. The anxiety may be chronic and sustained, but more usually comes and goes, each episode lasting a few minutes to hours or days. The chief complaint may be of intermittent attacks of panic; spells of choking, smothering, or difficulty in breathing; palpitations; rapid heart-beat; pain in the chest; nervousness; dizziness; faintness; a feeling of getting tired easily or of being irritable; or imagining the symptoms of heart trouble. Someone with these symptoms may run to different specialists for help, depending on the chief kind of complaint.

The most common feature is repeated episodes of anxiety coming out of the blue without any cause. The sufferer suddenly feels ill, anxious, weak, aware of his heartbeat, and light and dizzy in his head. He feels a lump in his throat and weakness of the legs, and he senses that he is walking on ground that is moving. It may seem to him that he cannot breathe properly, or he may overbreathe so much that he gets a sensation of pins and needles in his hands and feet. He fears that he may faint, or die, or scream out loud, or "lose control and go mad." His panic can become so intense that he may be rooted to the same spot for some minutes until the tension diminishes.

The anxiety attack may last a few minutes or several hours. It may pass off leaving the person feeling as fit as before until the next attack occurs the same day or weeks or even months later, or he may feel trembly throughout the day with the panic attacks appearing as periodic increases of this feeling. The attacks may occur only once in a few days, or come in successive waves every few minutes to become so troublesome that he is confined to bed. When these symptoms go on for long periods, they fluctuate so that there are periods when the person feels much better and other times when he gets worse again.

The intensity of the nervousness varies from paralyzing terror to mild tension. Some people are not even aware that they are anxious but simply complain of changes in their body due to anxiety, for example, that they sweat too much, that their hearts are fluttering in their chest, or that they can't take a deep breath. Anxiety may continue for long periods without being punctuated by discrete attacks of panic. Anxiety may be mixed with mild feelings of depression, desires to cry, and even occasional thoughts of suicide, but serious suicidal urges are not a feature of anxiety neurosis, unlike depressive disorders.

Breathing difficulties are common. The person may complain, "I can't get enough air" or "My breath keeps catching," and he may in fact show repeated catches in his breathing. He may also show the opposite problem of overbreathing. He may have choking and swallowing feelings which get worse in crowds, so that he has to open a window in crowded places.

There may be chest discomfort, including pain over the region of the heart, an awareness that the heart is beating, pressure over the upper abdomen, feelings of gas around the heart. With intense anxiety, there may be desires to pass urine or feces and thus the need to be constantly in reach of a toilet. Severe tension may also lead to nausea and vomiting; this can give rise to secondary fears of vomiting when one is in public places, and so the victims of anxiety attacks will eventually avoid such situations. They may lose their appetite, cease eating, and then lose weight. Occasionally they might have mildly loose stools.

People with this trouble may feel faint and dizzy, especially when walking or standing. These may lead them to feeling so insecure that they have to hold on to a nearby chair or walk close to the walls of nearby buildings. One man said, "I feel I am walking on shifting ground which is always falling or rising like the deck of a pitching and rolling ship."[3] A woman felt that "my legs are made of jelly and I'm walking on cotton wool."[4]

Acute feelings of choking, palpitations, and chest discomfort can accompany these symptoms and lead to fears of fainting, falling, having a heart attack, or dying. These feelings may be intensified in certain situations and lead to their avoidance. People anxious like this often avoid hot, crowded rooms or stores and will stay clear of a cinema, theater, hairdresser, or church, or if they do go to these places will sit near the end of the aisle to ensure that exit is possible with speed and dignity. Crowded streets, buses, and trains can become unendurable ordeals which bring on repeated attacks of panic, so that the sufferer may increasingly restrict his activities until he is virtually confined to his home. Strangely enough, such people often remain able to travel by automobile even when all other forms of transport are avoided and even when they may be unable to walk alone in the streets. The fears are often lessened by the presence of reassuring adults, so that someone may be able to do accompanied what is impossible alone. Sometimes the person may require company even at home, and husbands and wives may need to give up work and remain at home with their spouses.

Many people with these problems believe that they have heart disease or cancer. They may entreat their doctors repeatedly for reassurance on this score. In general such reassurance has but a transient effect, and many investigations don't convince the sufferer that doom is not around the corner. People with anxiety states are commonly very irritable, lose their tempers easily, snap at their spouses and children. They tire readily and find it hard to get through the day's work. Other complaints are of feeling strange or unreal, detached or far away from their surroundings. This feeling may come at the height of a panic, or at other times when there is no sensation of anxiety. Two contrasting case histories will show that anxiety states can strike people who previously have been quite calm and sociable, while in some persons they seem an exaggeration of a lifelong tendency to nerves.

The anxious mathematician

Let us look at a typical sufferer from an anxiety state, who previously had been well-adjusted.

A thirty-five-year-old mathematician complained of episodic palpitations [awareness of his heartbeat] and faintness over the previous fifteen years. There had been periods of freedom from these for up to five years, but in the past year his symptoms had increased and in the last few days he had stopped working because of his distress. At any time and without warning, he might suddenly feel he was about to faint and fall down, or tremble and experience palpitations, and if standing he would cringe and clutch at the nearest wall or chair. If he was driving a car at the time he would pull up to the curb and wait for the feelings to pass off before he resumed his journey. If it occurred during sexual intercourse with his wife he would immediately separate from her. If it happened while he was lecturing his thoughts became distracted, he could not concentrate, and he found it difficult to continue. He was becoming afraid of walking alone in the street or of driving his car for fear that the episodes would be triggered by it, and he was loathe to travel by public transport. Though he felt safer when accompanied, this did not abolish his complaints. Between attacks the patient did not feel completely well, and he remained slightly tremulous. The attacks would come on at any time of the day or night. He felt that he lacked energy but was not depressed and denied that he experienced any fear, anxiety, or panic during his attacks.

This man had had a happy childhood without nervous symptoms, led an active social life when free of his attacks, and had a contented marriage and vigorous professional life. No members of his family had had any psychiatric trouble.

During the interview, the patient gave a clear history of his problem but seemed unduly humble for a man of his achievements. His head and hands persistently trembled slightly and his palms were cold and sweaty. His heartbeat was fast. While his blood pressure was being measured he suddenly became very anxious, restless, and sweaty, and he would not lie down. He cringed when he stood up and immediately sat down, crying weakly "help, help." He tried to tear the blood pressure cuff off his arm, saying it was painful. After three to four minutes he calmed down again but wanted to remain sitting in an easy chair.

Over the next eighteen months this patient gave up driving alone or traveling by public transit, so that he stopped working. After treatment he managed to resume traveling and working. The episodes of free-floating anxiety which were not related to any particular situations persisted, though he felt better able to cope with them.[5]

The nervous administrator

Anxiety states can also manifest as an increase in anxiety which has already been present for most of a person's life. Another case illustrates this:

> A 52-year-old civil servant had been anxious all his life. As a child he had been timid and avoided rough fights and sports. Twice he had played truant from school when the school bully had threatened him. He did poorly in examinations, partly because he became very anxious in them. In oral exams he would stammer to a halt.
>
> His mother had been high-strung, and both his siblings had been treated for anxiety attacks during times of marital stress. As a young man the patient had been very shy but had fought against this by making himself do public speaking. He married when he was twenty-eight and worked as an administrative assistant. Any alterations in his routine threw him into a panic, and he would worry for days in advance over minor difficulties at work. He had visited his doctor many times over the previous twenty-five years and found that sedatives helped him over increases in his anxiety. The present episode had begun three months earlier when he had been given additional responsibilities at work and as examinations grew nearer.
>
> At an interview, this man complained of "all-pervasive feelings of anxiety," "tension in the neck," "palpitations, dry mouth, and sweating." He was treated by small doses of a sedative drug and by supportive interviews during which he learned to take a realistic view of his capabilities and shortcomings.[6]

Cultural aspects of anxiety

Anxiety states may be more common in certain cultural groups than in others. In Malaysia and Thailand psychiatrists see more Chinese than other groups with this problem. This may result partly from the marginal status of the Chinese in those societies.

Culture also affects how people express their anxiety. Among the Chinese of Southeast Asia, there is a strong belief that male genitals are essential for life, and semen is highly prized. The people have a folk saying that "100 grains of rice make a drop of blood, and 100 drops of blood make a drop of semen." Excessive sexual activity is regarded as unhealthy. Male Chinese with anxiety states commonly complain that they have lost semen, while in contrast Malay patients rarely have such worries.[7] (We should remember that until relatively recently in Britain and America, masturbation was regarded as a cause of insanity and countless adolescents went through agonies worrying about the consequences of their masturbation.)

The same worries about sexual activities also help us understand a curious phenomenon called *Koro*. This is a Malay word which describes a special form of acute anxiety affecting certain Chinese who have emigrated to other parts of Southeast Asia. The Chinese call the condition by a phrase which means "shrinking penis." Sometimes only one or two individuals in a community have this condition, but epidemics of such anxiety occur occasionally. The patient has acute panic in which he fears that his penis is shrinking into his abdomen, which might eventually kill him. To prevent this the penis is grasped by the patient or his relations and friends. Occasionally chopsticks or string are tied to the penis to prevent its retraction. Together with this acute fear, the patient is aware of his heartbeat; feels faint, breathless, and that he can't see properly; experiences pain in his body and tingling in his hands and feet; and may vomit. Strangely enough, Koro is sometimes seen in women, who complain of retraction of the nipples of their breasts or even of the vulva.

Not only industrial man is subject to worry. Anxiety about being bewitched was common enough in Medieval Europe, and a famous book called *The Hammer of Witches* was published as a detailed guide to the recognition of witchcraft. It includes a vivid description of how witches deprive men of their genitals. The terror of being under a spell is often found in preindustrial societies. An extreme form of this fear results in *voodoo death:*

somebody who thinks he has been "spelled" to death by pronouncement of a revered medicine man stops eating, goes into a decline, and literally lies down and dies within a few days. How this happens is still a mystery.

Anxiety is obviously not a privilege of Western man alone. A recent study of Australian aborigines living in primitive conditions showed that they have many physical complaints which are commonly found with anxiety, such as tiredness, inability to sleep, backache, and problems in breathing. The author has encountered the same kinds of agoraphobia, sexual worries, and obsessive-compulsive problems in India, Israel, Europe, North America, and South Africa. The pictures are similar whatever the race or religion. The main difference seems to be the language in which the anxieties are expressed.

Epidemics of acute anxiety

From time to time brief epidemics of acute anxiety sweep through some communities. These epidemics don't last very long and the sufferers aren't left with any lasting effects. Usually one can find some events beforehand which have led up to the epidemic. The form of the anxiety partly depends on the culture.

In Singapore one such epidemic took the form of Koro (imagined shrinking of the penis, occasionally seen in women concerning their nipples or vulva). In July 1967 there was an outbreak of swine fever in Singapore, and amid much publicity pigs were inoculated to control the outbreak. In October a few people complained of Koro and rumours spread that Koro could be caused by eating pork from infected or inoculated pigs. Over the next few days up to 100 cases of Koro a day appeared at general hospitals, and many more patients consulted their doctors. They worried that their genitals were disappearing into their bodies, and even attached wooden tongs to the penis to prevent this dreaded disorder. On the seventh day, at the height of the epidemic, a panel of experts appeared on television and radio, explaining to the public that Koro was psychological in nature and that it was impossible for the penis to retract into the abdomen. The day after this broadcast very few people complained of Koro, and the epidemic ended shortly after that. Most of the sufferers from this condition were southern Chinese and the great majority were male. Nearly all the sufferers recovered fully without any serious consequences.[8]

In Europe and America, epidemics of acute anxiety with overbreathing and faintness sometimes occur in young women, especially among those who are associated together in institutions, for example, schoolgirls and nurses. During such an epidemic in a girls' school in Britain two-thirds of 500 girls showed anxiety symptoms and one-third actually had to be admitted to the hospital. Many had repeated episodes.

The way in which this epidemic began was quite clear. Earlier in the year the town had received widespread adverse publicity during an epidemic of polio. Immediately before the epidemic of anxiety the schoolgirls went to a ceremony at which a member of the Royal Family was due. The ceremony was delayed by three hours because of late arrivals, and the girls waited in parade outside the building. Twenty of them felt faint and had to break ranks to lie down. The next morning there was much chatter about fainting. At assembly in school there was one faint, followed shortly after by three girls saying they felt dizzy. When a fourth girl was asked to get a glass of water for the original fainters, she said she felt faint. Over the next two periods more girls felt faint and were placed on chairs in the main corridor. A mistress thought that to prevent them falling from the chairs in a second faint they should lie on the floor. They lay thus in the corridor in full view at the midmorning break. The phenomenon now became epidemic. The chief complaints were excitement and fear leading to overbreathing and its consequences, faintness, dizziness, pins and needles in the extremities, and eventual cramps in the muscles of the arms and legs. Many of the girls looked alarmingly ill.

The epidemic began among the fourteen-year-olds and spread

to younger children. On the first day a quarter of the girls were affected. Each time school assembled, more cases appeared. The cases occurred during break twice as frequently as at any other time. However, by the twelfth day the nature of the epidemic was realized, and firm management prevented the problem from spreading further. The symptoms of anxiety slowly subsided over a few days.

SUMMING UP

When anxiety and fear exceed the usual response to stress and become a handicap, help is generally sought. Anxiety appears as part of many different patterns of psychiatric disturbances that we call syndromes or disorders. Depression is probably the most common problem, anxiety states the next common, and severe phobias and obsessions less frequent.

Nervous tension has many causes commonly acting together in varying degrees. These include heredity; loss of loved ones, status or ideals; and severe life stresses. The pattern of disturbance partly depends on age, and biological factors limit the range of stimuli which easily become the targets of fears. Trauma, overprotection by parents, and cultural taboos all influence the development of anxiety.

Depression can range from mild blues to serious illness and suicide and in one form can alternate with euphoria. Depressive illnesses usuall improve with time, and are eminently treatable. Anxiety states can be similarly fluctuating and might vary from mild tension to paralyzing attacks. Sufferers tend to attribute these to bodily problems. Accounts of how typical sufferers feel may remind you of your own difficulties. Anxieties are not restricted to modern societies but are also common in preindustrial peoples. At times short-lived epidemics of acute anxiety sweep through some communities, for example, fear that the penis is shrinking (Koro) among Southeast Asian Chinese, or episodes of overbreathing and faintness in Western young women. Intelligent and calm management can overcome these cultural waves of panics.

Anxieties discussed so far have no readily identifiable triggers. In the next few chapters we will look at phobias and similar problems which are cued by specific events.

5
Phobic Disorders:
Agoraphobia

A *phobia* is anxiety which is triggered by a particular situation. This situational anxiety is different from that of an anxiety state, which can occur without any obvious trigger and so is called free-floating anxiety. Phobias can occur in almost any situation, but in general some situations are more feared than others. Phobias may be minor complaints or handicapping disorders. We have already seen that they can occur as part of a depressive illness or an anxiety state. When phobias are the main problem that handicap a patient, we call the condition a phobic state or phobic disorder. Phobic states can occur in many forms—from an isolated fear in an otherwise healthy person to diffuse extensive fears occurring together with many other psychiatric problems.

AGORAPHOBIA

Agoraphobia, or phobic anxiety state, is probably the most common and distressing phobic syndrome which adult patients complain of. The word comes from the Greek root *agora,* meaning an assembly or marketplace, and was first used by a German psychiatrist, Westphal, a hundred years ago to describe the "impossibility of walking through certain streets or squares or possibility of so doing only with resultant dread or anxiety."

Today agoraphobia is still used to describe fears of going out into public areas such as streets, shops, or vehicles in variable combinations. At one extreme some people simply have a mild travel phobia or fear of closed spaces with no other problems. At the other extreme, people may not only have agoraphobia and other phobias but also much free-floating anxiety, depression, and many other difficulties.

The main features of agoraphobia are fears of going out into the open, into streets, shops, crowds, closed spaces such as elevators, theaters, cinemas, or church; of travel on underground trains, surface trains, buses or coaches, ships or airplanes (but not usually automobiles); fears of going onto bridges, into tunnels, having haircuts or hairdos, and of remaining alone at home or of leaving home. These fears occur in many combinations over a variable period of time and are commonly associated with other problems such as panic attacks, depression, obsessions, and feelings of being unreal.

Agoraphobia usually begins in adults between the ages of eighteen and thirty-five and for some unknown reason it is rare in childhood. Occasionally children who have severe phobias of going to school never improve in this regard and go on to show agoraphobia in adolescence. About two-thirds of agoraphobics are women. This statistic contrasts with those concerning anxiety states, which tend to occur equally in both sexes.

Agoraphobia often develops after some major upheaval in a person's life; for example, serious illness in oneself or a relative, acute danger or discomfort, leaving home, the death of a loved one, engagement, marriage, pregnancy, miscarriage, childbirth; or it may begin after an unpleasant scene in a shop, street, or bus. Agoraphobics often regard some trivial event as a trigger to the disorder even though such events might previously have occurred without undue trouble. Of course many other problems quite apart from agoraphobia can also start after some major calamity. Depression, schizophrenia, and even coronary thrombosis can be triggered by drastic changes in people's lives. Quite a few agoraphobics develop their agoraphobia without any obvious alteration in the circumstances in which they live.

Autobiographies of agoraphobics

It is instructive to read the autobiographies of agoraphobics who describe their problems. One such account comes from an American patient in 1890, whose agoraphobia began when he married at age 22.

> The first noticeable symptoms which manifested themselves were extreme nervous irritability, sleeplessness and loss of appetite. Any little excitement would throw me into a state of almost frenzy, so completely would I be overcome. Palpitation, spasmodic breathing, dilation of the eyes and nostrils, convulsive movements of the muscles, difficulty in articulation, etc., were the more prominent features. A sense of impending danger seemed to descend, spoiling every pleasure, thwarting every ambition. The dread of sudden death which was at first marked, gradually subsided, giving way more to a feeling of dread—not of dying suddenly—but of doing so under peculiar circumstances or away from home. I became morbidly sensitive about being brought into close contact with any large number of people. Finding myself in the midst of a large gathering would inspire a feeling of terror on my part. This could be relieved in but one way—by getting away from the spot as soon as possible. Acting on this impulse I have left churches, theatres, even funerals, simply because of an utter inability to control myself to stay. For 10 years I have not been to church, to the theatre, to political gatherings or any form of popular meeting, except where I could remain in the background, with means of egress convenient. Even at my mother's funeral, when it would be supposed that everything else would be subordinated to the impulses of natural affection, I was utterly unable to bring myself to sit with the other members of the family in the front of the Church. Not only has this unfortunate trait deprived me of an immense amount of pleasure

and benefit, but it has also been a matter of considerable expense. More than once I have got off a crowded train halfway to the station for which I was bound, merely from my inability to stand the jostling and confusion incident to the occasion. Times more than I can recall I have gone into restaurants or dining rooms, ordered a meal and left it untouched, impelled by my desire to escape the crowd. Times more than I recall I have bought tickets to theatres, concerts, fairs or whatnot, merely to give them away when the critical moment arrived and I realised the impossibility of my facing the throng with composure. To illustrate: I remember once going from Chicago to Omaha with my little boy. On entering the sleeper I found it crowded. I at once became ill-at-ease. As the train moved on I became more and more desperate, and finally appealed to the Conductor to know if I could possibly procure a section by myself. There was nothing eligible but a state-room. That I took, paying 10 dollars extra for it. Had it been 100 dollars and I had the money, I should have bought it without once counting the cost. . . .

[A fear of open spaces] has been at times very pronounced. Many a time I have slunk in alleys instead of keeping on the broad streets, and often have walked long distances—perhaps a mile—to avoid crossing some pasture or open square, even when it was a matter of moment to me to save all the time possible. The dominating impulse is to always have something within reach to steady myself by in case of giddiness. This feeling is at times so strong that even when on a steamboat or a vessel, I cannot bear to look across any wide expanse of water, feeling almost impelled to jump in out of sheer desperation. . . . This malady . . . has throttled all ambition, and killed all personal pride, spoiled every pleasure. . . .

. . . over this the will seems to have no control. At times buoyed up by stimulants or temporary excitement, I have faced situations which would ordinarily have filled me with extreme trepidation; but as a rule I have to yield or suffer the consequences. What those consequences would be, I do not know.[1]

Yet another autobiography illustrates how agoraphobia may gradually become increasingly restrictive as it spreads to different circumstances. Quite apart from the phobia itself there was a background of attacks of continual anxiety in this case.

> I am now in middle life and I have not seen a well day since I was about 12 years of age. Before I experienced any of the symptoms of agoraphobia I recall that . . . I was taken suddenly with "spells" which lasted about thirty minutes. During these attacks I was more liable to these attacks during times of excitement; for example, one of the worst attacks I ever had came over me while I was attending the funeral of a relative. . . . When my strange illness came upon me, I worried over it, fearing that I should die in one of the attacks. . . . [After a boy in the village was murdered] I almost feared to be alone, was afraid to go to the barn in the daytime, and suffered when put to bed in the dark. . . . During the months which followed . . . I experienced the first symptoms of agoraphobia. There was a high hill not far from my home in the country where we boys used to coast in the winter time. One evening, while coasting, in company with other boys in the neighborhood, I experienced an uncomfortable feeling each time we returned to the top of the hill. It was not a well defined symptom of this horrible . . . malady, but later experiences have taught me that it possessed the unmistakable earmarks. As the months went by I commenced having a dread of high hills, especially when the fields consisted of pasture land and were level with the grass cropped short like the grass on a well kept lawn. I likewise commenced to dread high things and especially to ascend anything high. I even had a fear of crowds of people, and later of wide streets and parks. I have outgrown the fear of crowds largely, but an immense building or a high rocky bluff fills me with dread. . . . Ugly architecture greatly intensifies the fear.
>
> The malady is always present. . . . I am conscious of it during every hour that I am awake. The fear, intensified, that comes over while crossing a wide street is an outcropping of a permanent condition.[2]

Most agoraphobias fluctuate a lot, sometimes, for no apparent reason. The same sufferer went on to describe this variability, clearly noting common tricks which helped his phobias—darkness, storms, changeable landscapes with a limited view, riding a bicycle, gripping a suitcase.

> At times my phobias are much more pronounced than at other times. Sometimes, after a strenuous day, on the following morning I find myself almost dreading to walk across a room; at other times I can cross the street without any pronounced discomfort. . . .
>
> Usually I feel better in the evening than in the morning, partly because the darkness seems to have a quieting effect on me. I love a snow-storm, a regular blizzard, and feel much less discomfort going about the town or riding on the train on such days, probably because one's view is obstructed. In fact, I welcome stormy days . . . on such days I make it a point to be out and about the town.
>
> I dread going on water in a boat, especially if the surface is smooth; I much prefer to have the waves rolling high. The most restful place in all the world for me is in a wood, where there is much variety in the trees and plenty of underbrush, with here and there little hills and valleys, and especially along a winding brook. . . . I love quiet, restful landscapes. . . . let the landscape be bold and rugged and bleak, and it strikes terror [into me]. . . .
>
> I ride a bicycle along the streets with comparative comfort where I should suffer agony were I to walk. In walking I feel least uncomfortable in passing along the street if I carry a suitcase or travelling bag—something to grip. . . . I have such a dread of crossing a long bridge on foot. . . .[3]

Much of the suffering caused by agoraphobia is hidden, since agoraphobics can conceal their disorder for long periods if they manage to hold down a job. Another autobiographical account was published after the sufferer had had this malady for forty-eight years. Only closest relatives and friends knew of the disability, and he continued as professor of English at a university during this time, living very close to the campus. The autobiography we have just read makes it clear that the sufferer never sought medical aid for his fears and led an active public life while concealing his disability.

Onset of agoraphobia

Many people have brief periods of agoraphobic symptoms which clear up after a few weeks or months without any special treatment. The onset can be sudden—within a few hours—or more gradual—over a few weeks—or slowly—over several years after an initial stage of vague intermittent anxiety. Some people start with an acute sustained panic, followed by phobias that cause them to remain confined to their homes within a few weeks. Others begin with vague fluctuating anxiety that gradually becomes agoraphobic in nature over many years. Many patients feel uneasy for decades about going about alone but dexterously manage to conceal their fears until the anxiety increases rapidly in new situations, when they seek treatment because the family cannot cope any longer. All kinds of variations between these two extremes are possible.

A girl of eighteen suddenly came home one day from her work as shop assistant and screamed that she was going to die. She spent the next two weeks in bed and thereafter refused to walk beyond the front gate of her home. She did not improve after four months in a psychiatric hospital and after discharge left her home only twice in the next seven years. She spent her time gossiping with neighbors, listening to the radio, and with a boy-friend by whom she had a child at the age of twenty-seven, though she continued to live with her mother. From the age of thirty-two until last seen at thirty-six she improved slowly and became able to go on short bus rides and shopping expeditions.[4]

Although this woman had wet and soiled her bed until the age of twelve, before her phobias started she was a good mixer, had many friends, and often went dancing. She was sexually frigid until she was thirty-two, after which she said she had normal orgasm with her boyfriend.

By way of contrast, agoraphobia developed very gradually in a girl of seventeen. She gradually developed fears of leaving home at seventeen, and these improved at twenty when she had psychiatric treatment. They became more marked after she gave birth, at age twenty-six, to a son, when she became afraid of meeting people and of getting lost in a crowd. For the next two years she was limited to traveling by bike or car to her mother's home one mile away, and thereafter she could not go beyond her own home and stopped all shopping. She improved when she was admitted to the hospital when she was twenty-nine, she became pregnant after discharge, and she made a further small improvement after her second child was born. For the next six years, until last seen, she was able only to do local shopping, to fetch her child from school, and to go out with her husband.[5]

She had always been a shy, dependent person who was dominated by her mother.

The panics of agoraphobia

Typically agoraphobia starts with repeated episodes of anxiety outside the home, of the kind already described for anxiety states. The panic can become so intense that the sufferer will be glued to the same spot for some minutes until the anxiety diminishes, after which he or she may just want to run to a haven of safety—a friend or one's home.

One woman described the panic clearly:

At the height of a panic I just wanted to run anywhere. I usually made towards reliable friends . . . from wherever I happened to be. I felt, however, that I must resist this running away, so I did not allow myself to reach safety unless I was in extremity. One of my devices to keep a hold on myself was to avoid using my last chance, for I did not dare to think what would happen if it failed me. So I would merely go nearer my [escape route] and imagine the friendly welcome I should get. This would often quiet the panic enough for me to start out again, or at least not to be a nuisance or use up any good will. Sometimes I was beaten and had to feel an acute shame and despair of asking for company. I felt the shame even when I hadn't to confess to my need.[6]

Once the panic attack is over the sufferer may be reluctant to return to the scene of the attack for several months.

The seizure of panic may go on for a few minutes to several hours. It can pass off leaving the person feeling as fit as before, and many months may go by before another such episode occurs. Episodes of panic can be followed by periods of normal activity, and a succession of panics may occur for years. Such episodes will lead the person to consult a doctor, who will not find anything abnormal except for some signs of anxiety. Eventually the agoraphobic, who is usually a woman will begin to avoid certain situations for fear that they might precipitate further panic. Because she cannot get off an express train immediately when a panic starts, she restricts herself to slow trains; when these too become the setting for a panic attack, she restricts herself to buses, then to walking, then just to walking across the street from home; finally she becomes unable to go beyond the front gate without a companion. Rarely, she may become bedridden for a while, as bed is the only place where she finds the anxiety bearable. Typically agoraphobics have periods when they feel much better and times when they feel much worse.

Conditions which affect agoraphobia

Agoraphobia fluctuates not only over time, but also with changes in the sufferers and in their environment. In the first full description of the problem a century ago, it was noted that the

agony was much increased at those hours when the particular streets dreaded were deserted and the shops closed. The subjects experienced great comfort from the companionship of men or even an inanimate object, such as a vehicle or a cane. The use of beer or wine also allowed the patient to pass through the feared locality with comparative comfort. One man

even sought, without immoral motives, the companionship of a
prostitute as far as his own door. . . . some localities are more
difficult of access than others; the patient [walked] far in order
not to traverse [the dreaded spaces]. . . . in one instance, the
open country was less feared than sparsely housed streets in
town. One case also had a dislike for crossing a certain bridge.
He feared he would fall into the water. In this case, there also
was apprehension of impending insanity.[7]

An agoraphobic usually feels easier in the presence of a trusted
companion, be it a human, animal, or inanimate one, and can
become dependent upon the relative, pet, or object for peace of
mind. Less commonly, agoraphobic persons may find it easier to
travel alone. Many become afraid of being left alone or in any
situation in which they cannot reach "safety" with speed and
dignity. Their need for constant company can strain relatives and
friends. Some tricks which people find useful include the grip of
walking sticks, umbrellas, suitcases, shopping baskets on wheels,
baby carriages, folded newspapers under the arm, a bicycle to
push rather than to ride, or a dog on a leash. Chewing gum or
strong sucking sweets in the mouth divert a few from their fears.
Deserted streets and vehicles are much preferred, and rush hour
is abhorred. Trains (and buses) are easier to go on if they are
empty, stop frequently at stations, and have a corridor and a
toilet. Some journeys are easier if they pass the home of a friend,
or a doctor, or a police station, when the patients feel that help is
at hand if they get panic-stricken. In such cases if the sufferer
knows the friend or doctor is not at home, the journey becomes
more difficult. It is the *possibility* of aid which helps such sufferers
in their acute anxiety before the journey. One patient was able to
go on a particular bus route because it passed a police station
outside which she would sit if the tension got too much for her.
Agoraphobics usually find it easier to travel by automobile than
any other way and may comfortably drive themselves many
miles even though they cannot stay on a bus for one stop.

Agoraphobics often feel easier in the dark, and move more

freely at night than in the daytime. Even wearing dark glasses can afford relief. Some sufferers also find that their fears improve during rain or storms and get worse during hot weather. A fear of heights is common, and agoraphobics prefer to live in a ground-floor apartment. This also avoids the need for elevators.

The nearer their home is to shops, friends, and helpful relatives, the easier their lives will be. They may ask for help in taking the children to and from school, or in getting to and from work. A patient may go to work if the place of employment is a short walk or bus ride away from home, but fail to manage if he has to cross a crowded main road or change buses in order to get there. He may find it easier to work at his own pace in a quiet room with a few other workers present rather than as part of a chain of workers or busy assembly line which requires split-second efficiency.

If agoraphobics go to a cinema, theater, or church they feel less frightened in an aisle seat near the exit so that they can make a quick getaway if seized by sudden panic. A telephone at hand to call a trusted person can afford similar relief and reduce their social isolation.

One phobic correspondence club jokingly put all these features together in a popular figure called Aggie Phobie—a woman walking at night up a dark alley in the rain while wearing dark glasses, sucking sweets vigorously in her mouth, with one hand holding a dog on a leash, the other trundling a shopping basket on wheels.

Quite a few other tricks have been helpful to different people. An agoraphobic man had to remove his belt whenever he had an anxiety attack; a woman had the urge to rid herself of all clothing when she panicked, could wear only garments which could be closed in front by zippers, and had to carry a pair of scissors and a bottle of beer in her purse when she left home. An army officer who felt anxious in crossing a square when in civilian clothes felt much better when he wore his uniform with his saber at his side. A man with a fear of crowds was able at times to face them when he clutched a bottle of ammonia in his hands in case he felt he was about to faint. A clerk also afraid of crowds carried a bottle of sedatives in his pocket, though he hadn't taken them for years; the bottle functioned as a magic talisman.

Minor changes in the view can also affect the intensity of agoraphobia. Usually the wider and higher the space walked in, the greater the fear. If a view can be interrupted by trees, or rain, or irregularities in a landscape, the phobia lessens. One agoraphobic felt anxious during a party on a private lawn and would have been relieved if he could have broken down the surrounding fence. A clergyman felt dizzy as soon as he went into the open, but he obtained relief by creeping around hedges and trees or, as a last resort, by putting up his umbrella.

Certain agoraphobics hate being confined in a barber's or dentist's chair or at the hairdresser because they cannot escape immediately. Somebody actually called this "the barber's chair syndrome." Again, because of the difficulties in making an immediate exit, some people may be unable to take a bath in the nude. While standing in the street or on a railway platform the agoraphobic may feel drawn to jump beneath an approaching bus or train and therefore have to look away from the oncoming vehicle. This fear is related to the impulse normal people often have to jump when looking down from a great height, a fear which is also found in some agoraphobics and is countered by withdrawal from the edge of such heights or by avoiding them completely. Fears of bridges are similar, especially long narrow bridges with open sides high above a river. Let there be a waist-high parapet between the agoraphobic and the edge of the cliff or bridge and the fear is diminished.

The fear of fear can be quite crippling. For weeks before a planned journey an agoraphobic may die a thousand deaths from anticipatory anxiety. Let the same journey be sudden and unexpected and she can do what she cannot do if forewarned. She might board a bus if she does not have to wait for it at the stop, but should there be any delay, panic rapidly builds up and prevents her from boarding the vehicle when it finally arrives.

Any stress can increase agoraphobia. A common event is depression, during which time the patient's phobias can become quite crippling. When the depression clears, the phobias improve again to their previous level of disability. Tiredness and physical illness make agoraphobia worse. So does confinement of the patient to bed, since this results in loss of practice at going out and makes it harder for the patient to resume her former activities when she gets up again.

As with any anxiety, alcohol and sedative drugs can give a lot of relief for a few hours. With the help of drugs sufferers can temporarily break new ground, but usually the effect wears off after the drug has been excreted. Patients often find it helpful to keep a stock of sedatives which they take shortly before a journey or some other anticipated stress. A small minority eventually get addicted to barbiturates or alcohol, but most people manage to stop the drugs or alcohol once their anxiety has gone.

Intense emotion sometimes arouses agoraphobics to activity for a while. They manage to go out again when they are intensely angry or during emergencies; for example, if there is a fire in the house they will jump through the window rather than be burned.

Impact on the family

Most agoraphobics live with their families. As their restrictions increase, the family inevitably becomes involved. More women than men have agoraphobia, and so the usual burden is on husbands, but wives of agoraphobic husbands suffer equally. Agoraphobics may require an escort to and from work or may have to give up their work; the spouse and children have to do the shopping; social activities become restricted or abandoned. A constant companion may be needed if the person cannot remain at home without anxiety. Even a child may be kept from school or a spouse from work, simply to keep the agoraphobic company. One woman had arranged her life so fearfully that she had never been left alone more than a few minutes over sixteen years of marriage, to the great inconvenience of her husband and daughter. When a patient drives a car, the disability may remain hidden for a long time, as even severe agoraphobics can feel safe in an automobile despite distress with any other form of travel. If the agoraphobic's work can be done at home and there is help, again the agoraphobia can be concealed for years. However, the restrictions to the patient's activities can cause many arguments between husbands and wives.

The role of willpower

Anything which heightens motivation can increase the phobic's level of tolerance for as long as the motivation continues. The limits of tolerance fluctuate readily in many circumstances; in an acute emergency, for example, an accident, patients can temporarily overcome their phobias and venture forth. Once the emergency subsides, the phobia reappears in its original form. A Viennese Jewish woman could walk only a few blocks from her home in Vienna. When the Nazis came to power she had the choice to flee or be placed in a concentration camp. She fled, and for the following two years traveled halfway around the world until she arrived in the United States. After she settled in New York City, she developed the same phobia of travel she had in Vienna.[8]

The fluctuating nature of agoraphobia makes it difficult for family and friends to accept that it is a disorder and not the result of laziness, lack of willpower, or a way of getting out of awkward situations. They often say that if the patient can master her phobias in an emergency, then she simply needs to exert herself more when there is no emergency, and so she just needs to be forced to go out. In fact nobody can be expected to muster his energies so as to treat every minor shopping expedition as he would a fire in the house. It is not only agoraphobics who can perform unexpected feats in an acute crisis. It is hard to demand such feats constantly of everybody as a matter of routine, and in an agoraphobic who has much anxiety, any minor sally outside the house requires great effort, trivial as it would be for the average person.

When there is a lot of free-floating anxiety and depression, agoraphobics find it particularly difficult to exercise their will-power. One woman of thirty-one described this state:

> I could barely get myself to the office or stay in it until it was time to go. I was always exhausted, always cold; my hands were clammy with sweat; I cried weakly and easily. I was afraid to go to sleep; but I did sleep, to wake with a constricting headache, dizziness, and tachycardia. To these now familiar symptoms were added waves of panic fear followed by depression. The panics almost overwhelmed me. I felt very much more frightened when I was alone and but little less frightened with other people. There were only three with whom I felt at all safe and able to relax, though even with them I was behind the screen of my fears.[9]

Once an agoraphobic feels reasonably comfortable away from the public places which evoke anxiety, it becomes easier to go out repeatedly to try and conquer the phobic situation. Sometimes she discovers by accident that she can in fact go out again. One woman had a modified lobotomy operation for severe agoraphobia and felt more relaxed thereafter, but she remained confined to her home for a year out of habit. By accident one afternoon a friend who had just visited left a handkerchief behind. The patient rushed into the street to return the handkerchief and to her surprise felt quite relaxed in the street she had previously dreaded; she proceeded systematically to do more and more, and remained relatively well four years later.

It is clear that high motivation or willpower is not enough to cure this disorder, but it is an asset to any agoraphobic, as it is in any disability. It can be of the greatest value once anxiety and depression have subsided. The trick is to reduce anxiety to a level that is low enough for the individual's willpower to allow him to complete his own treatment.

TREATMENT OF AGORAPHOBIA

In recent years effective behavioral treatments have been developed for the lasting relief of phobias. Unlike older psychoanalytic treatments, this approach does not explore the patient's unconscious fantasies. There is no search for hidden meanings. Details of the frightening situations are carefully elicited to plan the patients' reentry into them so that she can learn to develop tolerance instead of dread. Most behavioral methods use some way of persuading the phobic to enter and stay in her phobic situation until she feels better and to do this repeatedly so much that she becomes thoroughly used to it and it holds no more terrors for her. The principle behind these various methods is *exposure* of the phobic to her situation until she becomes accustomed to it. As we go along we will see how this principle is applied to the treatment of each kind of problem. This will prepare you for the detailed approach to treatment given in Part 3 of this book. Let us look, then, at the treatment of two agoraphobics.

Jean was a married woman of forty who had been agoraphobic for fifteen years and in the past year had not been able to leave her house without her husband. Before starting treatment she agreed with her therapist that there were two main targets she wished to achieve by the end of treatment, that is, crossing a moderately busy street alone and shopping in small shops nearby without crossing streets.

Treatment began with her therapist taking her to the road just outside the hospital and helping her across. They repeated this several times, the therapist gradually leaving her side, staying first a few yards away and then further away while she did the crossing on her own as he watched. By the end of the first 1½-hour treatment session Jean was very pleased and surprised with her own performance and at how much calmer she felt compared with the first time she had crossed the road. She was asked to practice crossing roads of similar traffic density near her home before she attended the next session. The following session she made similar trips outside the hospital, but this time more of them alone and further from the hospital. She reported that she still panicked in streets and held on to people, and during lunchtime at work a friend helped her cross the road. She was asked now to go to work and return by bus alone instead of relying on lifts from people. She and the therapist worked out a program of longer walks and bus journeys to complete between sessions. By the end of the eighth session Jean was shopping regularly alone on nearby streets without anxiety and had improved in crossing moderately busy streets. Jean was discharged at this stage but was asked to continue to set herself targets to accomplish and to return six months later for follow-up. Her improvement continued at follow-up and she became able to do even more things alone.[10]

Using the method of steady exposure to the actual frightening situation, agoraphobics can usually improve within ten sessions. Sometimes treatment can take longer. John was a fifty-eight-year-old professional man in a very responsible position. For twenty-five years he had been agoraphobic and driven to drink by his anxiety, so that his executive job was in serious danger. He found it impossible to get even beyond the gates of the hospital alone, and whenever he walked in open places he carried a heavy bag to "anchor" him to the ground. He found it very difficult to travel on underground trains or buses, to visit crowded places, to drive in a car over an overpass, to walk on the pavement with traffic passing him, or to climb stairs. This hampered his professional work, which required visits to clients and lectures.

John was treated by a nurse specially trained in the treatment method. First they agreed on five targets to achieve in treatment: using a stairway to the third floor in buildings, traveling by train, visiting any crowded place, walking along a narrow road with cars passing by, and driving over an overpass. At the start of treatment the nurse accompanied John beyond the gates of the hospital into a neighboring road; he often clung to the railings or rushed into the bushes, perspiring profusely. However, he became accustomed to this task and his walking boundary extended steadily further from the hospital toward a neighboring village. His first nine sessions concerned his walking toward and around the local village, which he gradually did without the nurse and with decreasing anxiety.

His problem with heights was then tackled. He was initially stationed up a stairway in a hospital building; this caused him great unease, but with the nurse's coaxing he stayed there. As he learned to endure this height, he was coaxed onto a higher and steeper staircase in an adjoining building. He gradually attained confidence in dealing with heights. The seventeenth session involved further stairs in public buildings and then a bridge which crossed a busy road near a train station. John found this almost intolerable; once they had to stop the session when the patient clung to the nurse in panic, frightened that passersby were looking at him. At the next session the nurse persisted gently in helping him get used to the bridge across the road, with increasing success. John then agreed to go across the footbridge across the river Thames, at first getting no further than ten yards. In the early phase of treatment, John had not completed the "homework" between sessions that the nurse-therapist had asked him to do, but now he cooperated increasingly in performing tasks set for him between sessions. He drove as instructed twice daily across an overpass, traveled by train, and visited busy streets and shopping centers alone as instructed by the nurse. Although frequently tempted to return to alcohol, he refrained from it and was praised by the nurse and his family for his efforts.

By the end of treatment he was well enough to be discharged from the hospital and returned to live at home while continuing to treat himself. John went alone to sit in empty lecture theaters and then attended actual lectures, first in a seat from which he could escape easily and then in the front where it was hardest to leave. He often feared he would disgrace himself by interrupting the lecture, but these episodes of panic gradually died down. He then resumed attending the conferences required by his work and reported that he was almost completely at ease in them. He kept in touch with the nurse-therapist regularly by phone. A year after discharge he was very much better, was back at productive professional work, had resumed all his former responsibilities, and had not touched alcohol. He had traveled hundreds of miles by train, had been with his wife regularly to parties, movies, theater, concerts, and professional meetings, and had lectured at a night school. His wife was most pleased with his progress.[11]

Using these methods of exposure, which will be described later in more detail, agoraphobics (and their families) can generally be helped to lead a more normal life in from four to fourteen sessions. The treatment can call for considerable effort from the patient and the therapist, but the improvement is usually worthwhile and lasting, even though some anxiety may remain.

In a program of treatment it is wisest to start with those activities which will help one resume normal work and social life. With progress, the tasks can be made more difficult. It is usually easier to enter phobic situations first in the presence of a reassuring person, and then alone and preferably when crowds of people are not expected. If phobics wish to practice going on a bus or train, they can avoid rush hour travel at the start, choosing trains or buses which stop frequently so that they feel free to get out whenever they wish. Then they can progress to more difficult tasks. In a cinema, theater, or church for the first time they will be more relaxed sitting on an aisle seat near an exit; as they get used to such places they can seat themselves in a more central position from which it is less easy to escape with speed and dignity.

SUMMING UP

When specific situations trigger anxiety, we speak of a phobia. Some phobias can be very mild, while others are socially crippling. The most common phobic syndrome seen by psychiatrists is agoraphobia, denoting fear of going into public places. This usually starts in young adult life, and two-thirds of sufferers are women. Regular features of agoraphobia include fluctuating fears of going into streets, shops, crowds, public transport, and places of entertainment. Entering these situations leads to extreme panics similar to those seen in anxiety states; sufferers then avoid these situations and may become totally housebound. As a result, family life is often severely restricted. Agoraphobia can strike out of the blue. More often it comes on in stages. It seems to fluctuate not only over time, but also with many other events; for example, it is usually less bad with a trusted companion and in places from which the sufferer can leave quickly without fuss.

We have seen examples of how agoraphobics can be treated by allowing themselves to be exposed to their dreaded situation and in remaining there until they become accustomed to it, a process which usually takes several hours. This is the central therapeutic principle of exposure, and applies equally to all forms of phobias. In the next few pages you will see how exposure treatments work in cases of social phobias, after learning what it is like to have such phobias.

6

Phobic Disorders:
Social and
Illness Phobias

SOCIAL PHOBIAS

Most people are often slightly anxious in social situations. This is perfectly normal; even prominent public figures have a slight fluttering in their chests before major public appearances. A little anxiety is often regarded as better than none at all since it can help keep the person alert and on his toes. It is only when the fear of social occasions becomes too great that it begins to disrupt activity. Hippocrates is said to have described someone who "through bashfulness, suspicion, and timorousness, will not be seen abroad; loves darkness as life and cannot endure the light or to sit in lightsome places; his hat still in his eyes, he will neither see, nor be seen by his good will. He dare not come in company for fear he should be misused, disgraced, overshoot himself in gesture or speeches, or be sick; he thinks every man observes him. . . ."[1]

Unlike most other phobias, which are more common in women, social phobias tend to occur as often in men as in women. Most of these begin between the ages of fifteen and twenty-five, as does agoraphobia. Generally they develop slowly over a number of months or years with no obvious cause. A small number do begin suddenly after triggering events, as with a

young man at a dance who felt sick at the bar and vomited before
reaching the toilet, making an embarrassing mess. Thereafter he
became afraid of going to dances, bars, or parties.

Many persons complain of phobias in a variety of social situations, the fears being of the people themselves or what they
might think, rather than of a crowd en masse in which the people
who make it up seem anonymous. Agoraphobics often have a
fear of crowds, but usually this is a fear of being crushed or
enclosed or suffocated by the crowd rather than a fear of being
seen or watched by people in the crowds. Most social phobics are
a bit different in that they are very conscious of being observed
and are able to do certain things only as long as nobody is
watching them. A glance from someone else will precipitate a
pang of panic.

Social phobias of this kind are not uncommon. Sufferers may
be afraid of eating and drinking in front of other people; the fear
may be that their hands will tremble as they hold their fork or
cup, or they may feel nauseous or have a lump in their throat and
be unable to swallow so long as they are watched. As one person
said, "When I go out to eat in strange places I cannot eat, my
throat feels a quarter of an inch wide, and I sweat." The fear is
usually worse in smart crowded restaurants and less in the safety
of the home, but a few phobics even find it impossible to eat in
the presence of their spouse alone. Such people become unable
to go out to dinner or to invite friends home because they are
afraid that their hands will tremble when drinking coffee or
handing a cup to a friend. Social life may then become very
restricted.

For fear of shaking, blushing, sweating, or looking ridiculous
some affected persons will not sit facing another passenger in a
bus or train, nor walk past a waiting line of people. They are
terrified of attracting attention by behaving awkwardly or fainting.
Some may leave their house only when it is so dark or foggy that
they cannot easily be seen. They will avoid talking to superiors,
and stage fright will prevent them from appearing in front of an
audience. They may cease swimming as it involves exposing their

bodies to the gaze of strangers. They will avoid parties and be too embarrassed to talk to people. "I can't have normal conversation with people. I break out in a sweat, that is my whole problem even with the missus," said a man who could nevertheless still have normal sexual relations with his wife.[2] In some people, the fear appears only in the presence of members of the opposite sex, but more usually it happens equally in front of men and women.

Social phobics are often afraid to write in public and so will not visit a bank or shop because they are terrified their hand will tremble when writing a check or handling money in front of someone else. For fear of shaking, a secretary may become unable to take shorthand dictation or to type; a teacher may stop writing on a blackboard in front of a class and cease reading aloud; a seamstress will stop sewing in a factory; an assembly line worker will find it impossible to perform the actions necessary for assembling a product. Harmless activities like knitting or buttoning a coat can induce agonizing panic when done in front of other people.

Generally the fear is that their hands or heads *might* shake, yet it is rare for such patients to actually tremble or shake so that their writing becomes a scrawl, their coffee cup rattles against the saucer, soup is spilled when they raise the soup spoon to their lips, or their head nods visibly when talking. Such people make a striking contrast to patients who have illnesses of the brain which actually cause them to shake quite vigorously but unselfconsciously. Patients who have Parkinson's disease, for example, often show prolonged repeated nodding of the head and shaking of their hands, yet they have no fear of doing anything in public despite this disability.

Vomiting phobias

Some people have a fear that they might vomit in public or that they may see other people vomiting. Usually this should not cause much incapacity, but in some social phobics this fear reaches such proportions that they avoid any situation which is remotely likely to provoke vomiting in themselves or in others, for example traveling on a bumpy bus or coach, going on a boat, or eating onions.

The following woman is fairly typical of a social phobic.

A secretary with a fear of vomiting

A thirty-four-year-old unmarried secretary had had a fear of vomiting for the past thirteen years.

> As a child my mother wasn't able to help the kids when they vomited and instead would ask my father to clean up the mess. I can remember being upset by other children vomiting when I was only about five years old, but did not develop the phobia until much later, at the age of twenty-one. At that time I became afraid that other people or I myself would vomit on the train, so I began avoiding traveling to some places. This fear has got worse over the last five years. I wake at 5:15 A.M. daily in order to travel to my office in the City before the rush hour. With a great effort I might rarely manage to return during rush hour. Over the last two years I've drunk a bottle of brandy a week to calm my fear of traveling, and also take sedative pills at times. I'm worried that I have to drink ever larger amounts of brandy. In the last five years I've avoided eating in public places, in restaurants, or in strangers' homes. I've also stopped going to theatres with friends if I can help it because it's easier to leave the theatre if I'm alone when I get this awful fear of vomiting. The funny thing, though, is that I've never vomited in a public place nor have I seen anybody else vomit for many years.[3]

When alone, the patient had no anxiety and was not depressed. She did her work well.

After treatment she became able to eat out in restaurants both by herself and in company without undue anxiety. She resumed travel in crowded subway trains and enjoyed mixing with people more than before.

Phobic Disorders: Social and Illness Phobias

A mother who dreaded vomiting

A mother of forty-six had suffered all her life from a fear of vomiting or other people vomiting.

> I am unable to mix with people as I constantly fear that they might be sick. My life is so restricted that I often take sleeping tablets in the afternoon as the days seem so terribly long. My only daughter is pregnant and has been vomiting almost ceaslessly over the last ten weeks. I go down and sit with her, but nobody knows the terrible fear and strain I feel. When she is vomiting I go out in the garden or turn up the radio (it seems to be the sound of sickness I am so frightened of) and have often wished that I would go stone deaf. I don't take sleeping tablets for the sake of sleep, but so that for a few hours I am released from my constant fear. Although I sleep with earplugs in, a sudden cough or movement from my husband is enough to make me start up sweating and trembling because I think it might be sickness.[4]

Intense feelings can sensitize a person to develop such a fear. Fears of trembling in public began for the first time in one young woman at her wedding service while she was walking up the church aisle with her father, wondering if her future husband was really good enough for her. The fear increased shortly afterward when her husband was in the hospital with tetanus and she went to a restaurant to eat alone after visiting him.

Some social phobics are not only afraid of social situations but are anxious and depressed at other times as well. Some of these cases are similar to quite severe agoraphobia; for example, consider the following:

A typist with depression and social phobias

A twenty-year-old unmarried typist had had social phobias for the previous three years which caused her to reduce her social activities. In the previous year she had not been out alone except to travel to work, and since stopping working two months previously she had not been out anywhere alone. She had to come to the hospital with her mother. She was afraid of people looking at her, of herself shaking while drinking in public, of walking out in public, or of any social situation. In addition to the social fears, even when she rested at home she was continually on edge, shaky and restless, and occasionally had panic attacks superimposed on this background of anxiety without any obvious trigger. She was free of tension only when she had alcohol or sedative drugs. In addition she had been depressed and wanting to cry at times over the previous two years.

Lack of self-assertion, shyness

Although one might not think so from the amount of violence reported in newspapers and on television, lack of self-assertion is a common complaint even in people who are otherwise well-adjusted. This lack creates problems when people become afraid of accepting promotion at work and lead more restricted lives than they need to. For instance, one young man had always been shy since childhood, but this became worse when at eighteen he was beaten up by some youths after an argument in a dance hall. He worked long hours in a garage and was so well thought of that he was offered the position of manager. He declined this promotion because he felt he could not assert himself sufficiently with his juniors. Nevertheless he could be quick-tempered at home and was more assertive with his wife than with other people. He had a happy sex life.

It is difficult to know at what point one calls shyness in particular situations a social phobia. When it is very pronounced in certain kinds of situations, the label *phobia* seems justified.

Extreme shyness can prevent people from making friends and can lead to great loneliness and social isolation. Lots of people lead very confined lives because they are afraid of making contact with other people; they worry that they might seem foolish, that they look silly, and so never make the first move that could bring them companionship. Such persons might tread a lonely path between their work in an uninteresting office where they keep to themselves and a room in lodgings where they speak to nobody but spend their time reading or watching television and going for solitary walks. In a few persons a fear of other people or a lack of social skills can lead them to become complete hermits—shut up, isolated, and unemployed in a dark room, living on a pittance from social security. Worry about contact with other people might even lead them to close their windows with blinds or dark curtains so that nobody can see inside. This degree of disability is also found sometimes in schizophrenics who have paranoid delusions that they are being persecuted and spend their time hiding away from imagined oppressors.

Worries about one's appearance

Worry about one's appearance can lead to handicaps rather similar to those of other social anxieties. Many of us think we are too fat or too thin, too short or too tall, and might be sensitive about the shape of our ears or our baldness. Women may think they are too flat-chested or too bosomy. However, most people learn to cope with the body they were born with, and some famous actors and singers even make a virtue of their huge nose or grotesque fat, turning these into an amusing and profitable trademark of which they are proud. An unfortunate minority seem unable to accept their appearance and spend endless hours preoccupied with minor or imagined defects.

One young man thought that his nose was bent, a fact not evident even to the keenest observer. So sensitive was he about it that he had not used public transportation for a year nor been on a vacation and had given up his friends. So anxious was he about the topic that it was only with great difficulty that he could be persuaded to write and say sentences like "My nose is ugly" as part of his exposure treatment.

Another man was concerned that his hair was falling out and developed the idea that if he didn't look at his reflection in the mirror his hair would not fall out. Gradually he became frightened of looking in mirrors or at photographs of himself and he became unable to put his own hand on his scalp because he thought other people scorned his appearance. He withdrew from company and became a loner.

Plastic surgeons have waiting lines of would-be patients who want to have their noses made smaller or bigger or straightened, or to have their bat ears retracted, or the excess rolls of fat removed from their bellies. When the defect is obvious to observers, some benefit might be gained from surgery to produce a more normal appearance. All too often, however, the physical defect is either invisible or so minute as not to seem worth bothering about; under such circumstances no surgery can help, and the patient has to become reconciled with his discomforting idea about himself and to test himself out as he is. Anxiety about one's body might not only be about its appearance but also about its odor. Occasionally some unfortunates begin to think that they smell excessively, however much they wash and use deodorants, and so they begin to avoid going out in company and gradually become more and more of a recluse.

Worries about one's body are related to those of illness. Concern about a little red spot on one's hand can become the focus of an idea that one has cancer, or a mark on the penis can trigger off fears of venereal disease. Worries about illness will be dealt with shortly.

A variant of social anxieties involves hearing rather than seeing people. Phobics of this sort may be scared of going through a door if voices can be heard on the other side or of answering a knock on the door. Occasionally people get worried about using the telephone. "I have a fear of answering the telephone so much," said one woman, "that I have a code with my husband and children so that if the phone rings I know it is them. If it is anyone else, I cannot answer the phone. I used to be able to when I was working because I knew then it would be about business, but I am frightened at home."[5]

Difficulty in using a telephone has led sufferers to give up their job as secretaries. The fear can be that one might stammer on the telephone, and the same worry can be aroused by having to ask for fares when traveling or ordering meals from a menu in a restaurant.

TREATMENT OF SOCIAL ANXIETIES

As with agoraphobics, the treatment is usually conducted on an outpatient basis and does not require admission to a hospital. The approach to the treatment of social fears is similar to that of agoraphobia in that the phobic is encouraged to actively enter the situation he fears and stay there until he feels better. Let us see how this was applied in the case of a young woman, Emma.

Emma was a single twenty-six-year-old secretary who for seven years had been anxious when she had to eat or drink in company. It began when she was working in a busy office. After a friend mentioned how she had felt nervous taking tea to her boss, Emma was asked to take tea to a group of accountants. Emma panicked and the group laughed at her. Thereafter she avoided eating and especially drinking in public. She was even uneasy drinking tea or coffee in the office with her friends. When Emma attended a social event like a meal with her friend, she could make the anxiety bearable only by having a stiff drink of vodka beforehand, and during the meal or a party would nip out to the ladies' room with a concealed half-bottle. Public places where she was not expected to drink, for example, the cinema, did not bother her.

She was treated over six sessions, always being persuaded to do those things of which she was frightened. During treatment sessions with her therapist, she drank coffee in a busy cafe for thirty minutes, then soft drinks in a moderately busy pub, and thereafter soft drinks in a very busy pub. At the end of that session, her therapist allowed her one alcoholic drink.

Between sessions Emma was asked to attend a restaurant every day for lunch and coffeehouses each afternoon, and to stay there until her anxiety had diminished. On her final (sixth) treatment session she was asked to spend 2½ hours making trays of tea and coffee in a hospital outpatient department and to carry these to staff and patients all over the building. She found this difficult at first, but it became easier as time wore on. Shortly after this she made her first panic-free visit to pubs and parties with friends. Her self-confidence soared, her spirits rose, and she no longer avoided any special situations. When last seen at six-month follow-up, she retained her improvement.

Exposure treatment—role playing

Sometimes treatment can be a bit more complicated when "role playing techniques" have to be used, as in the case of Pat. She was a nineteen-year-old office worker with social fears for four years. Pat was markedly anxious if she visited people in their homes and could not eat a meal with them. She could eat a meal in a restaurant or office cafeteria when alone but not while sharing the table with someone else. She had always been shy and reserved, and her social life was limited. She and her boyfriend visited each other's homes once a week, but no meal was taken in either.

Before treatment Pat agreed with the therapist that she wanted to achieve the target of eating a meal with three other friends, and of eating a meal at her boyfriend's home. To begin the treatment, Pat lunched with her therapist; she felt very anxious at the start of the meal, but by the end of it an hour later was feeling very comfortable. The next time she had a meal with the therapist, she felt comfortable but was still unable thereafter to have a meal with her boyfriend. It was not practicable to bring her boyfriend into treatment, and so instead Pat was asked to imagine the situation and relive it in her mind's eye. She was asked to describe to the therapist in great detail how she was picturing herself having a meal with her boyfriend. The therapist prompted her flow of talk when she flagged.

Pat was then taught to role play asserting herself when necessary. In a series of "playlets" to overcome her shyness, the therapist pretended to be a shop assistant and Pat was asked to act the part of a customer returning defective goods. This was recorded on videotape and played back to show her how she had performed. The therapist coached her in what to say as a disgruntled customer, and they played the same parts once more. They then switched roles, the therapist playing the customer and Pat playing the salesman, to give her the feel of what it was like to be on the other side of the fence. Other situations were then acted, for example, asking the way in the street from a stranger or refusing to carry out an unreasonable request from a colleague. The therapist showed Pat what to do first and then asked Pat to do the same thing. She responded well to this modeling and coaching and managed to have lunch with a strange man.

At this stage she was asked to join a group of five other patients with similar fears. These six patients took part in a day long group that lasted nine hours in all. When they met in the morning, the therapist outlined the day's program over coffee. The patients then played contact party games which encouraged them to mix together. In one game, one of their number had to "break out" of a circle made by the others. In another game, without using their hands, they had to transfer an orange held under the neck to another patient. These warm-up exercises led to the role playing of increasingly difficult social situations. Toward evening the group split into small parties to shop for the meal they were to cook together in the therapist's flat. During this period, they chatted a lot to one another and then ate the meal together. After their initial unease, the patients obviously enjoyed themselves and made plans to meet one another after the group's conclusion.

Pat felt she had gained a lot from the day long session with the group. All her other sessions were with the therapist alone. After eighteen sessions in all she felt she had achieved as much of the targets as she wanted to and was discharged from treatment. By the time of her six-month follow-up, she was able to eat with her fiancé and his family and had also eaten in selected restaurants

Forms of Nervous Tension and Their Treatment

with him and occasionally with a larger group of additional friends. She still did not enjoy meeting many strangers but could cope with them when necessary and no longer avoided them.

Social skills training

The group session in which Pat had participated was aimed at *social skills training*. This is a set of techniques for teaching people how to get on better with others. Individuals with social inhibitions can be taught to overcome some of them by carrying out social exercises in which they gradually learn to do increasingly difficult social tasks. Overaggressive folks can learn how to express their feelings in more acceptable fashion. Social problems like these can be treated either alone or in a group. In a social skills training group, the therapist's instructions might be:

> To unlearn the unpleasant feelings which you get in company it is necessary to carry out certain exercises. This will require much commitment and cooperation from you while you learn to master social behavior, learn to become less self-conscious, and to feel more accepted by your environment. In your program as you succeed in the easier situation, your training exercises will gradually become more taxing.

A group of people with similar social troubles will then act out with one another scenes like asking for the time in the street, asking a stranger the way to another street in the neighborhood, asking for a description of a complicated route to another city. Patients first act out these roles in the group and are then asked to do the same thing outside in real life. Other exercises they might be asked to perform would be asking in a shop for an item they cannot describe precisely or being a customer in a shoe shop and firmly turning down many pairs of shoes that have been tried on. Another role to be played might be having dinner in a restaurant and asking the waiter for a detailed explanation of the bill, or introducing oneself to a stranger at a party and carrying on a conversation.

Although social skills training has only recently come on the therapeutic scene, current developments look promising for the help of people who are shy, awkward, or who have difficulty in their dealing with others.

ILLNESS PHOBIAS

Fears of illness pass through the minds of most of us at one time or another. Who has not looked at a spot on his hand and wondered whether it was not a form of cancer or other dread disease? Hypochondriasis is typical of medical and dental students who think they harbor the disorders they happen to be studying at the time, and experience a succession of fears of illness as they progress through their curriculum. These, however, are short-lived, cause no handicap, and require no treatment.

In a few people, fears of illness are so insistent that they may go to a doctor for advice. When the fears are of multiple bodily symptoms and a variety of illnesses, the patient is said to have *hypochondriasis*. When the fear is focused round a single symptom or illness in the absence of another psychiatric problem, we speak of an *illness phobia*. The features of hypochondriasis were well described even in the seventeenth century:

> . . . some are afraid that they shall have every fearful disease they see others have, hear of, or read, and dare not therefore hear or read of any such subject, not of melancholy itself, lest, by applying it to themselves that which they hear or read, they should aggravate and increase it.[6]

Although a physical illness can occasionally trigger the phobia, or sensitize the individual to develop symptoms later, commonly there is no history of disease in the past to explain it. Indeed a few cases are recorded where development of the feared disease in fact led to resolution of the fear. One case is cited of a man who was almost beside himself with a phobia of venereal disease to the point where he needed to be admitted to a mental hospital. After he was discharged, he contracted syphilis with an ulcer which he could see himself. From that moment his fears disappeared, and he attended happily for regular antisyphilitic treatment.

Illness phobias are rather different from the phobias we have described until now because they are fears of a situation from which the patient cannot escape. The problem feared is in his body. He thus cannot avoid or escape the phobic situation, unlike people who are afraid of dogs, airplane travel, and the like. However, the fear of illness might be triggered by particular circumstances which the patient then starts to avoid, as in the woman with fear of epilepsy mentioned earlier who would not go out alone lest she have an attack. A man who had had so many x-rays that he thought he might get leukemia refused to be out of contact with his wife more than a moment because she constantly reassured him (page 113).

The endless quest for reassurance of people with hypochondriacal fears or obsessive-compulsive worries is a bit like an addiction. Being reassured reduces the anxiety transiently, but the tension soon builds up again to require further comforting within a few weeks, days, or minutes, the interval between reassurances growing progressively smaller. This is reminiscent of drug addicts who get withdrawal symptoms when their drugs are withheld but feel fine for a while after they have had their "fix." As the addiction deepens, the need for the drug increases in frequency and dosage.

Culture and family affect fear of illness

To some extent, illness phobias reflect worries about disease which are fashionable either in the culture at large or in the family subculture. In a campaign earlier this century to educate the American public about tuberculosis, many patients developed fears of that disease. Nowadays tuberculosis is rare and an unfashionable disease to fear, while cancer and heart disease are much more common worries.

Those who grow up in families which are very health-conscious are more likely to develop fears of illness. If somebody has had a disease in a particular part of his body, he may then be overaware of that part. A history of rheumatic fever can make a person worry unrealistically about his heart. Some people identify with a parent, brother, or sister who has a particular disease. Fear of a given illness may reflect problems of a psychological nature—fears of syphilis can occur in someone who feels guilty about sexual adventures. All these factors may be increased by an upbringing in surroundings where undue attention is paid to physical disease, or when public propaganda is being disseminated about a given illness. A young woman who had several relatives with epilepsy developed fears that she, too, would have seizures and became frightened of going out alone. Sometimes a fear of illness may result from a simple failure of the patient and doctor to communicate with each other. A patient may mistakenly misinterpret the silence of a taciturn doctor as an ominous sign that frightening information is being concealed from him.

Fears can lead to endless worry and search for reassurance

People with phobias of illness may in fact be perfectly healthy. The fear, however, is constant and distracts them from their everyday activities, more than might be the case if they actually had the disease they fear. As someone once said, "Fear is more pain than the pain it fears." The patient will constantly search his body for evidence of disease. No skin lesion or bodily sensation can be too trivial for the keen senses of a phobic patient. He will misinterpret genuine physiological sensations. His anxiety itself may produce fresh symptoms such as abdominal pain and discomfort due to contraction of the intestines and thus reinforce his gloomy prognostications.

While most of us have minor worries about illness at some time or another, these don't come to rule our lives to the exclusion of all else. The multimillionaire Howard Hughes was so terrified of dirt and infection that he went to extraordinary precautions to protect himself. He became a recluse, went on a strange diet, and refused to see doctors. In fact his fear seems to have hastened his death. When he became really ill and emaciated, a doctor could be brought to him only when he was unconscious and on the point of death. By then it was too late to rescue him, though elementary medical attention could have helped him earlier.

An illness phobic may make hundreds of phone calls and visits to doctors throughout his area in a vain attempt to seek reassurance. However, telling him all is well allays his worries only for a short time, and the search for reassurance soon starts again. The distress and handicap can be so dramatic that the average reader may find it hard to believe case histories like the following, yet they are about real people.

Extreme examples of illness phobia

A thirty-two-year-old woman has been to forty-three casualty departments in hospitals in the previous three years and had had x-rays in every part of her body. Sometimes she was scared she was going to die of cancer of the stomach, sometimes of thrombosis, sometimes of a tumor of the brain. Examinations never revealed any abnormality and she emerged each time from the hospital "rejuvenated—it's like having been condemned to death and given a reprieve."[7] But within a week she would seek out a new hospital "where they won't know I'm a fraud. I am terrified of the idea of dying, it's the end, the complete end, and the thought of rotting in the ground obsesses me—I can see the worms and maggots."[8] She was petrified of having sexual relations with her husband because she imagined she would rupture herself and burst a blood vessel, and afterward would get up at two in the morning and stand for hours outside the hospital so that she knew she was in reach of help.

Worries about illness can cause grave handicaps. A fifty-three-year-old man had had such worries for the previous twenty-eight years, during which time he had consulted doctors hundreds of times to seek reassurance about his health from them, and from factory inspectors and water supply officials about the purity of various substances with which he had come into contact. He had been off work from one-third to one-half of his working life. He made his wife telephone endless doctors and various authorities to give him reassurance. As he had had more than a hundred x-rays, he developed fresh worries about their having caused leukemia. His fears of illness and desires for repeated reassurance were also associated with compulsive rituals.[9] This association between illness phobia and obsessive-compulsive behavior is not rare, as we will see when we discuss obsessive-compulsive troubles shortly.

TREATMENT OF ILLNESS PHOBIAS AND WORRIES ABOUT ONE'S BODY

Treatment of illness phobias follows the same lines as those of other phobias, except that the stimulus the sufferer needs to be exposed to is in his own mind rather than in the outside world. Someone with a fear of illness has to be exposed steadily to the idea that he might have cancer, heart disease, or what have you. This exposure can be achieved in several ways. A patient who is frightened that he has a brain tumor may be asked by his doctor to

> imagine that in fact your doctor has just told you that you have a brain tumor and that you have six months to live and ought to start settling your affairs in order to provide for your family. You are shown an x-ray of your skull and the doctor points out the tumor. At first you cannot quite comprehend this but as you leave the consulting room and go down the outside steps you suddenly realize what he has said. . . .

The sufferer may be asked to imagine scenes like this for an hour at a time until they no longer evoke anxiety but they simply bore him.

A woman who is afraid of cancer might be given a specimen of cancer in a sealed bottle to keep by her side so that she can look at it every day until it loses its terrors for her. She might be asked to stick up articles about cancer and pictures of tumors on the walls of her bedroom and kitchen so that she gets used to them and stops running away from the mere idea of cancer.

What to do about constant requests for reassurance

Long-suffering relatives whom phobics have constantly asked for reassurance can help in the treatment. When a phobic asks for reassurance, he hopes to get a reply that he is not ill or contaminated or whatever. His anxiety then is reduced for a short time, only to surge up again later. What the illness phobic avoids is the thought all of us have sometimes that we might be ill and die. Unlike the rest of us, however, he avoids this ideas as much as possible, instead of facing it realistically. This leads to the principle of treatment, namely the withholding of reassurance so that the phobic's idea of illness is not immediately switched off; he then has to learn to tolerate the idea just as most of us do. In a way, the repeated requests for reassurance remind one of an alcoholic who wakes up with the shakes. He finds that a nip of alcohol settles him for a while, but soon the shakes start up again, more alcohol is needed, and so the vicious circle continues. Only coming off all alcohol will help the addiction in the long run. Similarly, addiction to reassurance will be broken by consistently withholding reassurance.

If an illness phobic has the habit of asking his wife, "Do I look pale, do I look ill?" his wife is taught to reply not, "No, you seem okay to me," but instead, "Hospital instructions are that I don't answer such questions." The therapist may several times rehearse a scene in which the phobic asks his wife for reassurance and his wife replies that she may not answer him. This is repeated until the couple knows exactly what to do. This simple transaction can be surprisingly difficult to learn and the two may have to rehearse the scene up to ten times in front of the therapist before they get it pat.

The principle of withholding reassurance is often easier to state than to carry out in practice. After all, relatives may have been trained for years to answer, "You're alright, honey." Nevertheless repeated rehearsal usually helps them to change course. The patient's doctor, too, may need to be taught to withhold yet further examinations and tests if he is satisfied these are unnecessary. Reassurance needs to be withheld because an illness phobic needs to become able to tolerate the discomfort of being uncertain whether he is ill or not. All of us sometimes wonder whether a spot on our hand might be becoming cancerous, but we are able to dismiss this idea from our minds. An illness phobic needs to develop the same facility, and he or she will not until reassurance is stopped. Early in treatment, when reassurance is withheld, the phobic's hypochondriachal worries may actually increase for a few hours or days; however, if the spouse consistently plays his or her role properly and does not give in, then the worries will gradually die down. Usually couples need to be in regular touch with the therapist for support, because it is naturally against our instincts to withhold comfort from our loved ones, even if it is in their best interests in the long run.

Treatment of a woman who thought she smelled

Worries about our body can lead us to avoid places which trigger our fears. Treatment then can follow the same lines as in agoraphobia or excessive social fears, that is, the phobic is persuaded to remain in contact with the feared setting, which he usually avoids, until he feels comfortable in it. An example comes from Mrs. Jones, a thirty-five-year-old woman who for sixteen years had intense worries that her perspiration smelled terrible.[10] It began just before her marriage when she was sharing a bed with a close friend who said that someone at work had smelled badly, and Mrs. Jones felt that the remark was directed at her. For the past five years, for fear of meeting people who might comment on her smell, she had been unable to go out anywhere except when accompanied by her husband or mother, and avoided the cinema, dances, shops, cafes, and private houses. Occasionally she visited her in-laws, but she always sat away from them. Her husband was not allowed to invite any friends home nor to visit any of them. His wife constantly sought reassurance from him about her odor, but his replies never satisfied her. If she watched television commercials about deodorants, she became very anxious. She avoided passing people in the street. Standing in a bus line with her husband made her sweat and feel too anxious to wait for the bus. She refused to attend the local church because it was so small and all the people who attended lived nearby. The family had to travel an extra eight miles to a church in which the members of the congregation were strangers, and they sat or stood away from the others. Her husband bought all her new clothes, as she was afraid to try on clothes in front of shop assistants. She had not spoken to the neighbors for three years because she thought she had overheard them speak about her to some friends. The front door was locked all day, and strangers who rang the bell were not answered. On rising each morning, Mrs. Jones washed completely from head to toe. She used vast quantities of deodorant and always bathed and changed her clothes before going out—up to four times daily.

When Mrs. Jones was assessed for treatment she was timid, blushed often, and would not look one in the eye. Treatment was designed to help her go back repeatedly and for long periods into places where she felt that she smelled until her worry died down. Mr. Jones nominated two targets on which to start treatment—walking past three neighbors in their garden alone, and sitting in the living room with friends talking about smells. Before her first session as an outpatient, she was asked to carry out tasks such as taking her son to the bus stop each morning and going shopping with her mother on two days. Her husband was asked to praise her when she had done these things but not to reassure her when she mentioned smell. By the start of her first session, Mrs. Jones and her husband reported that she had carried out most of these tasks. She had asked him frequently for reassurance, and he had found it difficult not to give in. In the first session the patient and the nurse-therapist traveled by bus to a shopping area and remained there for two hours. During this time, Mrs. Jones entered three shops and remained in each one until her anxiety decreased. She was asked to go into the most crowded areas and to stand in the longest lines. This was first done by the nurse with Mrs. Jones watching, and then Mrs. Jones was asked to do it herself with the nurse nearby. Over the next two hours her discomfort decreased greatly, though she sweated profusely, blushed, and often asked whether she smelled. She needed much persuasion to remain in the crowds, but the return to the hospital on a crowded bus caused her little anxiety and she no longer asked about her own smell.

She was instructed before the second session to carry out three tasks—shopping alone at local shops, taking her son for an hour's walk daily, and going to the cinema accompanied by her husband. She was also asked to come to the next session without having used a deodorant and without having washed—this also applied to all subsequent sessions. By the second session a week later, she had completed all these tasks and was pleased with her progress. Session two was staged in large stores in central London, again accompanied by the nurse. Slowly Mrs. Jones's discomfort diminished, and she was hardly anxious at all by the time she was traveling on a crowded train or bus.

The next three sessions were held at biweekly intervals; Mrs. Jones was again introduced to crowded places in central London; and the nurse gradually withdrew to leave her alone. By the fifth session Mrs. Jones was traveling by bus alone, remaining in large stores up to 1½ hours with only slight tension, eating in crowded restaurants, and standing in long lines. She made the two-hour journey from her home to London by public transport. At home she was doing more shopping alone, was waving to neighbors and visiting friends, but was still worried about shopping in her local town and traveling by bus. Her husband reported that she asked less often about her smell, was bathing less, and was using less deodorant. She did bathe before going to the hospital and could stop for a meal at a restaurant on the way home.

At session 6 Mrs. Jones was asked to accompany her husband on a shopping spree in London. She tried on clothes in two stores (the first time she had done this in four years) and took her husband into many crowded shops; in fact he had difficulty in getting her to leave. She was asked to shop more around their own area, first accompanied and then alone.

From this point onward the nurse did not participate in treatment sessions but simply monitored progress by weekly phone calls. Mrs. Jones began to visit friends after a long shopping trip, changed her clothes only when going out in the evening, and felt generally more relaxed. She was discharged and over the next year's follow-up improved even more. She became able to go to the nearby church with ease, to visit the neighbors and to attend a social gathering at her son's school for the first time. She and her family went on their first holiday together for years. Friends came to stay at her home for holidays and weekends, and she traveled freely despite slight unease. At her final interview, Mrs. Jones looked the therapist in the eye, smiled frequently, spoke freely about her past difficulties, and was much more assertive and cheerful. She remained well at follow-up a year later.

SUMMING UP

Unlike agoraphobia, social phobias occur equally in men and women. They also tend to start gradually in young adult life. The phobia may be of very specific social situations, for example, of eating in formal restaurants, or at the other extreme result in excruciating shyness everywhere, leading to severe isolation and loneliness. Worry about one's appearance is a common problem, and many people with this problem consult plastic surgeons for help.

Social anxieties can be treated effectively by prolonged exposure to those social events which trigger the fear. Where social anxiety results from ignorance about how to behave with people, we talk of a social skills deficit. In such instances treatment also includes social skills training. This involves demonstrating to sufferers how to react in different social contexts, with the patients then rehearsing such behavior in various role play situations. Patients can be treated individually or in a group.

Phobia of illness can be no more than mild hypochondriasis. On the other hand, it can be a crippling terror which results in sufferers getting addicted to endless and fruitless quests for reassurance and investigation by one doctor after another. Illness fears are fostered in families which are excessively health-conscious, and public fashion affects the choice of illnesses which are feared. Some fears simply reflect lack of knowledge. Triggers for the fears can be both external, for example, an article about cancer in a magazine, and internal, such as a pain or lump in the body.

Illness phobics may devote their lives to seeking reassurance. As with other addictions, only brief respite comes from yielding to the addiction, which in this case is to reassurance and investigation. The tension soon builds up again. In the course of treatment, relatives need to help as co-therapists by withholding reassurance from the sufferer. This can be difficult to learn, as it goes against one's natural inclination. The sufferer needs to learn to live with uncertainty about the status of his health and to develop a tolerance of talk about illness.

7
Phobic Disorders:
Specific Phobias

ANIMAL PHOBIAS

Most children aged two through four go through a phase when they are a bit afraid of animals. This fear may begin without the child ever having come to any harm or seeing anybody hurt by a dog or cat or other animal. It is almost as though the young of our species is programmed by nature to go through this stage with little or no special experience. However, the great majority of children rapidly lose this fear, and by the time they reach puberty, very few children have any fears of animals left at all. A tiny minority do retain their fears into adult life, the majority of this small number being women. It is most unusual for a fear of animals to start after puberty. Adults who complain of fears of animals usually say that their fears began in childhood before the age of six, or "as far back as I can remember." A few people can remember a brief period in early childhood when they were free of fears of animals before they developed their phobia at the age of three or four.

Naturally many people in our culture have mild fears of spiders, mice, dogs, and other animals, but such fears are rarely strong enough to be called a phobia and need treatment. Psychiatrists see far fewer adults with these phobias than with agoraphobia or social anxieties, which probably reflects a smaller incidence in the adult community. Many more animal phobias are found in young children than in adults, but most of these subside after puberty; those seen in adult life are usually the persisting remnant of these childhood fears.

Animal phobias in adults are usually quite distinct from agoraphobias. The disturbance they cause is much more localized and is associated with very few other problems. Once they have begun, they tend to run a rather steady course, unlike agoraphobia, which can fluctuate a great deal.

Reasons adults ask for help

Although adults who ask for help with animal phobias have usually had them for decades by the time they come for treatment, there is commonly some change in their lives which causes them to come for help at that particular time. A city dweller can avoid most animals and insects, but if she moves to some place where there are many animals, she can then become quite crippled. One woman managed well in a town flat but became anxious and sought treatment after she moved to a country cottage which was infested with spiders. She felt better again when she moved to a house which was free of them. Another woman began treatment when she could not take up a residential art scholarship in an old spider-infested hostel, and her career became jeopardized. Yet another young woman moved from a town with a few pigeons to a different city where they thrived; she had to ask for treatment because she became unable to walk to work through streets which contained pigeons.

Other people ask for help when they hear for the first time that treatment can be offered. Yet others come because they are afraid of passing on their own phobia to their young children. Some people see a doctor first for other problems such as depression, and the doctor then spots their animal phobia and suggests that it be treated. During depression, preexisting problems are often magnified and cause a patient to seek help with a minor disability which he could tolerate easily before. A few people ask for treatment of a simple phobia in the silent hope that other problems they find hard to talk about will also be dealt with. People who lead lonely lives are probably more likely to come with some minor problem, and social contact with the hospital can provide as much satisfaction in an empty life as relief of the mild isolated symptom. Given the same disability, people who are lonely seek medical aid more than do others.

Origin of the fear

In adults the origins of animal phobias are usually lost in the mist of early childhood memories, but a few can be dated to specific incidents.[1] One cat phobia began when a little girl watched her father drown some kittens. Occasional dog phobias begin after dog bites. A bird phobia started after a child posed for a photograph in London's Trafalgar Square, where there are thousands of pigeons. She took fright as a bird alighted on her shoulder but couldn't move because she was posing—the resultant photograph preserved the record of the origin of her phobias. A feather phobia began when an infant strapped in a baby carriage took fright as a strange woman with a large feather in her hat bent down to look at the baby.

Freud described the onset of these fears in children.

> The child suddenly begins to fear a certain animal species and to protect itself against seeing or touching any individual of this species. . . . The phobia is as a rule expressed towards animals for which the child has until then shown the liveliest interest, and has nothing to do with the individual animal. In cities, the choice of animals which can become the object of phobia is not great. They are horses, dogs, cats, more seldom birds, and strikingly often very small animals like bugs and butterflies. Sometimes animals which are known to the child only from picture books and fairy stories become objects of the senseless and inordinate anxiety which is manifest in these phobias. It is

seldom possible to learn the manner in which such an unusual
choice of anxiety has been brought about.[2]

It is surprising how seldom fears of animals are found in other
members of the patient's family, because one might expect these
fears to be modeled on the behavior of close relatives. Occasionally one does find the same fear in several members of a family,
and one can see how the fear is passed from one generation to
the next. However, this is the exception rather than the rule.

In most children, fears of animals disappear rapidly without
any apparent reason or sometimes because they have been
exposed to situations in which they can learn to get used to the
animal again. On the other hand, the fears can be stamped in to
become phobias when other children tease the child repeatedly
with the feared object. We usually do not know why a small
fraction of these fears continue after puberty. When the patient
comes for help, he or she generally complains of a longstanding
phobia of some animal or insect and is free of other problems.

What are animal phobias like?

Practically any animal or insect may be involved in a phobia. The
fears are commonly of birds or feathers. Pigeons seem to be
particularly feared, while smaller birds like canaries are tolerated
more easily. One woman described her fear of pigeons in detail:
"I would just be terrified. I put my hand up to my head—I am
frightened they will fly at my face, I suppose—and it's their
wings, the flapping of their wings."[3] Phobias of spiders, bees, and
wasps are quite common. "Spiders terrify me—its the way it
moves—stealthily. They're black and hairy and evil."[4] Some
people come to be treated for fears of dogs, cats, worms, frogs, or
flying insects. Sometimes the phobia is a nuisance rather than a
major problem, as in a woman living in the country who could
not go near ponds where frogs were plentiful, nor look at pictures
of frogs in books. With intense phobias of common animals, the

distress can be very great. One woman with a fear of birds could not go to work through the streets of London since they abounded in pigeons; she had to give up her job and remain indoors all day, venturing out only at night when pigeons no longer flew about.

Though a localized phobia might seem a trivial problem, striking distress does result when a severely phobic person comes into contact with the phobic object. During treatment, if sufferers are brought too close to the animal they fear, they show acute panic, sweat, tremble, and appear terrified. One woman with a fear of spiders screamed when she found a spider at home, ran away to find a neighbor to remove it, trembled in fear, and had to keep a neighbor at her side for two hours before she could remain alone at home again. Another patient with a spider phobia found herself on top of the refrigerator in the kitchen with no memory of how she got there—the fear inspired in her by the sight of a spider had made her lose her memory very briefly.[5] Another woman with a spider phobia had jumped out of a boat even though she could not swim to avoid a spider she found in the bottom of the vessel. Once she jumped out of a speeding car and on yet another occasion off a galloping horse to escape spiders which had come near her.[6] "I'm scared to go to any parks or even into my garden," said a forty-two-year-old woman with a fear of pigeons. "I've missed many appointments because if there are any birds near the bus stop I just have to walk away. Going shopping is torture for me—I have to cross and recross the road to avoid birds. I have nightmares about them."[7] Another middle-aged woman with the same phobia never had any windows open in her home in case a bird should fly in. The sight of one "reduces me to a jelly. If ever a bird flew at me I would have a heart attack from fright."[8] She sometimes arrived late for work because it took her so long to pick her way between all the birds near Waterloo Station in London.

People with spider phobias dread the approach of summer and autumn when spiders become more common and feel really happy only in the winter when these creatures are rarely seen. A few sufferers are plagued by recurrent nightmares of the animals they fear. They dream they are surrounded by large spiders or swooping birds from which they cannot escape. When they improve after treatment, these nightmares disappear. Phobics search for the feared object wherever they go. The slightest evidence of its presence will disturb them where a normal person may never have noticed it. One sign of improvement during treatment is diminished awareness of these animals in the surroundings. A dog-phobic woman had in her mind a "dog map" of her neighborhood concerning streets she could safely go in and streets she should avoid; once she recovered after treatment, she no longer thought about dogs and went freely everywhere.

TREATMENT OF A STUDENT WITH A PIGEON PHOBIA

Phobias of animals are usually easy to treat, generally needing only a few hours of contact with the animal concerned for the fear to subside. Where the contact is continuous for several hours, one or two afternoons may be all that is needed. If contact is only brief each time, many sessions may be called for.

Jane was a twenty-year-old university student who had been frightened of pigeons for at least seven years. She had nightmares of them attacking her and checked doors and windows at night so that pigeons could not get in. She could not sit in her room with the window open, and her fear was beginning to affect her studies. In the street she often took a detour to avoid walking past pigeons. She disliked watching them on television or looking at photographs of birds.[9]

In treatment Jane was encouraged to get used to pigeons by gradually coming closer to them, despite the terror which this inspired in her. Before active treatment began, she was asked to hang pictures of birds around her room and to buy and handle stuffed and dummy birds. In her first session she stroked and handled a pigeon which was being held by the therapist and then managed to be alone in a room with a caged pigeon a few feet away. The next session she managed to sit in a park with the therapist and feed pigeons which were about three feet away and sat outside a cafe in the park while pigeons were flying around and feeding near her table. In her third session she walked through the park accompanied by the therapist, looked at the pigeons, and sat three feet away from them feeding. Between sessions she became able to walk past many birds in the street and could look at them without shuddering. She began to keep pictures and models of birds and could handle these without fear. During the day she was able to keep the window of her room open while she went away. In further treatment sessions she learned to tolerate pigeons flying about her. She was discharged greatly improved after nine sessions, and at a year's follow-up reported that she was well and had no fear of pigeons at all. She slept with the window open during the summer and had been to parks and to London's Trafalgar Square, which has swarms of pigeons.

Early in treatment there had been one unexpected complication. In early sessions in the park in the presence of the therapist, whenever a pigeon came near Jane she screamed loudly, which disturbed other people nearby so much that the park attendant came up to the therapist and threatened to "make him unconscious" if he did not stop frightening the young lady! Further treatment sessions were held at 7 *a.m.* to avoid both the park keeper and the general public.

OTHER SPECIFIC PHOBIAS

Almost anything can trigger a phobia in some people, and there is really an endless list of phobias one could describe. *Phobias of natural phenomena* are not uncommon. One very unusual phobia a young woman complained of was a phobia for round arches and tunnels.[10] She had to shut her eyes as she went through them and this became a problem when she finally learned to drive. During her driving lessons she closed her eyes on approach to a tunnel and went rigid if her eyes were open. She also had nightmares about tunnels. Her anxiety was triggered only by *round* arches or tunnels. If they were square they did not bother her.

Other phobias for which people seek treatment can include being in the vicinity of anybody who smokes, of wearing clean white shirts, of hearing running water, of being grasped from behind, of reading books or letters, of dolls, or of firemen's helmets. A rare fear is of leaves. One phobic complained, "I'm terrified of leaves, especially rhubarb. I can't go near them. If I come close my heart thumps and I go all shaky. I've always been frightened and have memories of this since I was two. My husband can't stand it and I'm too embarrassed to go to a doctor for help."[11]

Heights

A mild fear of *heights* is not uncommon in many people, but severe incapacitating phobias of heights are rare. Whether or not people are frightened of a particular height depends largely upon the details of their surroundings. Patients with severe phobias of heights may not be able to get down a flight of stairs if they can see the open stairwell, but manage if it is closed. They will be frightened looking out of a high window which stretches from floor to ceiling but not if the window is obscured to waist level or higher. They have difficulty crossing bridges on foot because the edge is near, but they may be able to do so in a car. Anxiety about heights can also be evoked by looking at high structures. "Looking up at tall buildings, you feel as though they are leaning toward you—you get a dizzy feeling, a panicky feeling—always a feeling that you want to jump off and feeling that the ground is coming up to you," is how one sufferer described this anxiety.[12]

Fear of falling: Space phobias

Occasionally fear of heights is linked to an acute *fear of falling* if there is no support within a few feet and the phobic is afraid of being drawn over the edge of a height. This is similar to the feeling many people get when they are standing on the edge of a railway platform that they will be drawn down onto the rails under a train.

A fear of falling can become quite extreme. A forty-nine-year-old housewife was running for a bus when she suddenly felt dizzy and had to hold on to a lamppost for support.[13] This recurred, and gradually she became unable to walk anywhere without holding on to a wall or furniture to support her—she was "furniture bound." She could stand only if she could see a support a foot or less away from her. If this support was removed, she would become terrified and cry, although actual physical contact with the supporting object was not essential. She was perfectly calm when sitting or lying down. This woman had no trouble with her inner ears of the kind which sometimes produces an abnormal sensation of falling.

People with this falling fear seem to have disturbed perception of space. One woman like this felt she might fall down if unsupported and had to clutch on to something for support. For the previous six months she had had to crawl on her knees around the house. Despite this disability she was able to dance vigorously unsupported on a crowded dance floor, but had to be supported if the crowd went away. She felt no discomfort when swung around while dancing. She had difficulty getting on a bus because she would not let go of the railing but could board it if accompanied. She needed only light support when holding someone's arm but momentarily felt that she might fall and then clutched tightly. Twice within eighteen months she had fallen forward and hurt herself. Another woman had a similar fear if when she was driving she encountered a wide open road or hollows; upon seeing either of these she had to hand over the driving to her husband. She felt similarly anxious when she saw very steep slopes or stairs, heights or bridges. Real physical handicaps can be greatly aggravated by fears of falling. One vigorous elderly lady became quite incapacitated shortly after she recovered from a stroke which had left one leg weak. She had progressed very well and was quite independent until one day she tripped and fell over the edge of a carpet; after that she became terrified of venturing anywhere alone and had to have someone holding her wherever she went. Although she had good power in her legs, the collapse in her confidence prevented her from using them.

Darkness, thunderstorms, and lightning

Phobias of *darkness* are perfectly normal in childhood but rarely handicap adults. Some people have a phobia of *wind or storms* rather than of thunder. Others are phobic specifically of *thunderstorms and lightning*. A twenty-year-old female bus conductor with this phobia said, "I would give anything to be helped with my phobia because I'm afraid of losing my job if there is a storm while I'm on the bus. I scream and feel sick and have an upset stomach afterwards. People think I am crazy. I can't stop by myself when a storm is on, but I'm just as frightened and hysterical when I'm with people [during a storm]."[14]

People with this particular fear may become so terrified that they listen frequently to weather forecasts and become unable to venture out of doors when thunder is forecast in a few hours' time. They may dread the approach of summer and long for winter, when thunderstorms rarely occur. In some cities meteorological services are besieged by a constant stream of anxious inquiries about the weather from thunderstorm phobics.

Noise

Though most of us dislike intense *noise,* this dislike rarely goes on to become a phobia. Some people, however, are so terrified of balloons popping that they are unable to attend parties where this may happen. A woman complained of this terrible phobia about balloons being blown up. Because she was forty-two, she thought it was slightly silly. One unusual phobia of noise was concerned with a fear of whistling. This woman was not afraid of birds as such. She could hold a bird without fear and the sound of a cuckoo or parrot was easily tolerated. There had to be a defininte frequency before she became frightened. A high soprano voice made her tense, and she was sent into a frenzy of terror if a human whistled. She was greatly incapacitated in her work in filmmaking, because if anyone whistled at work this caused such fear and anger that she was unable to face going back to the same studio for the next few days.

Travel

Phobias sometimes develop of *driving* a car, especially after a car accident, or of other forms of *travel.* The most common fear of travel is usually part of the agoraphobic syndrome. However many people who lead otherwise unrestricted lives are afraid of traveling by airplane or underground train.

Enclosed spaces (claustrophobia)

The same applies to *claustrophobia,* which is commonly found in many agoraphobics but also often occurs as an isolated phobia. Claustrophobics are afraid of being shut in enclosed spaces like tunnels or elevators. In the words of one sufferer, "If the lift were to stop, I would just panic very rapidly. I would start banging the sides of the lift." One such sufferer had the misfortune to work as a roof expert and had to complete a job on the roof of London's 600-foot-high Post Office Tower. He walked to the top twice a day rather than go up in the elevator.

Fear of flying

Flying in airplanes has become increasingly important in modern living and as a result lots of travelers are discovering just how unnerving flying can be. More and more people are being forced to fly because of their jobs, and a flying phobia can prevent one from being promoted, as well as greatly limit where a family can go to for a vacation. One woman wrote for advice to a newspaper:

> My problem is that I am planning to move to California at the beginning of the New Year, but as I suffer from claustrophobia, I can't trust myself to think I can stay on a plane for 5 hours without getting panicky. . . . surprisingly enough, if I know there is a doctor around, I don't panic. . . . I am ashamed to ask for reservations on a flight when a doctor would be on the plane, but I am sure I would travel much better if I knew there was one around.[15]

Another woman was "terrified of flying. I have flown, but at great intervals, under great duress, and always suffer a thousand deaths."[16] A man said that his fear was "to be closed in, high and away from earth."[17] The mood was expressed by a transatlantic passenger who, breathing a sigh of relief on landing in London, said, "Well, we cheated death once more."[18] So common are flying fears and so few are the opportunities for treatment at the moment that an organization was formed in New York for " air fraidycats" which aimed to help them learn to fly without fear. This group chartered special aircraft to fly passengers under soothing conditions designed to help them overcome their worry.

As you might imagine, is isn't easy to arrange for people with flying phobias to be introduced gradually onto airplanes in a treatment program. One way of getting over this is by asking flying phobics to *imagine* themselves buying an airplane ticket, going to the airport, boarding a plane and going on a flight, and thereafter doing this themselves in real life. One young woman (a travel agent) got used to the idea of going on a plane by imagining it repeatedly in treatment. Finally she was escorted by her therapist to London airport and was put on a flight to Athens to begin her vacation. As she was waiting in the plane ready for takeoff, the pilot announced over the intercom that there would be an hour's delay due to mechanical failure—not the most therapeutic of events, and naturally our phobic felt that all her worst fears had been confirmed. She ran out of the plane back into the terminal lounge. Fortunately, an air hostess eventually persuaded her to return into the plane, she flew off, and her fears improved. However, this gives some idea of the practical difficulties involved in treating problems of flying phobias.

What about pilots?

Not only passengers but even pilots can get phobias of flying. These are especially common in wartime. The phobias of aircrew in World War II make little practical sense in that they often developed for safe maneuvers but not for dangerous ones. One outstanding fighter pilot took part in combat with delight yet was unwilling to fly over water. Several men refused to fly higher than 8,000 feet, although they risked with ease danger below that level. Some pilots had such a strong fear of parachuting that they rode severely damaged planes into a crash landing and were decorated for choosing the more hazardous course.[19] A navigator who was terrified of flying was shot down and soon afterward came upon a small group of dispirited infantrymen hemmed in by a large number of the enemy: his joy at being on the ground enabled him to lead the men out of a very dangerous position. Flying phobias increased a man's own danger, for they led to uncertainty and inefficiency in the air. Seized with a nameless fear before landing, a few men smashed their planes as a result; not a few bailed out unnecessarily or made serious navigational errors.

Swallowing

Rarely, people may have a phobia of swallowing solid food which will force them to resort to a liquid diet. The patients feel that they have a lump in their throat and find it difficult to swallow when they are intensely anxious. In the words of one woman of forty-nine, "Since I've been a child I've had this stupid phobia of swallowing. Whenever I drink or eat the muscles of my throat go into spasm and I make this crowing noise, my eyes water, and I get a terrible panic." This happened whether she was eating alone or with other people, and it so embarrassed her that she often wouldn't eat out, which hampered her job in public relations. She thought she had acquired the problem after watching her mother, whose stridulous noises while eating in front of other people caused many embarrassing memories. "I was born a placid child but had nervousness thrust upon me," she reasoned.[20]

A variant of this problem could be called *hypersensitivity of the gag reflex,* a reflex which we all experience when we stick a finger down the back of our throat. The stimuli which trigger this reflex can widen to include very minor pressure on the neck. One man of twenty had had this trouble since the age of six. He became unable to wear high-necked sweaters or a tie, which restricted his job opportunities. Sometimes he would gag while dictating letters on the phone, especially to strangers. When he gagged, he couldn't open his mouth or speak.[21] Sucking candies helped, but he had sucked so many that his teeth had rotted. He could not open his mouth for a dentist because this made him gag, and so he was on the waiting list for dental treatment under an anesthetic. He couldn't say "aaahh" during a medical examination, would have the reflex triggered if he had injections in the upper arm but not elsewhere, and might suddenly clam up when ordering a meal or tickets in a cinema. He had dreams of being choked and could not stand being under bedclothes.

When I interviewed this man, he seemed relaxed but took a candy to suck before speaking. He could not stick his tongue out beyond his teeth nor open his mouth widely. He wore an open-necked shirt and when he tried to close his collar at my request, he had to stop speaking. If he or I touched his neck, his eyes watered and he gagged intensely.

Food fads are terribly common, of course, but only rarely does this become so pronounced as to amount to a *food phobia.* People do become anxious or disgusted by special foods, especially by meat. Something similar is produced by religious taboos about eating certain foods. Many Hindus are vegetarian; Muslims and Jews are forbidden to eat pork. If religious people eat their forbidden food by mistake or coercion, they may vomit or feel nauseous for days. In his autobiography, Gandhi, a vegetarian, described this reaction after eating meat.

Medical procedures, blood, and injury

Many people are terrified of *dental treatment* or *injections*. They may get severe dental decay over the years due to their inability to go to a dentist, and appropriate medical treatment for other conditions may be delayed for fear of going to doctors. One young woman was so frightened of ambulances and hospitals that she remained confined to her home for nearly two years, lest an ambulance should appear. Asked what would happen if one day she needed an ambulance herself, she answered, "I know what my choice would be without a doubt—I would rather die than go in one of those."[22] Fears of needles and injections are not uncommon and sometimes are so severe that sufferers refuse major surgery and lifesaving antibiotics rather than have an injection.

A related common phobia is that of *blood* and *wounds*. It is of course quite natural to feel faint on seeing blood or severe wounds, but usually people are able to get over this squeamishness. In a few persons, however, the phobia of blood can be so intense that young women may refuse to become pregnant because they cannot bear the blood associated with childbirth. One young woman was afraid of becoming pregnant because pregnancy usually involves examination of one's body by a doctor, and this terrified her although she had normal sexual relations with her husband.[23]

Fears of blood and injury have one interesting difference from other phobias. With most phobias our heart rate goes up when we see the dreaded object, and only rarely do we faint. However, people who are afraid of blood and injury commonly faint on seeing blood or a gruesome sight, and this is associated with a marked slowing of the heart rate rather than an increase. The reason for this is not clear, though we might speculate whether it is related in evolution to the death feigning or playing possum found in some species of animals.

Treatment of blood phobia

Mary, age twenty-nine, had two children. Since age four she had fainted at the sight of blood or injury or even when hearing the subject discussed.[24] She was unable to fulfill her longstanding ambition to become a teacher because she might faint in dealing with children's cuts, which would inevitably be part of such work. She avoided films and plays which might include bloody injury scenes. She became ashamed of this problem and determined to overcome it after she fainted in a hospital emergency room with her son sitting on her lap while his scalded foot was being dressed.

At assessment, Mary and her therapist agreed on four targets for treatment: watching blood being taken from someone else and from herself, being able to cope with her children receiving first aid, and getting her own varicose veins treated. Treatment was by the usual principle of steady exposure to the troublesome situation until it no longer caused fainting; she was asked to look at scenes of blood and injury, fainting being prevented by her lying down at the first few sessions so that the blood supply to her brain would continue even if her heart rate slowed down greatly. At Mary's first treatment session she lay down and watched blood being taken from her therapist. She was delighted that for the first time she could remember she did not actually faint or feel faint at the sight of blood. She then had blood taken from herself while lying down and again remained conscious, but she felt very faint when she tried to stand afterward. She took home an ampule of her blood to keep in her bedroom.

In the next session, because of the inconvenience of arranging to see many real situations involving injury, she was asked instead to imagine these and watch them on films. She described scenes in which she had a car accident and received severe injuries to her legs, and later, that her fingertips were cut off in another accident. Then she watched films of operations, accidents, blood donors, blood transfusions, traffic accidents, and open-heart surgery; once she fainted while watching these films. She persisted in seeing them to the point of boredom. Finally she visited the hematology department of a nearby hospital and had her blood taken there.

Between sessions at home, she dealt successfully with several small emergencies with the children, and she had her varicose veins injected. At follow-up at eight months, she reported that she remained free of her problem concerning blood and injury, enrolled in a first-aid class, began to attend a teacher-training college, and went freely to films and plays depicting blood and injury.

Urination and defecation

Not uncommonly people are very frightened of being far away from public toilets. They worry that they might wet or soil their pants. Interestingly, despite this they might be quite unselfconscious about being in the nude or having sex. In some people these problems are rather like phobias, although they don't actually experience fear in given situations. Instead they have the physical feelings and signs associated with fear. People of this kind might have the urge to urinate or defecate whenever they are in social situations. They may run to the lavatory dozens of times a day as a result, or avoid social gatherings instead, or choose only those parties where they can easily reach a lavatory. In contrast some men may be unable to urinate in front of any other person, and may waste much time at work and other places waiting for the urinal room to become empty.

Sometimes worries about urination affect women as well. Joan asked for help at the age of fifty because for the previous thirty years she had not been able to pass urine outside her own home. As a result she was unable to go away to visit friends on weekends. Joan was able to retain her urine for up to forty-eight hours if necessary. Surprisingly she was able to have a bowel movement in a public toilet and to have normal sexual relations, despite her problem about urination.[25] Let us see how she was treated.

Treatment of a phobia of urinating away from home

Joan needed to get used to going into a public toilet and seating herself while trying to urinate: given enough time she would relax and perform the required act. She was asked to report for her first treatment session at 3 *p.m.*, not to urinate that morning, and to drink five cups of coffee before coming. Treatment consisted of sending her into the lavatory and waiting for her to pass urine, no matter how long it took. She was told that after a while her tension in this situation would reduce and she would then become able to urinate. She was aware that in time she would be placed in more difficult situations. In sessions 1 to 3 the therapist waited many yards away from the toilet. In sessions 4 to 8 he waited outside nearby. In sessions 9 to 12 he waited while talking with somebody, and in sessions 13 to 15 the doctor waited silently with another person (this was more stressful for Joan than having the doctor wait and talk outside). The first time it took Joan fully two hours before she could pass a few dribbles of urine. After a few more sessions she was able to pass water within ten minutes. By the twelfth session she was able to pass two litres (nearly one-half gallon) of urine almost immediately on demand. This gives you some idea of what a tremendous storage capacity her bladder had developed over the years.

Before treatment began, Joan had no desire to urinate outside her home even when her bladder was mightily distended. At session 10 of treatment she rushed to the hospital half an hour early with the urge to urinate, voiding eight minutes after arrival. Several days later she voided successfully at a friend's, who mentioned that it was the first time in their ten years' acquaintance that she had asked to use the lavatory. She then related her history, this being her first confession to anyone other than a doctor, and felt great relief. She voided again without delay at the home of another friend, who also expressed surprise at her asking to use the lavatory. She confessed her story once more, feeling pleased.

At a year's follow-up Joan continued to be able to urinate in public toilets without difficulty, though she still could not perform at the lavatory near her office at work, which had not been involved in treatment.

Asthma, sweating, and nausea

Occasionally people who suffer from asthma notice that the attacks are triggered by particular psychological circumstances, and if these are avoided they are free of attacks. They might get an attack after a row with the boss or the wife, but not at other times. Excessive sweating can be very embarrassing in social situations, and blushing can cause similar difficulties. Nausea and vomiting also are occasionally triggered specifically by certain environmental events. Some people avoid parties because heavy alcoholic drinking makes them nauseous.

Competitions and gambling

In the world of sport and work, contenders constantly jostle one another for position in the stakes for winning or promotion. Athletes may get very tensed up before an important race, and people at work might be very irritable with their juniors until they get the promotion they want. Life may not seem worth living in the family of a concert pianist the day before an important performance. *Examination anxiety* is a recognized problem that besets many students, some of whom fail to take the exams at all because they constitute such an ordeal for them. So-called test anxiety forms much of the bread-and-butter practice of counselors of students.

Compulsive *gambling* is another source of worry which has ruined the lives of numerous families. As the gambler loses more and more, the gambling becomes a persistent source of worry, and the tension it creates makes it more likely that he will go out and gamble again to relieve the anxiety. One thirty-three-year-old man came to me for help because he had been betting almost daily over the previous six years, had lost all his family's money, and was now in debt. Shortage of money caused frequent quarrels with his wife. He never bet by phone but always went into a betting shop, placing his bet in cash, eventually with borrowed money. Over the weekends he would not leave home for fear that he might bet more and his wife would discover him. Bets were usually on the horses, but he had bet up to $800 on the dogs. He was tense at work because he continually felt the urge to bet and was obsessed by the possibility of winning despite his losses. On his way to the hospital, he stopped in a betting shop to place another bet, eventually losing $1,000. This made him an hour late for the interview, and when I saw him, he was wringing his hands in agitation at his loss. Despite this, he had intense urges to go out and gamble again immediately in an attempt to undo the damage.

Anger avoidance

Quite a few repetitive difficulties are rather like phobias in that they are triggered by specific identifiable events which the sufferer goes to great lengths to avoid because he so much dislikes the unpleasant feelings which they arouse, though the feelings are not of fear but of other emotions, for example, anger.

An example of such a phobia-like problem comes from a twenty-five-year-old woman who wrote a clear account of her problem. She called it a "noise phobia," recalling that when she was nine years old, her father upset her a great deal by making a noise with his dentures while eating.

> Over the years the aversion has got worse, and has now extended to the noise of breathing, snoring, sniffing, etc., from almost anyone in my company. I really find these noises quite unbearable and have had to find more and more excuses for leaving the room. I can remember all through my teens eating on my own and sitting watching television with my fingers in

my ears to blot out the noise of my brother chewing his fingernails. My husband, from whom I am now separated, urged me many times to seek help, but I found it too embarrassing and I didn't really see what could be done to alleviate it. Towards the end of our marriage I would be constantly nagging my husband to breathe through his mouth, make less noise eating, stop snoring, etc., and although I don't pretend it was this that broke our marriage up, I'm quite sure it contributed very much to the decline of our relationship. At present I'm constantly having to find excuses for not eating with the family with whom I live and usually have to go to bed early to escape the noise of the light snorer in the house who dozes off in the evening.[26]

When seen, this lady was lonely and tearful, but not seriously depressed. She had married at seventeen, and when her husband left her for another woman, she had taken an overdose.

Treatment of anger phobias

"Anger phobias" can be relieved by exposure treatment along the same line as that given for more typical phobias, where the emotion experienced is one of anxiety. This was the treatment for a woman of twenty-seven, who complained of a revulsion toward pregnant women and infants.[27] Her baby had died when she was about four months pregnant. She carried the dead fetus for two months before aborting; during that time she made weekly visits to her obstetrician's office, where she saw obviously pregnant women who, ignorant of her problem, asked her about her own pregnancy. She developed a revulsion for pregnant women during this time. When she finally aborted she became mildly depressed, was hostile and abusive to pregnant friends, refused to attend socials for fear of losing her temper with pregnant women, and tore up invitations to baby showers. This curtailed her social life, and she avoided infant sections of stores. She began to have extramarital affairs and separated from her husband. Then she entered marital counseling with him, with some improvement in her attitude toward him, but with no abatement of her revulsion to pregnancy.

During two 1½-hour-long sessions of treatment she was now asked to imagine intense interaction with pregnant women and infants, some whom she knew, others hypothetical, and to cope with her resultant feelings. By session 3 she could no longer feel any more anger. Improvement continued during two months of follow-up, by which time with her husband she had resumed attending social activities at which pregnant women were present and could approach them again.

A slightly different approach was also successful, this time in a woman whose temper outbursts with her family were unmanageable. During nine sessions of treatment, she was asked to imagine anger-inducing scenes; then the therapist would suggest ludicrous developments of the scenes, which made the woman laugh, and she improved.

SUMMING UP

Fears of animals are normal, perhaps innate, in young children and rarely start afresh after puberty. Adults with animal phobias usually recall that they began before the age of seven. Sufferers are usually women, and they tend to have few phobias apart from one or two species of animals. They usually ask for help when some change in their lives causes them to become more handicapped from the phobia, or when treatment becomes available for the first time. Two or more sessions of treatment involving prolonged exposure to the real animal can result in rapid and lasting removal of phobias of even decades' duration.

Other phobias which are specific include fears of heights, of darkness, of noise, storms, and lightning, and of being in enclosed spaces (claustrophobia). The latter is often also found together with agoraphobia. Fears of flying are very prevalent and can occur even in experienced passengers and crews. A few people have phobias of swallowing solid food. Blood, injections, and other medical procedures inspire dread in many people.

Unlike those with fears of other situations, blood phobics commonly faint on seeing blood, with their heart rates usually slowing down rather than increasing, as is common in phobic situations. In treatment by exposure, the aim is to allow the patient to get used to the sight of blood and injury without slowing of the heart rate, so that fainting no longer occurs.

Some repetitive difficulties are rather like phobias, having identifiable triggers which the sufferer avoids because of the unpleasant feelings which they arouse, for example, anger. These can be dealt with like phobias; the sufferer learns to control his feelings while being steadily brought closer to the source of his discomfort.

So far we have dealt mainly with phobias in adults. Let us look at some of the special features of phobias in children.

8

Phobias in Children

Fears are much more common in children than in adults, and often start and die down again for no obvious reason. They fluctuate and are more intense than in adults. This is true for most children's feelings, which are generally more labile and keenly expressed. Because fears in children are so intense, it is more difficult to separate their normal fears from abnormal phobias.

Fear is an inborn response to certain stimuli that becomes differentiated from other feelings in the first year of life. The startle reaction which newborn infants show seems to be a precursor of later normal fear. Any intense, sudden, or unexpected stimulus to the infant will cause him to throw up both hands and feet and perhaps cry. After about age six months, fear becomes recognizably different from startle and is seen in response to strangers. Fear of animals begins a bit later.

The common fears change as the child grows. At age two to four, fears of animals are the most common, but thereafter children are more likely to have fears of the dark or of imaginary creatures. Fears of animals diminish very rapidly in boys and girls between the ages of nine and eleven, and after puberty very few people have phobias of these kinds.

Between age six and ten many children have normal little rituals which are harmless and don't develop into obsessive-

compulsive problems. These are not far removed from the counting and rhyming games and songs which are endlessly played by
children all over the world, for example, "One, two, buckle my
shoe; three, four, knock on the door; five, six, pick up sticks. . . ."
The rituals may involve touching every picket in a fence they pass
on the way to school, or avoidance of stepping on the lines made
by edges of paving stones on the sidewalk; the children feel that
this averts some awful danger. The spirit of this superstition was
charmingly caught in the poem "Lines and Squares" written by
A. A. Milne earlier this century:

> Whenever I walk in a London street,
> I'm ever so careful to watch my feet;
> And I keep in the squares,
> And the masses of bears,
> Who wait at the corners all ready to eat,
> The sillies who tread on the lines of the street,
> Go back to their lairs,
> And I say to them, "Bears,
> Just look how I'm walking in all the squares!"
>
> And the little bears growl to each other, "He's mine,
> As soon as he's silly and steps on a line."
> And some of the bigger bears try to pretend
> That they came round the corner to look for a friend;
> And they try to pretend that nobody cares
> Whether you walk on the lines or squares.
> But only the sillies believe their talk;
> It's ever so 'portant how you walk.
> And it's ever so jolly to call out, "Bears,
> Just watch me walking in all the squares!"[1]

Keeping to self-made rules staves off all kinds of imaginary terrors
and gives the child self-confidence.

Certain fears do not decline with age. General shyness and
worries about meeting new people continue into adolescence.
Such fears were present in slightly more than half of 6,000
children in London who were investigated, although they had

few fears of darkness or animals. Parents tend to underestimate the number of fears that children have. Out of more than 1,000 normal children in California at least one specific fear was found in 90 percent of the children at some stage between the ages of two and fourteen. The frequency of their fears diminished as they got older. The peak was at age three. In another study in Leicester, England, out of 142 children aged two to seven about a third had specific fears, most of these subsiding over the next 1½ years.

Although fears are very common in children, handicapping phobias are quite rare. Out of more than 2,000 children in the Isle of Wight in one survey, only sixteen had troublesome phobias of one or more objects. Five of these were of spiders and six of the dark. Out of 239 children referred to a psychiatric department, only ten had specific phobias.

Phobias in children can cause the same incapacity as in adults. A seven-year-old boy had had an intense fear of bees for two years. "I am very frightened of the bees and am scared they will sting and hurt me," he said. When he encountered a bee, his mother reported, "He used to go white, sweaty, cold, and trembly and his legs were like jelly."[2] He would blindly flee any bee, and his movements were curtailed. He would not play out of doors in summer and had to be driven to and from school during spring and summer. At least twice he had run across busy streets when he had seen a bee.

Most studies of fears in children have found that girls have more fears than boys. Whether this is because boys are expected to be brave and to suppress their fears or whether there is a biological difference which makes girls more easily frightened than boys is not yet known. It is quite possible, of course, that both explanations are true.

The place where the child lives also affects the things he fears. Children growing up in the countryside seem to fear animals more than do city kids. However, fears are often of objects the child has never met and which do not exist in the region. Sometimes fears are acquired by imitation of other people in the family who have the same problem. About one-sixth of adults with fears have a close relative with a similar phobia. During World War II in England, preschool children were more afraid of airraids if their mothers showed fear than if they did not. Conversely, children are less likely to develop fears if a trusted, reassuring adult is with them during a frightening experience.

For some reason, children with certain disorders also develop many fears. This it true for disorders like subnormality (mental retardation) and autism. Autism is a rare condition in which children become very withdrawn, avoid contact with people, and have weird repetitive habits. Fears in such children don't seem to die down as easily as in other children and can complicate their already difficult lives. One sturdy lad of seventeen whose brain had been damaged by inflammation following measles when he was four became terrified of dogs from that time onward. On seeing one in the street, he would make a grunting, frightened noise which caused the dogs to snarl at him and jump, which increased his own fear. Because of this phobia, he was unable to go anywhere alone, not even into the garden at home.[3] Another seventeen-year-old autistic girl was so terrified of certain noises that her life was endangered. If a dog barked suddenly or a child screamed or laughed loudly, she would escape immediately without thinking, even running across the road in front of cars. For this reason her parents were unable to let her go out alone.[4]

SCHOOL PHOBIA

The great majority of children have at some time or another shown reluctance to go to school. Very occasionally this reluctance culminates in outright refusal. School refusal can be a serious problem and is sometimes called school phobia. Although most children show anxiety about school at one time or another, this distress is generally short-lived and clears up without treatment. Long-standing cases of school refusal present a more difficult problem.

School refusal is different from truancy; in the latter the children do not refuse to go to school but use many wily tricks to stay away from school and wander alone or in the company of other truants, their whereabouts unknown to their parents, who first learn of the truancy from the school authorities. Truancy is often associated with other delinquent behavior, with frequent change of school, with a history of parental absence in childhood, and with inconsistent discipline in the home. At school, truants show a poor standard of work.

In contrast to truants, children with school phobias bluntly refuse to go to school, do not show other delinquent behavior, have no history of their parents being absent from the home, and more often keep a high standard of work and behavior at school. School phobics also have more physical symptoms of anxiety than truants, especially difficulties in eating and sleeping, abdominal pain, nausea, and vomiting.

The child will usually simply refuse to go to school. Young children may give no reason at all for their refusal, while older children will attribute their fears to various aspects of school life. They may complain of being bullied or teased or of being self-conscious about their appearance. They may be afraid of undressing in front of other children or of taking a public bath or shower after games. Anxiety about doing badly at games or schoolwork or fear of a teacher may be mentioned. A few children are frightened that harm may befall their mother while they are at school. Girls might also be anxious about menstruating, and both boys and girls might worry about reaching puberty or about masturbation. Other reasons some children give for not going to school include fears of fainting during school assembly or vomiting.

The child's fears are expressed not only directly but also in physical symptoms of anxiety, which may appear particularly in the morning when he is encouraged to leave the house for school. These symptoms include nausea, vomiting, headache, diarrhea, complaints of abdominal pain, sore throat, and leg pains. Eating difficulties, sleep disturbance, and various fears may be noted. The child's complaints may increase his parents' anxiety about him and lead sooner or later to open or tacit agreement that he should stay at home. Once the child is assured he can stay at home, his symptoms usually subside, only to recur the next morning when it is time to return to school. A typical picture is of a child who complains of nausea at breakfast and may vomit and who resists all attempts at reassurance by his anxious mother until a crisis is reached, at which she gives in and allows him to stay at home. Then he feels better unless the pressure to go to school is resumed.

In most children the school refusal develops gradually with a period of increasing reluctance to attend culminating in outright refusal. Before this point is reached, the child might be irritable, weep a lot, be restless and unable to sleep, feel nauseous, and complain of pains in the tummy when it is time to leave for school. Insistence that school be attended will produce fear, and the child may go pale, tremble, and sweat. In some children the fear begins suddenly on the Monday morning following a weekend, on the first day of a new term, or on the day of return to school following illness. A common trigger is a change to a new school at any level in the educational system. Less commonly, school refusal can begin after the death, departure, or illness of a parent.

The age of school phobics will naturally be the school-age years. The peak number of phobias usually occurs at those ages when there are changes of schools in a given country's educational system. In America and Britain this is about age eleven to twelve, which coincides with the period when most children move from a primary to a higher school.

The attitudes of parents can sometimes be important in cases of school phobia. Commonly the parents are overindulgent. Some mothers of school phobics develop unusually close dependence on their children as a compensation for their unsatisfactory marital or other relationships. When there is excessive emotional interdependence between the mother and her child, both of them may require treatment, for to treat the child alone may raise the mother's anxiety to the point where she may stop the child's treatment.

It is often held that school phobia is a misnomer for *school refusal,* on the grounds that the condition is not a fear of school at all but is rather a fear of leaving mother. This is too one-sided a view. Many children are more afraid of the school than of leaving their mothers. Some are afraid both of school and of separation from their parents.

Whatever the cause of school phobia, prolonged absence can lead to serious consequences which may be lifelong. The child loses touch with friends, social skills wither, and education suffers. The habit of avoiding unpleasantness may grow, so that in later years that person will cope more poorly with the slings and arrows of outrageous fortune with which we all must learn to contend.

TREATMENT OF PHOBIAS IN CHILDREN

Treatment of children's phobias follows lines similar to treatment of phobias in adults. Games are played which bring the child steadily nearer the thing that frightens him and keep him there until he no longer feels impelled to escape. One jokes with him meanwhile, gives him candy, and praises him for progress. It is helpful for fearful children to see other kids doing the same thing; for example, a dog phobic child feels more courageous on seeing another child of similar age and sex patting a dog. A useful way of helping children over a fear of animals is for them to acquire a pet puppy or kitten so that they can get used to playing with it. By the time the animal has grown up, the child has become desensitized to the animal and others like it. I treated my own daughter, who had a fear of cats at the age of 3½, by bringing a little kitten home and teaching her to play with it; she rapidly lost her fear and became deeply attached to it as it grew into an adult cat.

In the *treatment of school phobia,* one must first check that in fact conditions in the school are tolerable, that the child is not being bullied, and that unreasonable academic demands are not being made. Problems like those will need to be tackled directly. However, if the situation at school does not seem unsatisfactory and the main problem is that Johnny is scared of a normal situation, the most important point in treatment is firm insistence that he return to school and stay there, however much he dislikes the idea. Interest in what he does at school and praise for work he accomplishes can also help a great deal.

Returning the child to school may well require the cooperation of the teachers, who need to understand the situation. When the child is sent protesting back to school, crying and yelling, the parent may feel heartless. Usually crying stops quickly when the child is brought into the classroom. Until then the parent can earn angry looks from others accusing him or her of outrageous cruelty. This happened to me when my young son developed a mild fear of school after he had been out ill for a while with tonsillitis. Following the usual principles of treatment, which state that early return to the feared situation is the quickest way to reduce fear, I took my son by car to the school gates, his loud cries attracting malevolent glares from all around. When he entered the classroom, he quieted down and soon was busy enjoying himself in classroom activities. Within three days he was trotting off happily to school in the mornings without a murmur of protest. For a couple of years, each time he had to return to school after a long holiday, a few protests would ensue, but these disappeared increasingly rapidly after he was firmly taken to school.

CHILDREN CAN BE EDUCATED TO DEAL WITH ANXIETY

The attitude children need to learn is that anxiety is to be expected and that we have to be ready to face difficulties and overcome frightening situations. A courageous attitude is easier to nurture in a child of a naturally brave nature than one who is born timid, and we have to accept that some children are inevitably braver than others. Because the example of his parents is so important to a child, he will be liable to model their attitude. If he sees that his parents are consistently ready to master frightening situations, he will be more likely to do so himself, and he should be rewarded liberally for evidence of this mastery. However, a child should not be asked to do something far beyond his abilities. It also will not help him if seeing somebody else courageous merely strengthens his own convictions that he himself is a coward. When a child is sufficiently confident, gentle encouragement should be given to face mildly frightening situations until he has lost all his fear. While he faces his fear, he will need support until it has been overcome completely. Children and adults are more likely to show fear when weakened by illness, severe fatigue, or depression. Attempts should not be made to face fear while in such a state, as this may increase rather than relieve fear. Such attempts are best encouraged when the person is feeling well.

Children and adults cope better if they are prepared in advance for potentially stressful situations, taught what to expect, and learn what to do about them. In anticipation of dental work children could have preliminary visits to the dentist, as a game sit in the dental chair and have their mouths examined without any other procedures, and be given a treat afterward. The dentist can become a friend rather than the bogey man. The same applies to visits to a doctor. If children have to go into the hospital, they might visit it beforehand, meet nurses, and make friends with them before going in.

Intense separation anxiety can be prevented by having children go on vacations away from home with relatives and friends, first for a couple of days at a time, later for longer. They should be encouraged to go on trips and to camp with their friends. As for avoiding other common phobias, while children have to learn sensible hygiene, tidiness, and study habits, these should not be taken to extremes. Their sexual maturation can be anticipated by matter-of-fact sex instruction at an early age, with their inevitable questions being answered without embarrassment. Some schools now show films of sexual intercourse to children at or

arly sexual education might go a long way to
ysfunction in later life.

Changing nightmares into dreams of mastery

A fascinating example of the way in which children have been
taught to face their anxiety was reported by K. Stewart, an
anthropologist. He described how a tribe in Malaysia called the
Senoi handled a child who might tell them about an anxiety
dream, such as a dream about falling. When a Senoi child
reported a falling dream, the adults answered with enthusiasm:
"That is a wonderful dream, one of the best dreams a man can
have. Where did you fall to, and what did you discover?"[5] The
same comment was made when the child reported a climbing,
traveling, flying, or soaring dream. The child at first answered, as
he would in our society, that it did not seem so wonderful, that he
was so frightened that he awoke before he had fallen anywhere.

"That was a mistake," answered the adult authority,

> everything you do in a dream has a purpose beyond your
> understanding while you are asleep. You must relax and enjoy
> yourself when you fall in a dream. Falling is the quickest way to
> get in contact with the powers of the spirit world; the powers
> are laid open to you in your dream. Soon when you have a
> falling dream, you will remember what I am saying, and as you
> do you will feel you are travelling to the source of the power
> which has caused you to fall. The falling spirits love you, they
> are attracting you to the land and you have but to relax and
> remain asleep in order to come to grips with that. When you
> meet them you may be frightened of their terrific power, but go
> on. When you think you are dying in a dream, you are only
> seeing the powers of the other world, your own spiritual power
> which has been turned against you which now wishes to
> become one with you if you will accept it.[6]

Over a period of time the dream that started out with the fear of falling changed into the joy of flying. The Senoi also believed and taught that the dreamer should always advance and attack in the teeth of danger, calling on the dream images of his fellows if necessary, but fighting by himself until they arrived. Dream characters were bad only as long as one was afraid and retreated from them, and they would continue to seem bad and fearful as long as one refused to come to grips with them.

SUMMING UP

Most normal children have intense fears at some stage that start and die down again with no apparent cause. Newborn infants startle readily to noise, and by age one are usually frightened of strangers. From age two to four, fears of animals are the rule, and in adolescence shyness and sexual fears become manifest. Unlike fear, handicapping phobias are rare in children.

Youngsters are usually nervous when first at school, though they adapt readily within a few hours. School phobia or refusal is uncommon, but it can be a serious problem. Unlike truancy, it is not associated with other delinquent behavior, absence of parents, or inconsistent discipline at home. It occurs especially at times when children change schools, for example, at age eleven to twelve in the United States and Britain.

The treatment of phobias in children follows lines similar to treatment of those in adults, with the use of games, candy, and other stratagems to persuade the child to enter and remain in the phobic situation. With school refusal it is essential to firmly return the child to school, while ensuring there is no obvious bullying or other traumatic cause at the root of the anxiety. Return of the child to school may require the cooperation of understanding teachers.

Children can be educated to deal with threats with a courageous, though not foolhardy, attitude. They can be prepared in advance for potential stresses by being taught what to expect and what to do about them, for example, by playing games in the dentist's chair before formal dentistry is undertaken. Separation anxiety can be minimized by arranging increasingly long periods away from home with relatives and friends.

In the next chapter we will look at problems associated with anxiety that occur both in children and adults and have some features distinct from phobias. These are the obsessive-compulsive problems.

9

Obsessive-Compulsive Problems

Obsessive-compulsive problems can take the form of *obsessive thoughts* which intrude repeatedly into the mind against the will, despite all attempts to banish them. The ideas may concern contaminating oneself or other people, harming other people, or going against some other social taboo. Similar problems are *compulsive rituals*. These are repetitive actions carried out time and again although the person knows they are silly and tries to resist them. The classic example of ritual in literature is Shakespeare's Lady Macbeth's actions after the murder of Duncan (act 5, scene 1):

> *Doctor:* Look, how she rubs her hands.
> *Gentlewoman:* It is an accustomed action with her, to seem thus washing her hands: I have known her continue in this a quarter of an hour.
> *Lady Macbeth:* Yet here's a spot. . . . Out, damned spot! Out, I say! . . . yet who would have thought the old man to have had so much blood in him? . . . what, will these hands ne'er be clean? . . . Here's the smell of the blood still: All the perfumes of Arabia will not sweeten this little hand.

In real life, compulsive rituals do *not* usually depict an actual event. Unlike phobias, which are rarer in men than in women, obsessive-compulsive problems occur with equal frequency in both sexes. Usually the difficulties commence between ages sixteen and forty, but they can start at any age.

PERFECTIONIST PERSONALITY AND ITS OPPOSITE

Both obsessive thoughts and compulsive rituals tend to occur more in people who have always had meticulous and perfectionist personalities, though such problems can occur in the most slipshod of individuals. Meticulous habits can take many forms— you might be uneasy unless you use up that last tiny sliver of soap. One person might be a compulsive latecomer, while others can't bear to see a picture on the wall hang slightly askew. These are harmless quirks which are hardly abnormal, and people differ greatly in their habits. Some of us have always liked to be clean and tidy while others couldn't give a care if the house is sloppy or if there is a stain on trousers or dress. Lots of minor squabbles between husbands and wives occur because one likes to be more tidy or untidy than the other. There is a wide range of behavior in this respect. Dr. Elizabeth Fenwick, a medical journalist, caught the spirit of this beautifully in a series of vignettes:

> I once met a woman who ironed diapers. When I asked her why she did it she said it was because it made them square. Aesthetically, I can appreciate square diapers as well as anyone, but there are some things I am not prepared to make a good many sacrifices for. On a 0 to 5 Ironing Rating Scale I would probably score around 2, in front of the people who don't iron sheets and only do the bits of their husband's shirts which are going to show, but way behind the pajama and towel and vest and diaper ironers. . . .
>
> I suspect [my mother's] like me, but better at hiding it. She woke up once, clinging to my father. "I've had a terrible dream," she said, "I was in the kitchen, trying to make myself a drink, and I couldn't. There was rice in the tin marked coffee

and sugar in the tin marked tea." My father looked as if the world had stopped. "But there is," he said. . . .

[My grandmother] used to make ginger biscuits. Each biscuit was three inches in diameter and weighed half an ounce. It weighed half an ounce because she cut off a piece of dough and trimmed it and weighed it on her scales until that was what it weighed, and there was no cheating by weighing a two ounce lump and cutting it into four, either. All this sort of thing takes time, of course, which is one reason why I am not as obsessional as I might be. My grandmother never cut a piece of string in her life, no matter how enticing the contents of the parcel. She undid every knot and wound it into a neat little ball, and put it away in a Terry's Gold chocolate box labelled String (Oddments), and in the left hand front corner of the drawer next to the one marked Candles, which contained candles. Whenever there was a fuse or power cut at home it was always quicker to nip round to grandmother's and borrow a candle rather than hunt around in the dark for our own.

If I was obsessional I would be like that. I wouldn't sling the leftover garlic butter into an empty dish and bung it into the refrigerator. I'd put it into an old yoghurt pot with the lid on, and I'd label it Garlic Butter and I'd put it in the back right hand corner on the top shelf in the refrigerator, where the left over garlic butter always goes. Then I wouldn't make it into coffee butter icing when I came across it three weeks later.[1]

DISTRESS FROM OBSESSIVE-COMPULSIVE PROBLEMS

Although great neatness and cleanliness are virtues which help people in their jobs and everyday life, they can reach a point where they govern every action and at that point become an obsessive-compulsive neurosis. This can cause a great deal of suffering. A twenty-five-year-old married woman vividly portrayed her problem in the following words:

The biggest thing I've got is this obsession which spoils everything I do. If I had the courage I'd kill myself and get rid of the

Forms of Nervous Tension and Their Treatment

whole lot—it goes on and on, day after day. The obsession governs everything I do from the minute I open my eyes in the morning until I close them at night. It governs what I can touch and what I can't touch, where I can walk and where I can't walk. It governs whatever I do. I can touch the ground but I can't touch shoes, can't touch hems of coats, can't use the toilet without washing my hands and arms half a dozen times—and they must be washed right up the arms. If anybody touches their shoes I can't let them touch me—because then I would feel unclean and have to wash. Basically it all started from the toilet—first human dirt, then dog's dirt—now it's especially dog's dirt. I can't bear dogs—when I go out on the street I must be careful where I walk. It's always in my mind that I might have stepped in some dirt—the fear that I might have done so.

[And if you actually get contaminated?] That's the funny thing about it—it's not all that bad. My first feeling is panic, and my first thought is that I want to die—that's what first comes into my head, but I know you can't die just by wishing it, so then I've got to wash with a special procedure which is so long drawn out it never seems to come to an end—have to wash the tap and round the tap before washing my hands. I know it's all in the mind, I know it's ridiculous, but I can't accept it. I don't know why I'm so afraid of dirt all the time, but I am.

[Do you fight the feeling?] Yes, I do all the time, and usually succeed in the end after an hour or two, but the fear is still there. It frightens me because I don't know how to handle it, or what to think. Nothing in life interests me, I don't care what I look like, or what I eat. Mind you, I do get flashes where I care very much, but it lasts just a minute and it then disappears. I used to spend an hour washing every bit of me in the bath—washing all the time, but I only take half an hour, and now I can go and use a public toilet if it's clean. But the fear is more outside now—watching where I can walk. Things seem to change, and the fear slides over on to something else. What the fear started off with is still there, but it enlarges, and spreads to things I could have touched alright before. Once a long time ago I tried stopping washing for a week—but it was terrible, I

got awful nightmares, and was ready to scream all the time,
especially if anybody looked at me. After that I never tried
stopping it again. But I can't go on like this, I want to care, I
don't want to go on feeling life's useless.[2]

Obsessive fears of contamination usually occur together with
compulsive washing and rituals of avoidance.[3] Patients may feel
contaminated each time they pass urine or defecate, or after
being near dogs, and may have to bathe and wash for hours after
every such occasion. One woman felt that her son was contaminated and developed complicated rituals of washing his clothes,
his room, and everything connected with him. Another patient
felt that dogs were dirty and spent much of his life avoiding any
possibility of contact with dogs, dog's hair, or even buildings
where dogs may have been. He gave up his job when he heard
that a dog may have been on another floor of his office building.
Intense washing of his hands and clothes would follow the
remotest possibility that he might have been "contaminated."
Strikingly, he was as afraid of the hair plucked from a dog as of
the dog itself. An obsessive phobia is not a direct fear of a given
object or situation, but rather of the results which are imagined to
arise from it. This man would rather touch a dog with his hands
than let it touch his clothes, because hands are easier to wash
than clothes. Similarly, a woman obsessed with the idea of
possible injury from glass splinters was more afraid about frag-
ments she suspected but could not find at home than of the glass
splinters she actually found and removed with her bare hands.

Worry about harmful actions: Are they dangerous?

Obsessive phobias of harming persons include fears of killing,
stabbing, strangling, beating, or maiming, and these fears may
lead to avoidance of potential weapons and to complicated
protective rituals. A housewife may have to hide sharp knives in
her kitchen far out of reach to remove temptation, mothers may
need to have constant company for fear they will strangle their

babies if left alone, and so on. The concern may be about harming oneself rather than other people. Patients can be afraid of swallowing pins, broken glass, or other sharp objects, and go to ridiculous extremes to guard against the remotest possibility of this happening.

The risk of translating obsessive ideas into terrible actions is in fact very small. It is rare for obsessive-compulsive patients to actually perform the murders, stabbings, and stranglings which they dread. Out of the hundreds of patients with obsessive-compulsive troubles whom I have seen, only three patients yielded in any way to their impulse to harm someone. In one instance a young woman felt compelled to pick scabs off her young son's skin when they formed after he had scratched himself. So strong was the impulse that it was difficult to restrain her physically from lunging at a scab on her son's skin when she saw it. After treatment, this problem disappeared. A less happy outcome ensued in another woman, whose impulses were to kill her two-year-old child. She struggled against these urges painfully. They did not yield to treatment, and the danger that she might act out her urges became so strong that eventually she had to be separated from her daughter.

What it feels like to have obsessive ideas about harm was put in archaic language nearly 100 years ago.

Now, sir, I am a Homicidal (and sometimes Suicidal) Maniac. Up to the present time I have only thought these thoughts, I've never put them into action, but at the same time it is quite true that I cannot control them (the thoughts). . . . One night my mother was away from home, and I slept with my father. There was an old Dagger in the Room, my thoughts went unconsciously and without any will, wish, or control of mind to that, and I felt an almost irresistible impulse to get out of bed and murder my father with the Dagger, but I did not. I laid and trembled, and after that fell asleep. . . . Go where I will, be where I may, in Church, Chapel, Street, House or public meeting of any sort, the same ideas pursue me, I hear NO voices, it seems an IMPULSE. As in other people there is an impulse to go whoring, etc., where no object is present to give rise to the thought.[4]

More recently another person described the same problem.

One night after a number of weeks of fearful suffering, as I was lying in bed, tossing sleepless and despairing, the most horrible impulse seized me, an impulse impelling me to destroy one who of all living things, most deserved my love. I buried myself under the bedclothes, and struggled with the hellish impulse till the bed shook. It still gained strength. I sprang up, clung to the bedpost, sunk my teeth in the agony of despair into the hard wood. It was uncontrollable. I shut my eyes, bowed down my head for fear that I should see her, and rushed out of the house. Barefooted, with no covering over my nightshirt, I ran through the streets to a Police Office and implored them to lock me up. Fortunately the officer on duty was a humane and sensible man. He gave me a watchcoat to put around me, kept me under his own eye and, I suppose, sent notice to my friends, for my wife and sister came with clothing. The paroxysms had passed and panting for death in any form, I accompanied them home, steeped to the lips in despair.[5]

Family involvement in rituals

Quite often obsessive-compulsive patients drag their families into their rituals.[6] One thirty-six-year-old married woman was so frightened of tuberculosis germs that she would not sweep most of her house and left dust to accumulate on the floors because she thought that dust harbored germs. She could not feed her two-year-old son because she felt she might give him TB, which she had suffered decades earlier. Her husband therefore had to feed the child. She kept the child cooped up in a playpen all day, never allowing him the freedom to crawl around the house or walk. The child thus grew up as a stranger to the mother in her own home. His grandmother was never allowed to play with or even see him because of fear that the grandmother might bring germs in. Visitors were not allowed to come in, because they were potentially infective. The woman spent much of her day washing her hands—dozens of times—until they were raw and bleeding.

Another young woman was so distressed by "contamination" of her home that she forced her family to move five times in three years and totally avoided one town in the area which seemed particularly "dirty." Other wives were so worried by "dirt" that their families might bring into the home that they forced their husbands and children to strip naked in the entrance hall on coming home and to don fresh clothes there before entering the house. Many compulsives prevent other family members from bringing visitors into the home lest they disturb or untidy the oppressively neat, clean arrangements inside.

Obsessive-compulsive disorders sometimes run in families. In one family the mother and two daughters slept together in the same bed and all three developed similar hand-washing rituals based on fears of dirt. The father and brother slept together in another bed, and neither developed compulsive rituals.

Obsessions about hair and excreta

Some compulsive rituals center around hair.[7] One man of twenty-nine spent up to five hours a day washing and combing his hair, checking for hairs in his bed and on the floor around it. He felt uncomfortable if hairs came on his clothes and was impelled to remove them. Another young man, in addition to many other rituals, spent up to four hours a morning vacuuming and polishing his room at home, searching for hair, and worrying that it might have penetrated the electrical equipment. The worry was about hair from the head, not pubic hair or animal hair.

An unusual compulsion was complained of by another young woman.[8] She had intense urges to watch her lover's bowel action, though this did not excite her sexually. When her lover went to the toilet, she could not bear to be shut out and shouted at him if she could not watch him. When allowed to watch, she would stare at the feces for several minutes. Not surprisingly this compulsive habit dampened the enthusiasm of her boyfriends.

Severe obsessive-compulsive troubles greatly dislocate the lives of sufferers. An eminent jurist became unable to urinate or have a bowel action in his home for fear of contaminating it and would have to go elsewhere each time.[9] He could not endure sexual relations because they seemed dirty. When he came to see me, he had given up his job and was dressed in a shabby, stained suit. The breast of his jacket bulged from hundreds of paper tissues he kept in his inside pocket. He could open the door of the interview room only by using a paper tissue in his hand to grasp the "dirty" handle and could not shake hands for fear of contamination.

An obsessive paradox

The irrationality of obsessive-compulsive disorder was demonstrated by a woman who had been washing her hands up to 100 times a day until the skin was raw and bleeding. Though she spent endless hours at the tap washing her hands and arms, she would not take a bath or wash her body for weeks on end. The smell from her body became unbearable to people nearby, but this did not bother her in the least.

This lady required so many bottles of disinfectant and bars of soap a week that she could not afford to buy these out of her meager salary, and so she resorted to shoplifting soap and disinfectants. When she was caught in this action and taken to the police station, the police were unable to record her fingerprints as she had none—she had washed them completely away, and the skin on her fingertips was perfectly smooth.

Compulsive slowness

A special form of obsessive-compulsive neurosis is compulsive slowness. A man with this problem had been out of work for three years because it took him so long to do everything. He would take several hours to dress and have breakfast in the mornings. To be in time for his afternoon appointment with me, he had to shave the previous day. When I asked him how long it took him to have a bath he asked in reply, "Do you mean from the time I actually get into the bath, or from the time I start *thinking* of having a bath?"[10] Bathing took five hours. To cross a road would take another few hours, because he not only had to check that no cars were coming but he also had to look at every car parked along the road nearby in case they were about to move off. By the time he had finished looking inside the parked cars, he would have to start looking up the street several times once more, by which time he felt he had to look inside the parked cars again, etc. To switch off a light, he first checked that his shoes were insulated and would look many times at his soles before he dared to risk electrocution by putting his hand on the light switch. This slowness affected most of his everyday actions, but he rationalized it by saying that he could not take risks about being run over or electrocuted.

Compulsive hoarding

Another variant of obsessive-compulsive neurosis is compulsive hoarding. This can be combined with the rituals already discribed. People may find it impossible to throw rubbish away. They spend hours sorting out kitchen scraps before putting them in the garbage can lest they miss some useful food. Valueless papers from past decades will be stored until there is no room to move in the house. Vast quantities of food, cans, and other objects might be bought unnecessarily when there are no shortages in sight. Any attempt by somebody to remove some of the accumulation of ages will evoke great anxiety, and so the house might become quite unlivable as the rooms and passages become cluttered with old furniture, papers, food tins, and clothes that the sufferer cannot endure to have thrown away. One man could not bear to part with his old car, which had no wheels, and kept it rusting on blocks in his garage while his new car was left exposed to the elements outside.[11]

Number rituals

Number rituals are quite common and do not always interfere much with one's life. My colleague Dr. Leonard Cammer cited two clear examples of number rituals. One was the highly intelligent chief of a prestigious detective agency. He was attached to extensive counting and numbering rituals.

> I count the number of letters in the words spoken to me in any conversation, and I can tell you instantaneously the exact total of letters up to 350 or so. When you say "Good morning, John," I make an immediate mental note that this has 15 letters. When you asked me "Does your counting obsession interfere with your conversation with people," I answered "Not really," but before I answered I noticed that your question contained 63 letters. I also must count the number of letters on every street sign. That does interfere sometimes, especially when I am in a hurry to get somewhere in the car and there are lots of signs in the streets. If there are three numbers in a house or store window I must multiply them. For example, I see 275 on a building. I multiply $2 \times 7 \times 5$. Of course, I do it very rapidly. It equals 70.[12]

Similar rituals were described by a woman:

> I have to touch the venetian blinds four times, then all the *objets d'art* in the vestibule five times. That prevents harm to my older brother. He comes home safely, and proves that my ritual works. Maybe some people think it stupid, but if I don't go through with it, I start to stutter.[13]

TREATMENT OF OBSESSIVE-COMPULSIVE DISORDERS

Treatment of disorders such as those described above follows principles similar to those used in treating phobias, but it generally takes longer and more often requires inpatient admission for a few weeks, followed by brief treatment at home, plus involvement of the family where necessary. A good example comes from Ann, a twenty-three-year-old single woman employed in a bank.[14] For five years she had worried that she might become pregnant even during petting, although she was a virgin. For eighteen months she had feared that a small wart on her finger was cancerous, and eventually she sought treatment. She avoided any objects which might contaminate her with "cancer germs," and dreaded that she would pass this disease on to her family from her wart. She began to wash too much. Six weeks before treatment began, when her parents went on vacation and left her alone in the house with her teenage brother, her steady boyfriend moved into the house with them to ease her anxiety. It worsened instead. She became afraid to visit the lavatory after he had been to it in case she should catch "pregnancy" from it.

Before admission Ann checked electrical switches repeatedly because they seemed dangerous and frequently looked back over her shoulder to check for some nameless threat. She felt tortured lest she ever be the last to leave the bank at night and lest security checks became her responsibility. She washed her hands 125 times a day, used three bars of soap a day, took three hours to shower, and washed her hair repeatedly for fear of contamination with a cancer-causing germ. She felt that cancer took so long to come on that she could never be proved completely safe.

With her nurse-therapist Ann agreed on the following treatment targets: preparing and cooking meals for her parents without rituals to safeguard them, washing her hair without rituals, pricking her finger at the site of the former wart, and eating food with the pricked and bleeding finger.

In treatment Ann watched the nurse "contaminate" herself and then followed suit. The nurse then advised her what to do between treatment sessions, in a program designed to get Ann used to contamination and to systematically eliminate the checking rituals one by one. At first the nurse simply asked Ann to limit herself to using one bar of soap per day in whichever manner she preferred, but to eliminate washing under a running tap and to use a plug in a sink instead. Ann herself decreased the number of washes and the time they took. The nurse-therapist "contaminated" her bedroom, telephones, kitchen cutlery, and dishes. Ann went home most weekends with a program to contaminate herself, her home, and her parents and to restrict her rituals.

On the ward was another nurse who had had a breast removed years ago for cancer, which provided a focus of contamination for treatment. With this nurse's consent, Ann watched her therapist touch the scar where the breast had been removed and then touch herself and surrounding objects. Ann then did the same. After such "contamination," Ann was asked not to wash and later prepared meals and ate them with the nurse-therapist and the nurse. As Ann's fear of contamination improved, she was also asked to limit the items in her checking sequences one by one, restricting herself to checking each item just once.

The fear of pregnancy from the slightest contact with her boyfriend was then dealt with. The boyfriend's pajamas, towel, and underwear were brought into the hospital and put near to Ann. She was persuaded to touch and handle them to overcome her fear of becoming pregnant. She was given her boyfriend's pajamas to wear and his towel to use. She had to sleep with his underwear in her bed and under the pillow. The nurse-therapist discussed with her and her boyfriend a program whereby they would resume petting; this petting was increased from week to week until eventually Ann became able to touch her boyfriend's penis first through his trousers and then under them and became able to tolerate his masturbating her.

After forty-seven treatment sessions, Ann was able to return to work and was able to limit herself to using only one bar of soap every two weeks. She maintained this improvement over one year follow-up. She went abroad on her vacation without the contamination fear which formerly had made such a trip impossible. She was promoted at work and took charge of the normal security routine in her bank, which involved thirteen locks! She allowed her parents to go on vacation and leave her in charge of

Weekend of 18 August 1973.

Ann's tasks:

1. To either prepare a meal or else to help her mother with the preparation of a meal without any hand washing.
2. To touch all the dishes before having the meal.
3. To touch her father's pencils and pens, wallet and razor.
4. To touch her mother's rollers, handbag, and purse. Both of these are to be done without washing her hands either before or after.
5. To use her own soap for washing, and to wash only before a meal or after the toilet.
6. To put the plug in the sink when washing.
7. To eat something, yogurt or jelly, using her ring finger.

Parents' tasks:

1. To praise Ann when she does these things. Never to say that it was easy.
2. Not to give reassurance.
3. To show her fearless behavior, if there is anything that she believes to be potentially harmful, please, if it is possible, bring it to the ward when she returns from leave.
4. To leave a report, however brief, for the therapist on how the weekend progressed. Thank you.

Report on the weekend from parents to nurse-therapist

"Ann's day at home presented no great problems for her or for us. She still finds it difficult to wash with water in the basin and exaggerated the rinsing of hands and wrists after washing. We do not appear to have mastered your technique for persuading her to change her ways in this respect, and she was a bit rebellious over one incident but it was short-lived.

"Speaking generally we found that she was very much improved compared with her state when she went into hospital. She had little difficulty on a shopping expedition insofar as turning round, checking and worrying over electrical points in shops. She was quite relaxed and drove us all home in her own car.

168

She largely prepared the vegetables and dessert for Sunday's lunch, and if this caused her apprehension she didn't show it.

"I believe however that she still worries inwardly about cancer, hence the washing problem. (Visits to the toilet also create anxiety.) All in all we were pleased with her progress, and because she is very keen to overcome her problem she shows her disappointment when she fails to fulfill her tasks."

Weekend of 24 August 1973

Boyfriend's tasks:
1. Go to the toilet, do not wash hands, and contaminate (a) Ann's underwear, (b) Ann's knees, (c) Tampax.
2. Please send report to therapist about this. Thank you.

Report on the weekend from boyfriend to nurse-therapist

"Ann's underwear and Tampax were 'contaminated' twice over the weekend on Saturday and on Monday and her knees and thighs on a number of occasions (without tights). On no occasion was any anxiety apparent.

"Close proximity on the beach, which used to worry her, was no problem. A very successful weekend."

Report from Ann

Anxiety score: (8 = panic   0 = completely calm)

- Contamination of leg   Anxiety 1
- Contamination of underclothes   Anxiety 2
- Contamination of Tampax   Anxiety 2

SOURCE: I. M. Marks et al., *Nursing in Behavioural Psychotherapy*, Royal College of Nursing, London, 1977.

the home, which she could not have formerly contemplated. She was now able to shop regularly herself without her mother's presence being necessary to drag her away from checking rituals; at home she helped with the preparation of meals, which contamination fears had previously prevented her from doing. Sexual foreplay with her boyfriend was normal.

You can see from this description how closely the family may need to cooperate in treatment of some obsessive-compulsive problems. The flavor of the "home programs" over weekends can be given in the following sample for one weekend which Ann spent at home.

The following chart shows the tasks which the nurse-therapist prescribed for Ann, her parents, and her boyfriend to carry out separately that weekend when she went home. It also shows the reports which the parents and the boyfriend wrote to the nurse-therapist after Ann returned back to the hospital from the weekend. Note the meticulous detailed attention devoted to exposing Ann to the many different but connected problem areas which troubled her.

Exposure in real life preceded by modeling (the therapist first does what the patient has to do afterwards, demonstrating how to do it in detail) is thus useful in obsessive-compulsive disorders. Another patient had been bothered by numerous rituals which mainly involved attempts to ensure that he was not responsible for causing harm to others. He had been a truck driver for six years but was now afraid to drive as he tended to worry that he might have caused an accident. The worries could only be stopped by checking his route and on one occasion by checking with the police. He checked that taps were turned off, that razor blades were put away, that rugs were not ruffled, and he had numerous other checking rituals which made normal life impossible and interfered with his previously happy marriage.

During the first two days of treatment, he was encouraged to perform certain actions which he had avoided for at least four years. These included driving a car, bumping into people in a crowded supermarket, putting pins, matches, and stones on the floor of the hospital lounge, and turning on water taps, leaving them to drip. At each stage, the therapist performed the desired behavior and the patient copied him; all the most difficult tasks were included. After each forty-minute session, the patient was told that he must resist the urge to check and must not ask for reassurance concerning possible harm that he might cause. This patient felt sick for a short while after each of the first two days of treatment but recovered quickly and was symptom-free at the end of the three treatment periods. He remained well when seen for the last time two years later.

Family involvement in treatment

Obsessive-compulsive problems often have wide repercussions on the life-style of the patient and his family. These repercussions may also need to be dealt with carefully in treatment. One woman who was described earlier had many rituals which hampered her care of her infant son.[15] Before her treatment he was confined to a playpen all day lest he get tuberculosis from the dust on the floor; his food had to be ritually prepared by the father; his grandmother and aunt were never allowed to see him; and most of the house was never swept for fear of spreading germs. The patient lived 200 miles from London. Toward the end of her stay in the hospital, her husband lodged near the hospital and took part in treatment sessions so that the patient learned to feed her son herself, without rituals. A nurse escorted the family home on the train and ensured that the patient touched door handles and window sashes that she had shown initial signs of avoiding. The nurse spent two whole days with the family at home ensuring that the patient swept the whole house without fear of germs and that she fed her son properly and did not carry out rituals. Her husband had to be told to stop the many rituals his wife had taught him to perform. Once the patient had learned not to involve the family in her rituals and the husband had been taught how to cope with her remaining rituals, no further treatment was needed and she had no rituals when seen two years later.

Some compulsive patients repeatedly ask for reassurance from their relatives in a ritualistic manner, for example, "Darling, did I touch the dirt on the wall?" or "Are you quite sure I haven't put poison in the food?" The long-suffering relative has usually been trained to answer repeatedly with some reassuring noises like, "No, you didn't touch the dirt," or "Yes, honey, I'm sure there's no poison in the food."

As we saw earlier in the treatment of illness phobias, reassurances only damp down the patient's anxiety for a short while and prevents him from learning to tolerate the discomfort produced by his uncertainty about illness, dirt, or whatever. The patient will rapidly acquire the necessary tolerance and cease asking for reassurance if he is not reassured at any time. In treatment, therefore, relatives have to learn not to be reassuring, so that the questions are not kept going by repeated temporary reduction of anxiety through reassurance. In treatment the patient and spouse may need to rehearse a scene many times to teach the relative what to do; for example, the patient might ask her husband, "Is baby alright?" upon which the husband needs to respond, "Hospital instructions are that I do not answer such questions." It is surprising how much time it can take to learn this simple response after years of, "It's okay dear, he's fine, he's alright."

Families can solve problems together in a group

I have found it useful to conduct a therapy group in which several patients and their families come together to discuss the difficulties they cause for one another and ways of overcoming them. They meet about every five weeks. During meetings they review progress and work out tactics to reduce the remaining rituals.

Between meetings, some families phone one another to find out how they are getting on. In the group, families are often relieved to share their experiences with other people who have similar problems and are very helpful in devising solutions for one another's difficulties. It also aids them to learn what other people's norms for behavior are. Many patients are surprised to learn that most people take less than five minutes to brush their teeth, that it is not a general custom to spring-clean the house every day or to boil baby's bottles for three hours before every feeding.

Even quite young children can be taught to help their parents overcome rituals. In one family, children on their own initiative pinned the notice "touch me" on a laundry basket their mother used to avoid, and in another family persuaded their mother to come swimming in a public pool, an activity she dreaded for fear of becoming contaminated.[16]

In the therapy group, relatives are encouraged to praise their patients for undertaking difficult therapeutic tasks. This does not always come naturally. One husband consistently withheld approval from his wife's diligent homework to overcome her worries about fire; for example, at her therapist's request she left candles alight in secure holders in every room at home. When the group finally urged this husband to praise her, he refused, saying, "I can't—nobody in my family ever praised anybody."[17] However, he devised his own solution. Into a tape recorder he dictated, "That's very good dear, I'm pleased you managed it," and played the tape-recorded message to her. After a few trials of this he managed to say it himself without the aid of a tape recorder—he had overcome his inability to praise his wife.

Eighteen-year-old Helen used to drive her family mad by lining up mom, dad, and sister in a neat row every night at home so that she could be sure she had kissed them all good-night systematically, usually doing this several times.[18] Helen also insisted on her mother holding a glass of water for her to dip her toothbrush in repeatedly—this could go on for an hour. In front of the family group Helen was requested to start these rituals, and her mother and father were then told not to comply, saying the routine phrase, "The hospital has told us not to do this." At home they were able to stay firmly out of Helen's rituals, which then greatly diminished.

Compulsive slowness can be treated with an approach we might call "time and motion" treatment. Here the patient is prompted to carry out his slow rituals with increasing speed until eventually he is able to complete his actions in normal times. As an illustration, a man who takes three hours to get up and ready for breakfast would be given a stopwatch and asked first to complete these tasks within 2¾ hours while being advised which actions to cut out so that he can speed up. Then he will be encouraged to complete his actions in 2½ hours, 2¼ hours, and so on until he eventually takes no longer than the average person, say half an hour. The patient can take home a tape recording of the therapist's instructions to play at the appropriate times as a reminder.

Obsessive hoarding can be treated by encouraging patients to get over their fear of throwing things away lest vital information be missed. A therapist may accompany the patient to his home and together they will slowly throw away ten-year-old newspapers to let him get used to the idea that even if information has been lost it does not matter. It is amazing how resistant a hoarder might be to throwing away old potato peelings or a broken chair which has no hope of being repaired. With gentle encouragement, however, a hoarder might be taught to part with many objects and to clear the living space at home so that visitors can be entertained once more.

Provided people with compulsive rituals carry out treatment instructions faithfully with respect to contaminating themselves, not checking, and so on, the chances of getting better and remaining well are good. For instance, one man who had been unemployed for years because he spent most of the day washing himself repeatedly was encouraged in treatment to touch articles the therapist had first touched, ending up with touching spots of urine and dried excrement, which were the focus of his worries.

This man improved dramatically, and two years after treatment his mother wrote a letter of thanks: " . . . he was married last September and has bought a house. He and his wife have settled in well, and it is a pleasure to call on them and see him gardening and doing various odd jobs around the house. This is a thing we would have thought impossible a few years ago."[19] Though treatment of this condition is not easy, the results are well worthwhile and enduring.

SUMMING UP

Obsessive thoughts are those which intrude repeatedly into one's mind against one's will, while compulsive rituals are repetitive actions we feel compelled to carry out even if they seem silly. Like most phobias, obsessive-compulsive problems usually start in young adults, but, unlike phobias, are equally common in both sexes. Often these problems occur in people who have always been meticulous and perfectionist, but this is not always so. Obsessive thoughts about potentially harmful actions are usually groundless. It is very exceptional for thoughts to be carried out as acts.

Relatives are frequently dragged into helping patients with their rituals, which tends to increase them, and the family life-style and child rearing can be gravely disrupted. Common rituals involve repeated washing and checking for contamination or harm, and doing things by numbers. Less common are worries about hair, serious slowness, and hoarding of all kinds of useless objects.

Treatment of obsessive-compulsive problems follows similar principles to those used in treating phobias, but it can take longer because the ramifications can be so much more extensive in the sufferer's life. The patient is asked to deliberately face those situations which bring on the rituals and to refrain from ritualizing for as long as possible, while learning to tolerate the ensuing discomfort. Great attention is needed to all the detailed circumstances which may be involved, and relatives can be valuable helpers in management by monitoring and praising progress while withholding reassurance and refraining from participating in any rituals. Families can help sort things out by meeting together in a problem-solving group.

We proceed now to a very different but frequent source of worry—sexual anxiety.

10

Sexual Anxieties

Worries about sex are among the most pervasive problems of adolescents and young adults. They are all the more troublesome because people are often ashamed to talk about them and find it hard to turn for advice to anybody, including doctors. In years gone by, sex was such a taboo topic that many sufferers never got the help they needed, but today attitudes are changing and aid is easier to get.

In the past normal activities like masturbation were regarded as sinful and as the cause of numerous hideous ailments from venereal disease to insanity. Though 99 percent of boys masturbate at some stage and those who do not are in a tiny minority, many of them—and girls who masturbate as well—endure endless hours of suffering from guilt. With the spread of information about normal sexual behavior, guilt feelings are probably less common today. However, some adolescents do still believe that their pimples result from their masturbation and that their habits can be read on their faces in some vague way. Guilt not only about masturbation but also about other sexual behavior is still a source of torture to many people who grew up with restrictive

177

sexual attitudes in their homes and schools. Girls who pet or have premarital intercourse even now will sometimes be depressed and worried by a perfectly normal sexual experiment. Adolescent boys and girls often lack confidence in approaching each other and die a thousand deaths from embarrassment when they meet the opposite sex in a potentially sexual situation like a party or a date.

Somehow most of us eventually get over our sexual hang-ups through a normal process of trial and error and of more or less successful experimentation. By the time people are married, the majority of them are leading fairly happy sex lives, though there is a wide range in norms. A love-nip for one woman becomes a sadistic hurt to someone else. One couple might veto oral intercourse as perverted, while another might feel deprived if their sexual menu lacked it. Initial stimulation may be superfluous for the woman who loves a fast "flyer" because she achieves orgasm rapidly with deep penetration. Lying on the bed, she calls to her partner, "I am ready whenever you are, honey." Another man might be made impotent by this.

SEXUAL INFORMATION AND ATTITUDES

A big difficulty in the past was inaccessibility of reliable sexual information for lay people. This deficiency is being remedied as an increasing number of instructive books come on the market explaining and showing what sex is about together with helpful photographs and diagrams. Good films of sex are also becoming easier to get. It is best to choose materials designed to instruct rather than titillate. Straight pornography can be misleading. Moreover, although it generates excited interest from censors in various countries, pornography can become very boring after the initial novelty has worn off.

Though sexual attitudes seem to have changed remarkably, actual sexual behavior may have changed less than the media would have us believe. One study of young German students showed little difference in sexual patterns over the years except that nowadays students seem to begin having actual intercourse a year or two earlier than in the past and are a bit more tolerant of their partner having other affairs. Nevertheless by far the dominant sexual pattern is "monogamous romantic love," with steady dating between one boy and girl who plan eventually to get married. Much is written in the papers about wife-swapping or "swinging," but a recent survey of a Midwestern community found that only a tiny minority of people had practiced this. The usual sexual norm even in these permissive days is one of fairly conventional, steady sex between stable partners, though fewer women are virgins when they marry, and more oral genital sex is practiced among young adults than used to be the case.

SEXUAL JEALOUSY

Marital jealousy can ruin people's lives. Othello and Desdemona are tragic models of the misery jealousy can bring. Sexual jealousy is more common among men than women and is often associated with alcoholism or with impotence. In its extreme form, morbid jealousy can lead to murder. More typical is one couple who had been on the brink of divorce because the husband had repeated "funny imaginations" that his wife was unfaithful to him. This caused frequent quarrels, although they both denied that they had ever been unfaithful to each other. Despite all this, they had sex together regularly.[1]

The danger of homicide being provoked by jealousy is recognized in the legal systems of certain countries, which do not punish severely crimes of passion in which one partner is found *in flagrante delicto* by the other. In such instances, in a man's world a man may murder the wife with impunity more often than the reverse. This reflects the double standard of morality still present in many countries where the man is free to have as many mistresses as he wishes, but the woman may not openly take a lover.

TYPES OF SEXUAL PROBLEMS

Sexual problems secondary to physical or psychological causes

Loss of sexual interest by either sex can be a sign of severe depression. A few physical diseases may cause reduced sex drive or poor sexual performance, especially failure to attain erection or orgasm. The same effects can be caused by not a few drugs and from excessive intake of alcohol. Sexual deviation refers to the desire for unconventional sexual activity such as homosexuality, cross dressing, sadomasochism and so on. Sexual deviation can be associated with impotence, but this is by no means invariable.

Marital disharmony

A common source of sexual difficulties is marital discord. If you are at war about a thousand and one things, the chances are that bed will be part of the battleground. There is then little point dealing with the purely sexual arena if at the same time you are quarreling endlessly with your spouse about the housekeeping money, the children's education, the color of the curtains you are buying, and which show to see tomorrow night. Until you can sort out your relationship to a level of mutual toleration, it will be difficult to work with your spouse in a sexual skills program.

It is sometimes difficult to know whether the sexual problem of a couple is primarily sexual or, rather, the result of getting on each other's nerves in other respects. One woman who had ceased sexual relations with her husband flounced into my consulting room and announced, "You're the phobia king. Well, I've got a phobia of wearing tight clothes in the presence of my husband."[2] She then launched into a narrative which made it obvious that the main problem was marital discord about matters having nothing to do with her phobia or with sex, but then spilling over into sexual issues.

Unconsummated marriage

Fewer than 1 percent of marriages have not been consummated by successful intercourse within the first year. Occasionally a husband and wife may never have had sex together despite years of marriage. This can be because of problems in either partner. In one couple I saw, the problem was that the husband preferred young boys to women.

Another couple I treated had petted together to climax frequently before marriage and afterward masturbated each other to orgasm three times a week over ten years of marriage. The man would have a normal erection, but whenever he tried to have intercourse, his wife would thrust him away. She didn't mind his touching her breasts or genitals but would not touch his penis nor walk about in the nude in front of him, although he could watch her having a bath.

Equally striking was another young couple who had never had normal intercourse over three years of marriage.[3] As a child the wife had had an excruciatingly painful abscess of her genitals, and when she was nineteen she was virtually raped by a man who then blackmailed her into repeated sexual relations. When she married, these painful memories prevented her from having normal sexual relations with her husband, and they restricted their sexual activities to mutual genital caressing to climax. Although she did not mind her husband's penis touching the outside of her vulva and could even have an orgasm in that way, if he tried to insert his penis into her she would have painful contractions of her vagina, and he then found it impossible to achieve penetration.

SEXUAL PROBLEMS IN WOMEN

Painful intercourse

A common complaint from women is that intercourse hurts them. They find themselves squeezing their pelvic muscles into spasm while hating every minute of it, a condition called *vaginismus,* meaning spasm of the muscles around the vagina. As we just saw, in its extreme form vaginismus can prevent coitus by stopping the penis from entering the vagina. Occasionally pain on intercourse may indicate physical disease due to infection, hormone disturbance, or benign tumors, and these should be excluded at the start by medical examination.

Anorgasmia

A frequent problem and one that can take several forms is anorgasmia. A woman may fail to reach orgasm even though she might enjoy insertion of the penis and be perfectly relaxed about it. On the other hand, anorgasmia is often found together with vaginismus. Some women have never experienced orgasm, either with masturbation or during coitus. Others may readily achieve orgasm through masturbation but not during intercourse. A few have multiple orgasm with coitus, but not with masturbation. Anorgasmia is more likely where the man is inexperienced, clumsy, or can't sustain his erection. It can also result from the woman being too timid to guide her mate to do what turns her on, for example, "A little more to the left. Press harder. Yes, do that again. Lovely!"

SEXUAL PROBLEMS IN MEN

Lack of social skills

The lack of certain social skills can stop a man from ever finding a sexual partner. Although women's liberation has produced changes in sexual behavior, men are still usually expected to take the sexual initiative and they have to learn how to relate to women before sex becomes a realistic possibility. They have to know how to talk with a woman, the rules for dating, and how to make sexual approaches that are acceptable. Having done all that, a man still needs to have an erection before intercourse can be achieved, and excessive fear can prevent an erection. A typical example is nineteen-year-old Dick, who complained that he was still a virgin and got very uptight when he was with women, especially if they seemed to be rejecting him.[4] Although young women found Dick attractive and approached him, such approaches made him tense, and he would break off the relationship. Petting with women gave him strong erections, and Dick often masturbated while thinking about women.

Failure of erection (impotence)

Inability to get an adequate erection for intercourse is called *impotence*. On a honeymoon, failure at first attempt is not uncommon, but practice makes perfect. Impotence is common when men are tired or anxious for any reason, or when they are on certain medications, like those designed to lower high blood pressure. That ubiquitous drug, alcohol, can also hinder performance. Shakespeare recognized this relationship when he wrote in *Macbeth* that alcohol provokes desire but takes away from performance. The English phrase "brewer's droop" paints the picture clearly. Although relatively rare, impotence can be caused by physical illnesses like diabetes and diseases of the brain or spinal cord may result when the endocrine glands do not produce the right sort of hormones. People with sexual deviations may also be impotent. A homosexual male may be turned on by men but not by women, although many gay men and women also have regular heterosexual relations.

Premature ejaculation

Early ejaculation is a frequent problem. Here the man climaxes (ejaculates) too soon and cannot delay his emission of semen until the woman is satisfied. She may then feel understandably frustrated and let down. The problem is often combined with a failure to get a proper erection, or the man may have only a brief erection and then ejaculate suddenly before he wants to.

How soon can ejaculation occur without being called premature? It depends a bit on how long the woman takes to reach orgasm. If she climaxes within a minute or at the same time as her partner, he is less likely to ask for help. However, if she never attains orgasm even though he sustains an erection and delays ejaculation until 20 minutes of coitus, it would be misleading to say he has premature ejaculation.

Failure of ejaculation (ejaculatory incompetence)

Failure to ejaculate is the opposite difficulty and is rarer. The man is able to have an erection for hours on end but is unable to attain a climax with ejaculation of semen. His partner may have climax after climax during this time.

Failure of erection and premature ejaculation happen more often if the woman is irritable or dislikes sex. Unless he is unusually capable, her mate might be put off by attitudes such as "get it over with fast" or "alright, if you really have to. I will still love you, dear, despite it." Equally, a sexual demanding woman might make him think, "You think it's a battery-operated toy where I push a button to make it stand up for you?" and his "toy" will hang limp.

Although at first sight one might think that having good sex is simply doing what comes naturally, in fact it is a complicated set of skills which people have to learn. It is not surprising that things often go wrong, especially in the beginning until the couple learns to perform adequately. An experienced partner can be a very good therapist. Twenty-year-old Ralph asked for psychiatric help because he could not get proper erections with women he knew, nor with prostitutes. Nevertheless he masturbated regularly. While on the waiting list to see a psychiatrist he met a sexually experienced girl five years older than he. She was very patient. She knew about his problem and let him try to approach intercourse slowly and repeatedly without hurrying or laughing at him. With her support within a few weeks Ralph was leading a vigorous, normal sex life.

TREATMENT OF SEXUAL ANXIETIES

Before sexual problems are treated, it is necessary to exclude obvious causes such as marital discord, severe depression, alcohol, drugs, physical disease, and lack of social rather than sexual skills. For treatment to succeed, a cooperative partner is necessary. This is the first essential, and shy people may have to embark on a program to develop their social skills to this end. When a young man worries that girls will laugh at him or a young woman refuses a date because she feels gawky, the solution lies in prompting oneself to make the date or accept the offer of going out and learning to handle the situation. If shyness is your problem, you might practice talking to others in the canteen at work, telling stories to them, chatting with them, offering them coffee, going out with them on a walk in order to be able to make progress. As each new step becomes easier, you will grow more comfortable and be able to proceed to the next stage.

Principles of treatment

We are fortunate to live in an age when sexual worries are understood and dealt with much better and more openly than in the past. Sexual fears can be dealt with in the same way as other anxieties, but in addition to overcoming fear, you need to learn what to do to have enjoyable sex, and this skill takes time to develop. Sexual skills programs are effective, given a cooperative couple willing to work hard at overcoming the problem.

The principle of the program is literally graduated exposure and the learning of sexual behavior. Sexual anxiety slowly subsides through steadily increasing contact of the partners with each other's bodies. Gradually increasing intimacy allows them to become comfortable with each other, learn what turns each other on and off, and acquire fluent sexual skills. In clinics couples are first encouraged to talk about their sexual difficulties in detail and to learn a sexual vocabulary which will enable them to tell each other clearly about their sexual activities and feelings. The couple needs to know what words to use to describe the genitalia and various aspects of intercourse.

A good idea for self-help is to read a reputable book about sex which describes and shows pictures of the genitals and people having intercourse in different positions. Read this together and discuss your problems in the light of what you have learned. Then explore your bodies and examine your genitals, first your own, then each other's. For women, unless you are especially agile, you may need a hand mirror to see your vulva properly. Although you don't have to, you might wish thereafter to stimulate your own genitals with your hands, a vibrator, or both, eventually masturbating alone to climax. After doing this enjoyably a few times, you can proceed to the next stage of mutual caressing. If you already enjoy touching each other's bodies and have no anxiety about this, but only have one of the specific problems described earlier, you can skip the next stage on sensate focus and proceed immediately to the special techniques described for them which follow.

Sensate focus

The first stage of treatment is based on the principle of gradual exposure. It consists of getting used to touching each other's bodies, while being banned from coitus. This stage of treatment is called *sensate focus*. What it means is that the couple has to set aside time (say fifteen minutes) several times a week to caress each other's bodies without clothes on, learning to give each other pleasure without touching the genitals or breasts, on the understanding that neither party will move toward sexual intercourse. To aid the caressing, some couples like to apply lotion or oil to the skin. Certain therapists invite the couple to inspect one another's bodies and genitals in the clinic so that they can overcome their squeamishness and get accurate information.

Simply lying together in the nude can lead to great anxiety. When I instructed one couple to proceed on this course, no matter what they felt, I got the message the next morning from the wife via my secretary: "Tell Dr. Marks that I did what he asked and I could kill him for it, but I did it." The task in question was to sleep in the nude all night next to her husband. After doing this for a week, this woman had no qualms at all about doing so or about engaging in mutual caressing in the nude. Within six weeks she and her husband were having intercourse regularly for the first time in their three years of marriage.

Only when a man and woman are happy about caressing each other's bodies freely without anxiety is it advisable to start on the steps that lead to sexual intercourse. Specific problems call for specific ways of overcoming them. In the descriptions which follow, you will notice that when the time comes for intercourse it is assumed that the woman is on top of the man. This is the usual advice, as it is said to give the woman greater control. Some couples I have treated disliked this and preferred to start coitus with the man on top. The answer is, "Try whatever sexual position you find most comfortable."

Problems in men

Failure of erection

When the problem is that the man cannot achieve an erection, the woman is taught to caress his penis gently until he slowly attains an erection. When this happens she lowers herself gently onto him, inserting the penis into her vagina. If he loses his erection, she raises herself up again, resumes caressing him until he has an erection once more, and then again lowers herself onto him. This is repeated time and again until the man can tolerate being erect in her for, say, fifteen minutes, after which time they can carry on normal intercourse movements to climax.

The man has to learn that losing his erection is not a disaster—it will come back if the couple just continues love play and he does not feel flustered. You can see from this description that the man and woman are learning quite a complicated motor skill and also how to read each other's feelings and to communicate freely about them.

Premature ejaculation

If the difficulty is too-early ejaculation, then the technique is slightly different. It is designed to teach the man to inhibit ejaculation while his penis is being stimulated. In brief, there are two very similar variants, either "stimulate, pause, stimulate," or "stimulate, squeeze, stimulate."

The wife is asked to caress her husband's penis until he has a full erection, and continues this stimulation until he feels that ejaculation is almost imminent. He tells her this point is near, whereupon she ceases caressing him. Now they can just pause for a few minutes, or if they wish they can also use the squeeze technique. Here she stops caressing his penis and instead firmly squeezes the glans (the bulbous tip of the penis) between her thumb and second finger. Pausing or squeezing stops the desire to ejaculate. When the man feels there is no longer any danger of ejaculating, he tells his wife, who then resumes caressing his penis.

This masturbation is continued until the man can sustain an erection for fifteen minutes without danger of ejaculation. At that stage the wife lowers herself onto him, inserting his penis into her body. If he feels ejaculation is close, he tells her immediately. All motion must now stop, to reduce anxiety and excitement. If this is not enough to inhibit the desire to ejaculate, she withdraws for a minute or two until the urge has passed, after which they come together again. The rule is thrust, stop, separate if need be, thrust again, and so on, until good control is achieved.

The important point is for the couple to work steadily together toward the desired target behavior at a speed which they find comfortable, feeling free to experiment as they achieve control of their sexual behavior.

One variant is worth considering. Instead of penile stimulation being carried out by the wife at the start, there is no harm in the man masturbating himself, pausing when close to climax, and resuming masturbation when the urge has subsided. When he has acquired control by himself, the same exercise is repeated, but with his wife doing the stimulation.

I was most surprised with one couple I was advising about the husband's premature ejaculation.[5] They had listened carefully to my outline of the treatment program at the first session. At the second session the wife complained that she found it a bit difficult to stimulate her husband's penis for as long as fifteen minutes. On inquiry it turned out that instead of using her hand she was in fact stimulating his penis with her mouth by fellatio, rather than using her hand. She and her husband had regularly practiced oral sex in the past despite his problem. After a few sessions the husband became able to keep up an erection for fifteen minutes outside and inside his wife. At that point the wife began to tire of treatment, and ways had to be found to keep up her flagging interest. Boredom does occur, and you can arrange to reward yourselves for targets reached by activities you find enjoyable—a weekend holiday, a night out, or a present you've wanted to buy for years.

Failure of ejaculation

Ejaculatory incompetence is an uncommon problem. The man is able to maintain an erection, for hours at a time if necessary, but is quite unable to reach a climax even though his partner may reach orgasm many times. For this trouble, start your program with mutual caressing of each other's bodies without intercourse. Then the woman starts stimulating the man's penis vigorously *outside* her body until he has achieved ejaculation through this masturbation. Once this has happened, during the next erection, when the man reports that ejaculation is imminent, the woman lowers herself onto him rapidly, inserting his penis into her so that he can ejaculate inside her vagina. The couple then moves the time of coming together (insertion) earlier and earlier in their sexual stimulation. This helps to make it easier for him to subsequently ejaculate inside her through intercourse alone.

Don't be discouraged by early failure

Some men think they are impotent simply because they fail a few times, or because they are deviant sexually. A middle-aged clergyman and his wife once came to me complaining that they had not been able to achieve successful intercourse during their four years of marriage.[6] It turned out that the clergyman had for years been attracted to little boys. While he lived in another country, he had masturbated boys regularly. He had not engaged in this practice since he and his wife returned to England a year earlier, although he still retained his penchant for young lads. During his honeymoon four years earlier, on trying intercourse he had failed to obtain an erection three times in a row. He and his wife never tried again thereafter, giving up in despair.

Treatment of this couple turned out to be remarkably easy. I pointed out to them that many couples fail at their first few tries at making love and that as they hadn't tried for four years it might be worth trying again. First, at home they had to sleep nude next to but not touching each other. This they achieved, and before the next session they were asked to start caressing each other daily at home, but without intercourse, no matter how much they wanted to. By the third session they were given permission to have intercourse if they so desired. By the fourth session a few weeks after seeing me they were having regular normal coitus, which gave them both much pleasure. The man's desire for boys had disappeared entirely. The wife soon became pregnant and a few months later another impotent clergyman was referred to me on the advice of this couple.

Problems in women

Vaginal spasm (vaginismus)

When the woman has vaginal spasm each time penetration is attempted, quite a few approaches can be helpful. Once you are used to sensate focus with your mate, that is, mutual caressing in the nude, you can start experimenting by first putting the tip of your little finger inside your own vulva and vagina, and as you get used to this, the whole finger, and then two fingers. When you can accommodate two of your own fingers comfortably, allow you partner to insert his finger into your vagina slowly, gently, and repeatedly, until you are used to it. An alternative at this stage is to pass little rounded dilators of progressively increasing size into your vagina until you can move them about quite freely and easily tolerate one a bit longer and broader than a man's penis. Your partner can then do the same to you, after which you can proceed gradually toward intercourse, with you allowing him to move more vigorously as time goes on.

Anorgasmia

If you are a woman who does not have orgasm, you need to learn to move more vigorously during intercourse to stimulate yourself, and to teach your mate to move in ways which satisfy you. Before coitus is attempted it might be useful for you to start by masturbating yourself manually to climax in a systematic program.[7] You can use a vibrator as well if you enjoy the sensation—it is not expensive and many women find it useful.

A virgin couple ten years after marriage

It is quite common for both partners to have some sexual difficulties. This was the case with Jean and her husband Jack. Jean is the lady of forty whose treatment for agoraphobia we glimpsed on pages 92–93. Her husband was six years older, and they had never had intercourse during ten years of marriage. Part of the problem was Jean's vaginismus, complicated by Jack's occasional premature ejaculation. Neither of them had had any sexual experience before their marriage. After marriage they frequently tried coitus unsuccessfully, and five years later had their marriage annulled on the grounds of nonconsummation. Later they remarried, knowing their sexual problem would continue. They came eventually for treatment because they wanted to have a child.

Jean and Jack were interviewed twice together to get a detailed picture of their sexual behavior. This brought them much closer together. They masturbated each other on five nights to the point where Jack had an emission but Jean did not reach orgasm. They were asked by their therapist to carry out homework before the next session. This was to caress each other's bodies, including their genitals, for fifteen minutes daily but under no circumstances to attempt sexual intercourse. By the next (third) session two weeks later both reported increased sexual arousal and less anxiety during sensate focus. Both partners had a very enjoyable week, and Jack felt very relaxed and pleased. Jean enjoyed the sensate focus and was also much more relaxed. Jean had exceeded instructions in allowing Jack to insert one finger into her vagina, which caused her slight discomfort but great pleasure. They were asked now to prolong their sensate focus from fifteen to thirty minutes, to buy a vaginal lubricant such as KY or petroleum jelly, and with its aid to increase vaginal exploration, which was to be undertaken first by Jean and then by Jack. They could use different finger widths as dilators to gradually increase the stretching. Actual intercourse was still banned, but mutual masturbation was allowed. There was no need to hurry.

By the fourth session a week later progress had been a bit less satisfactory, and they had practiced finger-insertion into the vagina on only one night. They were encouraged to continue and were told, "There is no haste—you will have bad weeks as well as good ones, but with persistence you will overcome these troubles and succeed." Two weeks later they reported further advances. The KY lubricant made everything easier and more exciting. Jack had managed to insert his penis for one inch into the vagina and to ejaculate inside Jean. They had continued their sensate focus and finger insertions to stretch Jean's vagina. More homework was set with further mutual caressing and finger exercises to dilate the vagina together with the help of plastic dilators. Jack was to try deeper and more prolonged penetration by the penis, but not to move during intercourse.

Gradually Jack became able to penetrate Jean more deeply and to stay inside for longer, though he still tended to ejaculate a bit too soon. Both partners enjoyed sex more and felt very content. Neither showed high sex drive, and intercourse tended to occur only about once a week. After the seventh session both said they were satisfied with the incomplete progress they had achieved and did not want further treatment. At follow-up six months later, they were continuing to have intercourse about once a week with pleasure to both of them, and no problem of vaginal spasm.

In summary, the principles of sexual skills programs are that the couple should be well informed about sexual matters, learn to discuss them freely with each other, be able to handle each other's bodies without shame or fear, and to experiment gradually as they get used to different things until they reach a compromise that satisfies them best and enables them both to reach climax. A lot of homework is needed before this happy state is attained, and it is always easier to do it under guidance of a therapist to whom one reports regularly about progress. It is also helpful to read suitable books on the subject and, when these are available, to see films as well. The idea is to overcome traditional taboos and the veil of silence that surrounds the subject of sex. It is surprising how highly intelligent people often lack basic knowledge about sex, and of course it is difficult to succeed at anything one knows little about.

Anxiety concerning menstruation and the menopause

Nowadays the onset of menstruation in girls at puberty usually leads to no problems. However, when girls have been kept ignorant about their bodies and sexuality, the sudden appearance of menstrual bleeding can be worrying. The proper approach is to reassure the young woman that monthly periods are perfectly normal, to explain what they mean, and to give her simple advice on the use of sanitary napkins and tampons.

Premenstrual tension

In the week before menstruation and the first few days of actual menstrual discharge, many women feel irritable and a bit depressed. (We are not talking here about pain during menstrual bleeding.) Some research workers report that women have more accidents, suicide, and other mishaps during the premenstrual week than at any other time during their cycle. A few days before menstruation, women also often complain of tenderness and swelling of their breasts and sometimes swelling of their hands and feet. This fluid retention may also cause an increase in weight by a couple of pounds.

Although premenstrual tension seems to be pretty common, scientists know remarkably little about its cause or treatment. We do not know how much premenstrual tension is due to hormonal changes and how much to worries about the flow itself. Some research suggests that the tension can be reduced by taking low-dose oral contraceptive pills which contain estrogen and progesterone compounds together.

Menopause

The menstrual cycle ceases in women in middle life. This is the *menopause,* and it has been unfairly blamed for a multitude of ills in middle age. Terms like "menopausal depression" are gradually fading away, and people are beginning to realize that the menopause need cause no special anxieties. Menopausal hot flashes are often inconvenient but are not responsible for psychiatric disorder. Treatment by giving female hormones (estrogen) is said to be helpful for troublesome physical changes which can follow the menopause, for example, for dryness of the vaginal skin, which can cause pain during intercourse.

SUMMING UP

Sexual worries are common in adolescents and young adults, but are usually overcome by discussion and normal experimentation. Recent changes in social attitudes have made this easier. Sexual problems can be secondary to physical or psychological disorders, and to marital disharmony.

Dysfunction in the sexual arena takes several forms. Unconsummated marriage is rare. Frequent problems in women are painful intercourse, vaginal spasm, and failure to reach orgasm. In men, common difficulties are lack of social skills preventing any form of relationship with women, failure to have an erection, and premature ejaculation. Rarely, men cannot ejaculate despite adequate erection.

Management of sexual problems involves two principles—learning about normal sexual behavior and reducing sexual anxiety by gradually engaging in increasingly intimate sexual relations. Husband and wife need to be treated together as a couple and to learn to tell one another what turns them on and off. Reading sexual books and seeing sexual films together can be very useful. They can explore one another's genitals and learn to caress one another at leisure. In addition they can learn specific ways of overcoming particular problems such as failure of erection, premature ejaculation, vaginal spasm, and anorgasmia. Some setbacks should be expected in the course of treatment, but patient persistence by both partners will lead to success.

The Treatment
of Anxiety

11

Professional Treatment

Many different techniques have been used in the past to treat phobias and anxieties. When agoraphobic members of a correspondence club were asked in a newsletter what treatment they had had, their replies included drugs, psychoanalysis, narcoanalysis, group therapy, and other therapies including occupational therapy, leucotomy (lobotomy), LSD (lysergic acid), hypnosis, autosuggestion, ECT (electroconvulsive therapy), deep relaxation, yoga, spiritual healing, acupuncture, behavior therapy, psychology correspondence courses, homeopathy, naturopathy, and many others. Broadly speaking there are are three classes of treatment of severe anxiety and fear: (1) psychological methods, (2) drugs, and (3) in a few cases only, other physical methods such as electroshock therapy and psychosurgery. At the moment psychological treatments offer the most hope for lasting improvement, except where there is marked depression, in which case antidepressant medication is useful.

The Treatment of Anxiety

PSYCHOLOGICAL MANAGEMENT

Remember anxiety is normal and can be helpful

Perhaps the most important thing to understand about anxiety is that it is perfectly normal for all of us to feel anxious from time to time. Moreover, tension can be constructive. It can spur us on to deal with the problems that are the cause of our tensions. We all feel unhappy if we are threatened with serious illness, by loss of a job, by failure on important examinations, by arguments with our wives or tiffs with our children. We may be faced with financial demands we find hard to meet, or our car might break down on the way to an important engagement. In fact, our hardships cease only with death.

The aim should not be to abolish anxiety. That can't be done. Instead try putting it in perspective. Cease regarding it as an enemy and instead recruit it as a spur to necessary action. Learn to roll with every stress. If you can't beat it, join it and transform it from foe to friend. Living in the real world of difficulties which crop up every day, we all have to learn to cope with stress and deal with problems as they arise. There is a grain of truth in the saying, "It isn't what happens to you that matters. It's how you take it."

A little anecdote makes the point that fear as such is less crucial than the way we act. During World War I a Jewish military doctor in the Austrian Army was sitting next to a colonel when heavy shooting began. Teasingly, the colonel said, "Just another proof that the Aryan race is superior to the Semitic one! You are afraid, aren't you?" "Sure I am afraid," was the doctor's answer, "but who is superior? If you, my dear Colonel, were as afraid as I am, you would have run away long ago."[1]

Discussion with other people can help

An important aspect of dealing with stress is being able to talk about it and to ask for help when necessary from our relatives and friends. Talking about our fears to someone we can trust can be valuable for some of our difficulties. Simply chatting about our problems calmly to someone who can listen to us can help put them in a new light and suggest helpful ways of dealing with the thing that's bothering us. Sometimes it is useful to do this talking to members of the caring professions, who are professionally trained to help sufferers. There are many helpers such as doctors, psychologists, social workers, nurses, probation officers, and the clergy. Lots of people in trouble can be helped by workers of these kinds. More complicated problems may require quite skilled intervention by members of these professions who have specialized in the necessary treatments.

We must distinguish between those problems we can eventually master and those which will not go away whatever we do. Sometimes we are reduced to making the best of a bad job. A woman who has a drunken husband who beats her and the children every day might have to find a job that takes her out of the house and brings in the money her husband refuses her, which might eventually enable her to set up a separate household.

Supportive psychotherapy may be all that is needed for many people who are suffering from anxiety. In others, however, what we call exposure treatments are necessary to overcome tension. Whatever method we use to deal with anxiety, it is important to know that it is we ourselves who have to learn how to live with it. The job of a therapist is not to abolish our anxiety by magic, but to teach us what is necessary to learn to cope with distress. Learning how to do this can be enjoyable and interesting, but one should not expect sudden miracle cures. Such an expectation will lead to disappointment and discouragement. Improvement with exposure treatment tends to come gradually, and only by looking back over several days or weeks may one realize what progress has been made. What are exposure treatments? They are a form of behavioral psychotherapy, which it is now time to describe.

THE BEHAVIORAL REVOLUTION: EXPOSURE TREATMENT

In the last ten years there has been a revolution in the treatment of persistent fears and obsessions. Until then the most common psychological approach derived from Freudian models of psychoanalysis and psychotherapy. These assumed that phobias and rituals usually symbolize other hidden problems which need to be discovered and that when these were revealed through free association and worked through, the anxieties would disappear. This form of treatment is time-consuming and can go on for years. Moreover, research has found that the psychoanalytic approach is not especially helpful for relieving specific anxieties and that certain behavioral methods are superior. Furthermore, behavioral treatments can be effective within a few days or weeks, or at most a couple of months.

Behavioral treatment does not assume that phobias are symbolic transformations of hidden difficulties. It does not rake about for unconscious dirt. Instead it regards the phobia or obsession itself as the main handicap, and tries to eliminate it directly, not by trying to uncover unconscious meanings, but by teaching the sufferer how to face those situations which trigger his discomfort so that he can eventually come to tolerate them. There is now a wealth of research which shows that this approach works in most cases. Even phobias which have been present for twenty years have been overcome in three hours of treatment, though usually ten to twenty hours are necessary, spaced over sessions one to two hours long.

The principle of exposure to the anxiety-evoking situation

Not all behavioral methods are equally effective. Relaxation is often called a behavioral treatment, but it does not reduce obsessions or phobias. Effective behavioral techniques known under various names have in common the principle of *exposure to that which frightens you until you get used to it.* Another name for exposure is confrontation. Once we confront our fear determinedly it will diminish. Research shows that provided exposure continues for long enough, the anxiety eventually goes down.

"How long is long enough?"

There is no quick answer beyond *longer is better.* In a lucky minority of sufferers just a few minutes' exposure to the things which terrify them lead to a reduction in fear. This might be especially true for those who have not had their phobias for long and are really determined to get the better of them. More commonly, the fear starts to diminish within half an hour after the start of the exposure, even in people with very long-standing phobias. Rarely, several hours may be needed for the fear to start abating. The important point is to persevere until the anxiety starts to lessen and to be prepared to go on until it does.

"How rapidly should I tackle my worst fears?"

"Should I go little by little, slowly from my easiest to my worst fears, or should I grab the bull by the horns?" In general *the more rapidly you tackle your worst fears the more quickly you recover.* The faster and longer we embrace the monster of our panic, the more rapidly it will fade in our arms to become a shadow of itself, the old familiar friend of mild tension rather than the monster of terror.

"Can anxiety during exposure be harmful?"

The answer is usually, No, contrary to popular belief. In the past doctors and psychologists were scared to allow patients to become very frightened because they thought serious harm would result. Now we know that the great majority of patients who allow themselves to experience extreme panic eventually become unable to experience more than mild fear. If we try to panic, paradoxically the odds are that we won't be able to, or that we will produce only a pale reflection of the real thing. Even if severe panic does strike, it will gradually evaporate and become less likely to return in the future. In a curious way, really effective exposure treatments for anxiety could develop only as therapists learned to endure the anxiety of their patients, secure in the knowledge that it is unlikely to harm but instead to lead to their improvement.

Early exposure prevents phobias from growing

The golden rule to nip phobias in the bud is, *Avoid escape! Encourage the facing of fear.* After a sudden accident, there is often an interim lag phase before a phobia develops. If during this phase you are immediately reexposed to the original situation, this protects you from getting frightened of it. It has long been said that people should reenter a traumatic situation immediately after the original trauma. Airplane pilots are encouraged to deliberately fly again as soon as possible after a flying accident. Car drivers are recommended to resume driving as soon as they can after a car crash. If you fall off a horse, it is best to mount it again right away.

While fears are still mild, people can be helped to overcome them by warm reassurance that it is perfectly in order to go back to the frightening situation and experience fear in it until it dies down. Numerous tricks of suggestion have been used successfully to encourage people to face their fears. One man was bet $1,000 by his doctor that he would not die of a heart attack should he venture forth from home, and he promptly found himself able to go out alone for the first time in months. Professional actors who were suddenly struck with stage fright managed to overcome this on stage by constantly looking at and repeating to themselves messages of encouragement written by their doctors.

Once we avoid a frightening situation, we are more likely to steer clear of it again the next time we meet it, and gradually a phobia builds up. It is better to take risks and face slightly frightening situations rather than have the opposite risk of developing a phobia because you avoid the unpleasantness. While children with heart disease must not be extended beyond the physical limits set by their heart disease, one would not wish to make them invalids. The fewer restrictions children are hedged in with, the less likely they are to develop hypochondriacal anxieties in later life.

The general attitude which an anxious person needs to have can be summarized in a short verse:

Which epitaph shall be mine?

She couldn't try		She couldn't try
For fear she'd die		For fear she'd die;
She never tried	or	But when she tried
And so she died		Her fears—they died[2]

Established phobias need structured exposure

Once phobias are causing persistent avoidance of the phobic object, simple exhortations to bravery and willpower alone may not be terribly helpful. Your phobia can be aggravated if you enter situations with which you cannot cope and from which you then escape. Before severe phobics confront the source of their terrors, it is vital that they first understand what is likely to happen and then structure their exposure so that they can deal properly with the problems which will arise. They must be determined to get the better of their fears and not run away from them. The fear won't disappear by magic. *It usually takes time to lessen—up to several hours* if the phobia is very severe, and this must be allowed for. Rather than briefly poke her nose into a dreaded crowded store, feel the surge of panic, and rush out again, it is better for the agoraphobic to reserve a full afternoon for the adventure. She should take with her a book or knitting or materials to write a letter, and when the panic strikes, sit in a corner of the store and ride out the panic by reading, writing, or knitting during the thirty to sixty minutes which may elapse before the panic passes. When she feels better, she can continue her shopping.

Overcoming fear takes time

This is clear from the example you have just seen and should be taken into account in planning treatment of any anxiety. Enough time should be arranged for anxiety to subside in the situation you are trying to get used to. This time may be several hours if the fear concerns animals or airplanes. Longer and more delicate negotiations may be needed for sexual anxieties. If you are impotent, there is little point propositioning a sexy woman you have just met at a party and jumping into bed with her without further ado. Your vital part will be limp and your partner irritated that you can't perform as promised. Shame at your poor performance will make you anticipate failure next time around, and so the problem will go on. Overcoming sexual anxiety needs patience even if you have an understanding partner, and careful preparation is necessary. Your partner needs to know about the problem and to be prepared to cooperate in the stages to be gone through before regular success is attained.

Determination and patience

Two qualities that are essential to conquer fear rather than be ruled by it are determination and patience. This is true as much for helping others as for helping yourself. Parents who want to help a child overcome a school phobia must be prepared to tolerate the child's almost inevitable crying the first few times he or she is returned to school. You will need to steel yourself to ignore the complaints of headache or pain in the stomach with which the child will greet you in the morning just before it is time to go to school. Obviously if the child looks ill it might be wise to check his or her temperature, but if this is normal for the fourth consecutive morning the chances are that you needn't carry on with this precaution. Firm but loving and consistent pressure toward school should help the child overcome the fear within a couple of weeks.

It is generally easier for treatment to be carried out by trained therapists rather than by relatives or oneself. Perhaps this is for the same reason that it is easier to learn to drive from an instructor rather than by oneself or from lessons with a spouse. Like the driving instructor, the therapist is more detached and less thrown by the anxiety which usually occurs during the process and knows more about the possible snags and how to overcome them. However, many people teach themselves skills or overcome fear without other people's help (see Chapter 12).

A patient's view of qualities needed for success

Here is what Lisa, age fifty, said of her experiences in treatment of her height and train phobia. Though to start with she had quite a lot of help from her nurse-therapist, determination played a crucial role.

Your willingness to trust your therapist through thick and thin is essential, as well as your willingness to follow his instructions, however weird some of them seem at times. You need to realize that the early part of treatment is the hardest. You will experience some real shocks during the sessions and they won't be softened by tranquilizers. It will take everything you've got to hang on when you feel like giving up. Very soon you will find yourself going over the edge between the safe and the panic making. I shall never forget (I had a fear of heights) being asked to look over the edge of the bannister on the first floor landing, and nearly chickening out with fright. The therapist stood by me—in more ways than one—coaxing me, firmly encouraging me to stay in my panic, fight against my urge to draw back from my fears. We made it. I was then taken into even more anxious-making situations, after which leaning over the bannister became child's play. These experiences were hell, but there were also the occasions when I learned that my will to win was stronger than my fears; that it worked at the severest point of my panic with the help of techniques I had been taught; that I had it in me to conquer my fears. After each such experience I was left with the memory that I had made a breakthrough, that I had achieved the impossible and with confidence that I could do it again and more.

Each further step in the treatment was carefully prepared for, working towards targets agreed at the beginning of the treatment. In between the sessions I was set tasks to be done entirely by myself. These were a very important part of the whole thing, as they proved I could cope on my own. At times in between sessions I felt anxious, at times rebellious, at times despondent. It was often a running battle between the part of me that said, "I can't," "I won't" and the part that replied, "I have done it before; I will do it again in spite of my anxiety." There were the memories of the agonies already suffered as well as of the victories already won, plus the prospect of more to come—and anyone who has had panics and avoided them knows what it feels like knowingly to expose oneself to more. But the good memories together with the will to win and the knowledge that the therapist knew what he was doing, helped to keep me going.

The treatment has taught me how to cope positively with my anxieties, which have not completely disappeared but are now manageable. More, it has really changed my attitude to life in a more positive direction. Instead of saying "No" to my hangups and some of the ups and downs of life I can now say "Yes" with much more confidence, having learned during treatment that I could cope with terrifying things. When the therapist's part was done it was over to me. The "impossible" can be done if you are prepared to stick it out during the treatment come what may. You will then find yourself the winner even if it's not a knockout victory.[3]

Lisa then offered her services as co-therapist for other phobics.

Failure is likely if you feel treatment is unnecessary

For treatment to be successful we may need to give up some cherished ideas, and this can be very difficult, as one obsessive hand-washer complained when she was told that it was perfectly in order to put her infant's dirty diapers into the washing machine without bothering whether they touched the edge of the door hatch. She put her doubts in verse:

Coming to Terms with the Germs: An Inmate's Complaint
(to be sung in melancholy tones to the tune of
"Oh My Darling Clementine")

> To be clean was once a virtue
> Next to godliness sublime
> But when they put you in a nuthouse
> You are told that it's a crime
> I wish the doctors and head shrinkers
> Would get together and agree
> Whether urine is really harmful
> Or as pure as cups of tea.[4]

Sad to say, this woman never accepted that washing sixty times daily was abnormal, failed to do much in treatment, and improved very little.

Contrast this with the positive attitude of another woman who improved dramatically, losing all her obsessions and rituals in a few weeks. "I'm trying always to follow the golden rule 'never avoid,' and working hard at things until the fear goes. I am so very grateful to be able to go about my daily life, without having to do extraordinary things."[5]

WHAT FORMS OF EXPOSURE TREATMENT ARE THERE?

In its simplest form, exposure treatment consists merely of advice to patients to expose themselves every day to a situation they find slightly difficult and to record their daily actions in a diary which the therapist reviews at the next visit. As they gain confidence, they can set themselves fresh targets to achieve from one week to the next. They have to define weekly targets which will be useful for them to attain. An agoraphobic man who is unable to go to work because he cannot travel on a subway might be asked first to practice standing outside the subway station every day for a few days and to record his reactions, lengthening the time he spends at the station each day. Then he would be asked to go and buy a ticket several times and finally to go down on to the underground platform. Thereafter he would be asked to jump on and off the train before it departs, to get on the train for one stop, and then for ever-increasing distances. Relatives can help greatly in such programs of retraining by helping the patient work out details of his program, monitoring it, and praising him for any progress which he is making.

Many phobics find it easier to follow advice about exposure after they have had several periods with a therapist showing them how to do it. This exposure with a therapist can be experienced in many ways. In some forms of exposure treatment the approach to the frightening situation is very slow and gradual—this approach is called *desensitization.* Other kinds of exposure persuade the patient to tackle his fears more quickly—these are the methods known as *flooding.* Exposure to the phobic situation can be purely in one's mind's eye (in *fantasy,* in imagination), may occur by viewing slides and films of the phobic stimulus, or may be to the real live situation itself (exposure in *practice,* or in vivo exposure).

In general, the more rapidly somebody allows himself to approach his phobic object and stay there until he feels better, the more speedy his recovery. The quicker he deals with the real situation, as opposed to merely thinking about it, the more rapid the improvement. During rapid exposure to live situations patients usually experience more fear than during slow approach in their mind's eye only, but this price may be well worth paying for the time it saves in getting better more quickly. In fact phobics who were treated by rapid exposure to their really frightening situations later said this was no worse an experience than going to the dentist.

Desensitization

In the method known as *desensitization in fantasy* the patient is first asked to draw up a list of all the situations which frighten him and to list them from the most terrifying to the least disturbing.

He is then made to relax and is asked to imagine himself very slowly coming steadily closer to the phobic situation for a few *seconds* while he is relaxed. He imagines easy scenes first until he feels comfortable with them and is then slowly given more difficult situations to imagine repeatedly until finally he can contemplate his most terrifying scenes without anxiety. After each session he is asked to practice in real life that which he has successfully visualized in fantasy.

As an example of desensitization in fantasy, a patient with a phobia of birds might be relaxed and then asked to imagine herself first looking at a small pigeon 100 yards away in a cage. She holds this scene in her mind for a few seconds and is then asked to drop it and relax. If this caused her no anxiety she is then asked to imagine the same pigeon 90 yards away in a closed cage; and in subsequent scenes the pigeon will be drawn gradually nearer until after many hours she is able to handle the pigeon in her mind's eye without fear. This treatment is an easy one to learn, but it can take many hours before sufferers learn to overcome their fear with it. It is of some value for people who suffer from a very specific phobia. However, if they are also anxious for much of the day wherever they are, it is not of particular value. Desensitization in imagination is also not of great use for patients with obsessive-compulsive disorders.

Flooding

A form of rapid exposure is *flooding*. If desensitization is compared to wading slowly into a swimming pool from the shallow end, flooding is equivalent to jumping in the deep end. *Flooding in imagination* is often called *implosion*. Here patients are asked to imagine themselves in their most frightening situations continuously for one to two hours, and the therapist helps them to do this by giving a running commentary on phobic scenes they are to imagine. The patient can elaborate these scenes further by himself if need be.

By way of illustration, an agoraphobic being flooded in imagination may be asked to imagine herself leaving the house alone, tremulously walking down a busy road to a crowded high street, entering a crowded supermarket, and waiting for ages as part of a slow-moving line while she feels faint and fearful.

A young man with examination anxiety was helped by having him make a deliberate effort to feel and experience fully his fear without trying to escape from it.[6] He was a student with examination panic forty-eight hours before an examination. He had already failed a previous examination because of a similar attack of panic. The student was made to sit up in bed and to try to feel his fear. He was asked to imagine all the consequences that would follow his failure—derision from his colleagues, disappointment from his family, and financial loss. At first as he followed the instructions, his sobbings increased. But soon his tremblings ceased. As the effort needed to maintain a vivid imagination increased, the emotion he could summon began to ebb. Within half an hour he was calm. He was instructed to repeatedly experience his fears. Every time he felt a little wave of spontaneous alarm he was not to push it aside but was to enhance it and try to experience it more vividly. The patient was intelligent and assiduously practiced his exercises methodically until he became almost unable to feel frightened. He passed his examinations without difficulty.

Paradoxical intention

A variant of flooding is *paradoxical intention*. As an example of paradoxical intention, a man who was afraid that he might die of a heart attack was asked to try as hard as possible to make his heart beat faster and die of a heart attack right on the spot. He laughed and replied, "Doc, I am trying hard but I can't do it."[7] He was instructed to go ahead and try to die from a heart attack each time his anticipatory anxiety troubled him. As he started laughing about his neurotic symptoms, humor helped him to put distance between himself and his neurosis. The patient was instructed to die at least three times a day of a heart attack, and instead of trying hard to go to sleep, try hard to remain awake. The moment he started laughing at his symptoms and became willing to produce them intentionally, he changed his attitude toward his fear and it improved.

Paradoxical intention can overcome the tension some people feel in trying to fall asleep. When one man complained of terrible insomnia, that he just never could get any sleep, his doctor advised him instead to "try lying awake in bed all night. Don't get up. No sleeping pills. Just lie there with your eyes open as long as you can."[8] The next day the man apologized to his doctor for not being able to follow instructions, as he fell asleep so quickly!

Rapid prolonged exposure to the public situation in real life

The most common approach used in my department is rapid prolonged exposure to the actual situation as it yields the quickest lasting improvement. In this method an agoraphobic might be asked to enter a crowded shopping area, remain there for several hours until his desire to escape disappears, and then report back to his therapist.

Prolonged exposure to the real phobic situation is a quicker therapy than exposure in fantasy, though occasionally the latter might be a necessary preliminary to it. Sessions lasting two continuous hours are more effective than several shorter periods adding up to the same total exposure time. Patients with specific phobias can virtually lose their phobias in three afternoons, while agoraphobics require rather longer. Patients usually become very anxious in the early phases of treatment, but this dies down as the session continues.

Before treatment begins, the patient must fully understand what will be required of him and agree to complete the treatment without avoidance; otherwise he may escape during the session, which might make him worse. Full cooperation is essential, and without it only slower exposure, such as desensitization, is possible. Desensitization can also be used where physical disease may make excessive anxiety harmful, as in people with asthma or heart disease.

Exposure to the phobic situation in fantasy or on film

While exposure to the *real* situation yields the most dividends, sometimes the phobic stimulus can't easily be brought into the treatment situation while the therapist is present. Thunderstorms are an example. Under such circumstances the phobic can be asked to imagine a thunderstorm, or be shown a film of one. Watching specially prepared films of sexual intercourse can help people with sexual problems not only acquire much-needed information but also lose their discomfort about coitus. Sometimes patients prefer to experience their fears in fantasy or on film first before exposing themselves to them in real life, as we see in the next example.

Case example: Rapid improvement in a woman with cat phobia

A young woman had had a phobia of cats since childhood to the extent that she avoided them at all costs and required a companion to help her through streets where cats might be present.[9] After two 2-hour sessions of imagining cats close to her and scratching her, she thought she was able to face real cats. A black cat was then brought into the room and held on the table about 6 feet away from her; looking at the cat made her heart rate go up and she felt very anxious, but this anxiety died down after about five minutes. Over the next few minutes the therapist gradually brought the cat nearer to her. Each change in position of the cat led to a short increase in her heart rate and anxiety, during which she was reassured and encouraged to keep looking at the cat. After fifteen minutes she was able to touch the cat, and as the session proceeded she became able to stroke the cat and hold it on her lap. She was praised liberally for each step forward she took. If she hesitated, the therapist showed her how to touch the cat by doing it himself first. This is called *modeling*. She spent the last fifteen minutes of the two-hour session cuddling the cat on her lap without anxiety. After two sessions of treatment lasting six hours in all, this woman was able to handle cats normally and her life was no longer restricted by fear.

Patients of this kind can overcome their fears so rapidly that it takes them some time to realize that they are no longer phobic. One spider-phobic woman who watched spiders running up her arms for the first time in her life without feeling anxiety said that she just could not believe this and took some weeks to get used to the idea that she could now handle spiders with equanimity.

Case example: Loss of a dog phobia after two treatment sessions

Further flavor of the way in which many phobics improve rapidly with treatment can be gathered from a twenty-year-old woman who had had a fear of dogs at least since she was four.[10] She would cross roads to avoid dogs, would not visit friends who had dogs, and being a painter, she wanted to go out to paint landscapes but could not do so because of her fear. She was treated over two sessions, each two hours long. In the first session a gentle little dog was gradually brought nearer to her; the therapists patted and stroked the dog and then encouraged the young woman to follow suit. At first she was terrified, cried, and backed away, but slowly as the session went by she acquired confidence. After a few minutes she touched the rump of the dog for the first time and said, "It is so horrible and ugly, the whole dog seems like a head to me." As the minutes ticked past, however, the fears gradually died down and she stopped crying, began cuddling the dog, and said she didn't know why she had thought dogs were ugly before. Her attitude changed within a few hours. In the second session a larger dog was brought in and the same process was repeated. By the end of the four hours of treatment, she no longer had more fear of dogs than the average person. At follow-up she reported that she visited friends who owned dogs, played with them, and no longer avoided them in the street, though she remained wary of large Alsatians. So much had she gained in confidence that this also spilled over into another area where she had had slight difficulties, in her dealings with her parents. She had become more assertive with them and as a result got on better with them.

An unusual twist: Imagine eating a dog and you'll feel better

Six months after treatment this same young woman had one unusual complication. At that time a newspaper report was giving wide publicity about a European couple touring Hong Kong who took their pet dog with them into a Chinese restaurant. The waiter did not speak very good English, but they indicated to him that they wanted him to serve some food for their pet as well. He disappeared in the direction of the kitchen with their dog under his arm. Dinner took an unconscionably long time to appear, and they became very restless. Eventually the waiter appeared with a large platter which he uncovered with a flourish to display their pet poodle cooked in expert fashion. Clearly the waiter's English left room for improvement, and the horror of the couple can be imagined. When this patient heard the story at a party, she became upset and preoccupied with visions of cooked dogs which haunted her wherever she went. After these had persisted for a few days, she asked to see me again. To help her, in the consulting room I asked her to "imagine yourself eating a cooked dog. Try just a little bit of the leg first, please." She hesitated and said, "I feel sick," but I persisted. "Just take a knife and fork in your hand and cut a tiny sliver of meat off the haunch, just chew it properly." She followed my instructions, appeared to be chewing, and then nearly vomited. On my instructions, with persistence she swallowed the meat in fantasy, accompanying this scene with swallowing movements, and within twenty minutes had polished off the dog and was smiling with relief at her accomplishment, in contrast to her earlier tears. The visions of cooked dogs disappeared after this. A year later she wrote a letter saying that she was very well, had married, and had given birth to a son.

Rapid exposure in groups

Recently it has been found that agoraphobics can be treated in groups, which first meet together to discuss useful ways of reducing their fear and then under the guidance of the therapist go into their frightening situations. As they get used to this as part of a group, they then send one another out on individual sallies and report back to one another on their progress. Phobics seem to get comfort from one another in this setting and encouragement to redouble their efforts to master their feelings in phobic settings. Group experience also affords the chance for shy patients to learn new social behavior and shed their fears of other people. Those who before treatment were ashamed to have their handicap, would not talk about it, felt uniquely ridiculous, were inhibited about eating in restaurants, could not look at other people in buses or subways, or were unable to ask strangers for directions in the street had to cope with these situations as part of their treatment exercises and so overcame these problems by the end of their treatment.

Social gains were especially clear when patients were sent out by the group to carry out exposure exercises on their own. Several got used to speaking to strangers when they were anxious. A patient, fearful of elevators, was on her third run up and down in the elevator when the operator asked her why she was doing this. Feeling ashamed she told him the problem. He sympathized and immediately told her about his flying phobia! This gave the patient heart to talk to other people when she became frightened again thereafter.[11]

A patient who was phobic of underground trains panicked when one stopped in a tunnel. She admitted this to a neighbor, who responded sympathetically and started talking about her own particular problems. The patient calmed down and thereafter whenever she went by train looked for people whom she thought she could talk to in case of a panic and chose them to sit beside in the coach.

A patient with a social phobia panicked in a shop and started to chat to the saleswoman who was giving her change. The sales-clerk politely told her to see a psychiatrist.[12] The patient left the shop shaking, ashamed, and angry with the therapist. She was persuaded to return to the shop immediately and tell the same clerk that she had just seen a psychiatrist, who had told her to go back to her. The patient did so and after twenty minutes went back for a long talk with the saleswoman, who then admitted she disliked customers trying to make small talk with her, as she felt so inhibited. She invited the patient to come as often as possible, so that she might learn with her how to chat with the customers.

Nightmares can be treated like phobias

Nightmares are sometimes the expressions of waking fears and can be reduced by exposure to the frightening stimuli. On page 152 we saw examples of children being taught to transform bad dreams into experiences of mastery through deliberate confron-tation with the unpleasant content and by being persuaded to change it by rehearsal into more positive material. I found a similar approach useful in a woman of forty who had had a very difficult relationship with her mother, who had died fourteen years earlier. For twelve years she had been plagued by recurrent nightmares in which she pushed her mother off the roof of a house, went downstairs to check that her mother had been killed, and found the head severed from the body. She put on jackboots and then jumped onto the head to make sure her mother was really dead. But as she did so, something streamed out of the head's eyes toward her own eyes, pursuing her as she retreated, and just as this thing pierced her eyes she woke up trembling and thinking, "My bloody mother, she always wins!" For the whole morning after these nightmares, she would feel so depressed she would be unable to go into work.

I treated this problem by asking this patient over twenty minutes to retell her nightmares three times over, and to write them down afterward at home and read them repeatedly. At first she cried and was very agitated, but she then calmed down and was able to retell the nightmares more easily next time. On her second visit with me, which lasted about forty minutes, I persuaded her to retell her nightmare with a triumphant ending, which consisted of her succeeding in smashing her mother's skull and squeezing the brains to a pulp in her hands and flushing them down a toilet. She was then instructed to write out the dream three times more, but this time with triumphant endings over her mother. With difficulty she was also persuaded to swear aloud repeatedly against her mother and me and other people, something which she could not bring herself to do previously, much as she wished to. When I saw her for the third time two weeks later, she managed this, felt far less depressed, and was able to talk about the nightmare with equanimity. Over the next year she remained well and free of nightmares.

A more gentle kind of exposure can also help people over nightmares. An example is that of a nineteen-year-old woman who had had nightmares for the past four years.[13] All these bad dreams contained the fear of falling from a bridge. She had had a conscious phobia of bridges for as long as she could remember and was also afraid of heights. She lost her fear of bridges after seven sessions of desensitization in imagination, during the course of which her nightmares ceased. Toward the end of treatment she instead experienced two pleasant dreams about bridges. She remained well when seen six months later.

STRESS IMMUNIZATION

Learning to cope

Medical inoculations produce immunity to an infection by exposing the individual to a related but less harmful germ that stimulates the body's immune defenses without overwhelming them.

A similar idea has been suggested to help people resist stress. Experiments suggest that stress inoculation is a real possibility, that individuals can be protected against emotional stress by experiencing similar but less extreme versions of their stress. The principle is "a hair of the dog that might bite you tomorrow." As an example, children were prepared for later dental procedures by getting them to play in a dentist's chair and with dental equipment, and to undergo mock examinations of their teeth. When it came to real dentistry, these children showed less fear than others who had not played these dental games before.[14] Preparing adults, too, for distressing situations can help them reduce their suffering when the trauma comes. When surgical patients were given preoperative explanations about the problems to be expected after surgery and descriptions of the kind and duration of pain they would have, they recovered more quickly and with less pain and discomfort than similar patients who had not been prepared in the same way.

In another study by an American psychologist, Richard Lazarus, experimental subjects were shown a gruesome film about the circumcision of Australian aborigines during a puberty initiation rite.[15] In the film boys, without benefit of anesthetic, were stretched back over a boulder while the underside of the penis was slit in two lengthwise. While watching the film some subjects heard a sound track which either gave a detached description of the operation or said that it wasn't painful or harmful but on the contrary was desired by the boys as an essential part of becoming an adult. Subjects who heard this sound track were less disturbed by the film than others who saw the film in a silent version, or with a sound track which emphasized how painful the procedure was.

Our mental set thus influences whether we will perceive something as threatening. Surgery patients have been helped by being told that some anxiety was natural before the operation but that it could be controlled if they knew how to. They were asked to rehearse realistic positive aspects of the surgical experience.

An extreme example of mastery

Some people learn coping methods so well that they can endure even the most gruesome torture without showing undue distress. Few persons, however, could develop the degree of control described by a Spanish Inquisitor in 1629. He was less than pleased at the indifference shown by some victims to his torture.

> Some rascals trusted so strongly in the secrets they possessed to make themselves insensible to pain, that they voluntarily gave themselves up as prisoners, to cleanse themselves of certain sins. Some use certain words pronounced in a low voice, and others writings which they hide on some part of their body. The first one I recognized as using some sort of charm, surprised us by his more than natural firmness, because after the first stretching of the rack he seemed to sleep as quietly as if he had been in a good bed, without lamenting, complaining or crying, and when the stretching was repeated two or three times, he still remained motionless as a statue. This made us suspect that he was provided with some charm, and to resolve the doubt he was stripped as naked as his hand. Yet, after a careful search, nothing was found on him but a little piece of paper on which were the figures of the three kings, with these words on the other side: "Beautiful star which delivered the Magi from Herod's persecution, deliver me from all torment." This paper was stuffed in his left ear. Now although the paper had been taken away from him he still appeared insensible to the torture, because when it was applied he muttered words between his teeth which we could not hear, and as he persevered in his denials, it was necessary to send him back to prison.[16]

Fortunately most of us have to contend with less trying ordeals, and programs have been devised to help this along.

Programs for stress immunization

A Canadian psychologist, Don Meichenbaum, has evolved a program of stress immunization with students.[17] They are taught that when they are frightened they should recognize the signs of fear, such as rapid throbbing heartbeat, sweaty palms, and tense muscles. Next, they are helped to become aware of all the anxious things they say or think to themselves when in a difficult situation, with a view to changing these self statements.

All of us silently say worrying things to ourselves when in trouble, although we may not be aware of this until we think about it. If we are anxious, say, about giving a chat to an important audience and some people walk out of the room, we might say to ourselves, "I must be so boring. No one's interested in what I am saying. I knew I never could give a speech: I'd better dry up quickly." This reaction increases our anxiety until we become paralyzed with fear. On the other hand, if we are self-reliant, when members of the audience leave, we might think to ourselves, "I suppose they have another appointment they have to keep. What a pity that they have to miss my good talk," or, "What a rude bunch."

Another example might occur when taking a driving test for a license. A worrying person would glance at the examiner and think, "Why is he frowning like that? I'm making a fool of myself. I know I'm a terrible driver." A more confident individual would say to himself, "I suppose he's frowning because he had an argument with his wife before he started today. I'll have to be careful to show him that I can manage this car. I may not be an expert driver, but I'm good enough to pass and I have to convince him that I can do it."[18]

In each of these examples, the same event is seen differently by anxious and by confident people, and what they say or think to themselves reflects this anxiety or confidence. Part of stress immunization is teaching people how to "speak" differently to themselves. When the agoraphobic leaves her home on a practice exercise she needs to say, "One step at a time, relax, good, I can get myself to do it if I try hard enough. This giddiness in my head and fluttering in my chest is exactly what I knew I would feel. I am supposed to label my fear from zero to ten and watch it change. That's it, I'm breathing heavily, that's a sign that I must bring in my coping techniques. Let's see, I'll try slow deep breathing—one, two, in, out . . . that's the way old girl, you'll pull through yet."

So habitual does our worrying thinking become that we may not even be aware of it, and we have to learn to recognize that what we might be saying is, "Heavens, I'm going to have a heart attack" or "I'm sure I'm going to lose control—I'm going to go mad." When we say these things we make matters worse, and so we have to change what we say or think to ourselves. The therapist teaching stress inoculation might say, "We are going to work on ways to control how you feel, on ways of controlling your anxiety and tension. We will do this by learning how to control thinking and attention. The control of our thinking, or what we say to ourselves, comes about by first becoming aware of the negative things we say, of the prophecies of doom we make, of the way we fail to attend to the task in hand. Recognizing that we do this is the first step toward change. When we realize what we are saying, this will act as a reminder, a bell-ringer for us to produce different thoughts and self-instructions to challenge and dispute our worrying thoughts. This way we can learn to do things more confidently and attend to what needs to be done.

Most of us have in fact developed ways of coping with stress such as that caused by visits to the dentist or taking exams. What we need to do is to use these coping mechanisms more systematically. After learning self-instruction, a phobic woman reported, "It makes me able to be in the [phobic] situation, not to be comfortable but to be able to tolerate it. . . . I don't talk myself out of being afraid, just out of appearing afraid. . . . you immediately react to the thing you're afraid of and then start to reason with yourself. I talk myself out of panic."[19]

Another young woman who was scared of snakes, while trying to master the problem by approaching a snake, started speaking to it, saying, "I am going to make a deal with you. If you don't scare or hurt me I won't scare or hurt you." She went on to touch the snake. Other people who got thoughts they didn't want dealt with them by saying, "Screw it! I'm perfectly normal."[20]

Each of us prefers to use methods which are tailored to our own personal needs. Meichenbaum listed a selection of coping self-statements which various students chose to rehearse during stress inoculation training. In the first phase of *preparing* for a stressor, the students chose some of the following things to say to themselves: "What is it you have to do? Try to make a plan to deal with it. Just think about what you can do about it. That's better than getting anxious. No negative self-statements; just think rationally. Don't worry; worry won't help anything. Maybe what you think is anxiety is eagerness to deal with the stressor."[21]

When *confronting* and *handling* a stressor, statements might include "just 'psych' yourself up—you can meet this challenge. You can convince yourself to do it. You can reason your fear away. One step at a time; you can handle the situation. Don't think about fear; just think about what you have to do. Stay relevant. This anxiety is what you knew you would feel. It's a reminder to use your coping exercises. This tenseness can be an ally; a cue to cope. Relax; you are in control. Take a slow deep breath. Ah, good."

At some stage in a frightening situation one is bound to feel *overwhelmed*. In coping with this one might say, "When fear comes just pause. Keep a focus on the present; what is it you have to do? Label your fear from zero to ten and watch it change. You should expect your fear to rise. Don't try to eliminate fear totally; just keep it manageable."

Finally, when we succeed in making small advances in dealing with fear we deserve to *pat ourselves on the back* by saying things like, "It worked; you did it. Wait until you tell your therapist/husband/wife/mother/father/friend about this. It wasn't as bad as you expected. You made more out of your fear than it was worth. Your damn ideas—that's the problem. When you control them you control your fears. It's getting better each time you use the procedures. You can be pleased with the progress you're making. You did it!''

Ways of handling anxiety along these lines have been written about extensively by Dr. Claire Weekes. Here's an example of instructions to an agoraphobic going down the road:

> We are off. But, oh my goodness! Here comes Mrs. X from down the street! What are you going to do about it? You advance towards her with your heart in your mouth. You can feel your heart pumping in your throat, banging in your chest. . . . *your sensitized nerves are recording and amplifying each beat. Does it really matter if you feel your heart beating?* It doesn't matter in the least. It certainly does not harm your heart, so don't be afraid to feel your heart pounding while you talk to Mrs. X.
>
> But she is settling in for a good old gossip. What if she were to continue for another 10 minutes, *half an hour?* You tremble at the thought and think, "I can't stand it. I'll make a fool of myself. She'll notice! . . ."
>
> Take your hand off those screws. Let your body slacken. Loosen. Loosen. Take a deep breath; let it out slowly and surrender completely to listening to Mrs. X, she'll eventually stop.
>
> Now we're off down the street again. You feel a little better. You made it! But now you must cross the main road, and just when you need your legs most they suddenly turn to jelly. Those old jelly legs—you stand rooted to the pavement sure your legs will never carry you across.
>
> But here again I whisper, "Jelly legs will get you there if you will let them. It is only a feeling; not a true muscular weakness. Don't be bluffed by jelly legs . . . let them wobble. They can carry you across the street whether they wobble or not. And don't think you must hold tensely on to yourself from collaps-ing. *It's the holding on that exhausts, not the letting go.* So let your legs wobble. It's only a feeling, not through muscular weakness. . . ."[22]

The essence of dealing with fear is learning to ride it until the storm passes. In stress immunization how to do this is taught as a deliberate skill. It is like learning how to drive a car.

The secret of coping with stress is not just to mutter good things to oneself. One has to become aware of all the worrying things we say or do that impair our style and upset us. Then we have to systematically generate a set of positive rules and strategies we can adopt when in trouble. Finally we must learn to use these repeatedly in a whole variety of different problem situations. We need to practice these again and again until we can automatically bring them into play whenever we feel frightened or upset.

The students of Meichenbaum managed to learn coping skills in about three hours of training. They imagined themselves repeatedly having unpredictable shocks, keeping their hands for long periods in cold water, seeing stressful films, being made to feel embarrassed, and so on. While these situations were imagined repeatedly, the students rehearsed methods of dealing with them. Rehearsal of dealing with experimental pain was done by imagining a scene along the following lines:

> In your mind's eye you are volunteering for a pain experiment. You watch apprehensively as a blood pressure cuff is inflated around your upper left arm. You are asked by the experimenter to tolerate as long as possible the pain you are about to experience. Soon the tourniquet will induce a dull, aching, slowly mounting pain. How long are you going to tolerate it: 5 minutes, 20 minutes, 40 minutes? What coping techniques will you use to tolerate it and endure the pain? How would you train someone to cope better with exactly this sort of pain?
>
> You can try and reduce the pain by relaxing your muscles and attending to your breathing while you breathe slowly and deeply. Start this breathing now. See that you don't go over 14 breaths a minute—that's it. Just let your muscles go loose while you are doing this.
>
> You don't need to focus on the pain. Just focus on other things. Let's see you doing some mental arithmetic. How about subtracting 7's from 100 in order? When you have done this

you can count the number of tiles there are on the ceiling. That took quite a time—now let's see what we can look at through the window.

That worked for a while, now let's try something different. Let's watch and analyze the change in my arm and hand as the tourniquet continues to press tightly. Yes, there is some pain but it's interesting—my arm also feels numb. It seems a bit swollen. The color is also different. It seemed rose pink in the beginning. Now it seems more white.

Another way you might deal with the pain is by manipulating your imagery. Let's transform the pain. You can imagine yourself lying on a beach and the sun warms your arm, or you can imagine your arm as being cold or numb after the injection of a local anesthetic.[23]

Students were offered these various possible coping tactics and encouraged to choose in "cafeteria style" whatever happened to suit them best. They were asked to use these at critical moments when the pain seemed most unbearable and when the subject was likely to give up. Each student thus developed his own individually tailored coping package to employ in times of trouble. They also role-played the teaching of these skills to the trainer. Their job was to tell him what to do when he was in pain or frightened.

After brief training in stress immunization along these lines, college students became able to endure a tourniquet on their arm for twice as long as other students who did not have such preparation in imagination.

Can I carry out my own exposure treatment?

Yes, self-help is often possible without the intervention of experts like doctors, psychologists, or nurses. A detailed guide for you to help yourself appears in Chapter 12. Many people have discovered by themselves the principle of exposure to their feared situations until they feel better about it. This process may start when some change in their lives gives them a fillip to do so, as you can see in the following examples.

The agoraphobic who described her problem on page 91 found the impetus to change one day when

> my husband came flying home and said I've found the very place—it's a nice shop for you and it's a Post Office for me but there's only one thing—it's in the open—open spaces. And I said I'll try, I'll go, because anything is better than this. When we got settled in this shop, I made a list of everything that I wanted to do and I ticked off when I had done it. I couldn't go up the garden when I first came, but now I can go all around the garden, and ticked that off. I can go on long walks with the dog. I can go on car rides. So my husband and I again had a talk and he said: "I will enroll you at a driving school." To me that was a panic again. I just couldn't do it, but he enrolled me and—er—the first three times were terrible. I was so tense that I was away from home and with a strange person and in a strange village that I couldn't concentrate on driving, but he encouraged me and he said, "Don't worry." Just for today we will go in small circles and the circles got bigger and bigger. We went one mile, two miles, three miles, and now it's 40 miles and now I don't care if it was 50 miles. I would go.[24]

Accidental exposure

Another young mother who had compulsive washing rituals concerning her baby's diapers was treated by accident, so to speak. When her daughter was sexually assaulted she had to leave her baby boy in the house unattended to deal with the emergency.[25] On returning she found that he had urinated all over the carpet and elsewhere, but she was so agitated about the other matter that she did not carry out her usual ritual of cleaning. Shortly after this she was again unable to do the cleaning and had to remain exposed to urine. After these events she found that her compulsive ideas and rituals had so reduced that she could be taken off the waiting list for treatment.

Self-exposure carried out without help

In patients who feel relatively comfortable while at rest, repeated efforts to master their fears on their own are well worthwhile. This was described by the same woman who wrote on page 91 about her acute anxiety and depression years before:

> For three years I had been unable to make a train journey alone. I now felt it was essential to my self-esteem to do so successfully. I arranged the journey carefully from one place of safety to another, had all my terrors beforehand, and traveled as if under light anesthesia. I cannot say I lost my fears as a result, but I realized I could do what I had been unable to do.
>
> Soon after this I had to learn to drive. I passed the driving test without difficulty. . . . Waiting in traffic blocks brought at first a return of panics—and there was no running away. . . .
>
> Now, like others who are disabled, I have my methods. The essentials are my few safety depots—people or places. The safety radius from them grows longer and longer. I am still claustrophobic; that rules out underground trains for me, and I use the District Railway. I find it difficult to meet relations and childhood friends, and to visit places where I lived or worked when I was very ill. But I have learned to make short visits to give me a sense of achievement and to follow them when I am ready for it by a longer visit. Both people and places are shrinking to their normal size. Depression usually returns about a week before menstruation, and I have learned to remind myself that life will look different when my period begins. . . . I am also learning that it is permissible to admit to anxiety about things I have always sternly told myself are trifles to be ignored. Many of them, I find, are common fears.
>
> If I am fearful of going anywhere strange to meet my friends, I invite them home instead, or meet them at a familiar restaurant. . . . Strangers, too, can be more helpful than they know, and I have used them deliberately; a cheerful bus conductor, a kindly shop assistant, can help me to calm a mounting panic and bring the world into focus again. If I have something difficult to do—to make a journey alone, to sit trapped under

the drier in a hairdresser's, or to make a public speech—I know I shall be depressed and acutely afraid beforehand. I avoid trying myself too high meanwhile. When the time comes I fortify myself by recalling my past victories, remind myself that I can die only once and that it probably won't be so bad as this. The actual experience now is not much worse than severe stage fright, and if someone sees me to the wings I totter on. Surprisingly, no one seems to notice. . . .

I dare not accept my sickness—fear—because it never stays arrested. My very safety devices become distorted and grow into symptoms themselves. I must, therefore, as I go along, break down the aids I build up; otherwise the habits of response to fear, or avoidance of occasions of fear, can be as inhibiting as the fear itself.[26]

This woman treated herself years before behavioral principles were worked out. Now that these are known, many other people can follow suit more easily. The last chapter of this book is intended to help you to help yourself, or cooperate better with a therapist. Meanwhile, you may wish to know a bit about other kinds of treatment that are sometimes given.

ABREACTIVE METHODS

The problem about abreactive treatments is that they are very uncertain in their effects, although rarely they can be surprisingly helpful. *Abreactive treatments* are designed to help a person express his feelings freely with much emotion, after which he experiences relief of tension. Many religious ceremonies have something in common with medical abreactive methods. One need only think of the talking in tongues during voodoo sessions. The confessional in some faiths is another useful way of helping people talk out their problems and anxieties. Doctors find that sometimes it is helpful to inject intravenous drugs of certain kinds to aid the process of talking, but this is seldom necessary.

Another method is known as *induced anxiety*. The patient is relaxed and instructed to turn his attention inward, to forget everything outside of himself, to let a small feeling way down inside start to grow. Continued suggestions are given that the feeling is growing stronger and stronger. The therapist sits on a chair next to the patient's couch with one hand on his wrist and one hand on his other arm, monitoring the patient's appearance and tension. When the patient contracts his muscles, the therapist says, "Good, let it out," and so on. Gradually intense emotion develops along with muscular tension, rapid breathing, and sobbing, sometimes with intense anger, fear, and even laughter. The patient will remember past events associated with his emotion and be encouraged to talk about them. This method has been found to be helpful in relieving some people's anxiety and fears.

In wartime, soldiers who have become shell-shocked are encouraged to describe their horrible experiences and often feel better after describing them. Sometimes hypnosis helps them to recover the experiences. *Primal scream therapy* is a form of abreaction in which people are encouraged to relieve their tension by screaming; how useful this drama is remains to be seen, as it has not been carefully evaluated.

LEARNING TO RELAX

Anxiety in some people is helped, at least briefly, by training in *relaxation exercises*. Relaxation is not necessary at all to overcome phobias or obsessions, but it can temporarily help people relieve tension. One way in which relaxation can be achieved is by developing a muscle sense through tensing one muscle group, for example, the biceps of one's arm, feeling the tension in the biceps, letting the muscle relax, then tensing and relaxing it once more. The same is then done with other muscle groups until all of them can be easily relaxed together. These flexing and relaxing exercises can be practiced at home twice daily for fifteen minutes at a time. It is usual to start with the muscles of the arms and legs and then to move to the head and neck muscles. When a patient has successfully relaxed each important group of muscles, he then learns to coordinate relaxation of all these different muscle groups together. The achievement of good relaxation is indicated by stillness of the body, looseness of the muscles, regular breathing, and motionless eyelids.

When a therapist relaxes a patient, he might say something along the following lines, which you could equally well say to yourself:

> Settle back as comfortably as you can. Let yourself relax to the best of your ability. . . . Now, as you relax like that, clench your right fist, just clench your fist tighter and tighter, and study the tension as you do so. Keep it clenched and feel the tension in your right fist, hand, and forearm . . . now relax. Let the fingers of your right hand become loose, and observe the contrast of feeling in your muscles. Let those muscles just relax completely. . . . Once more, clench your right fist really tight . . . hold it, and notice the tension again . . . now let go, relax; your fingers straighten out, and you notice the difference once more. . . . Now repeat with your left fist. Clench your left fist while the rest of your body relaxes; clench that fist tighter and feel the tension—relax and feel the difference. Continue relaxing like that for a while. . . . Clench both fists tighter and tighter, both fists tense, forearms tense, study the sensations . . . and relax: straighten out your fingers and feel that relaxation in the muscles of your hand and forearm. Continue relaxing your hands and forearms more and more. . . . Now bend your elbows and tense your biceps. . . .[27]

Another way in which one can relax is by *autogenic training*. In this technique the person is asked to visualize one part of his body, to hold the image of that part and then to relax it. As an example: "Get a clear picture of your right hand, see the outline of the fingers, the color of the skin and nails, the wrinkles on your knuckles. Now relax your right hand as you think about it, keeping the image in your mind all the time. Now try to see your right forearm in your mind's eye . . . , etc." It does not seem terribly important which mode of relaxation is used, provided the person feels completely relaxed both muscularly and mentally.

In the East various kinds of *meditation* have been developed which are also relaxing for people who practice it successfully. Some forms of meditation are said to be mastered quite quickly, for example, *mantra meditation*. In this method the subject is asked to think about a secret word and to keep that in his mind continually while he blots out all other thoughts, sitting motionless meanwhile. Various other methods are used in the practice of Yoga and Zen meditation. Some of these approaches are said to take years to master, and people who are successful report serenity as a result. Unfortunately we do not yet know whether very anxious people can use these techniques therapeutically.

A further method by which some people relax is by *hypnosis*. It does not matter much which method of hypnosis is used. Only a minority of people are good hypnotic subjects, though in them these methods can be helpful to achieve relaxation. It can be very difficult to hypnotize those patients who are extremely anxious and need relaxation most of all. While hypnosis has dramatic effects in a few people, in general hypnosis is not a reliably predictable method of overcoming fear in a lasting manner.

Methods of relaxing can help reduce free-floating anxiety for a while. However, this effect is not usually long-lasting. For the relief of phobias and obsessions which have endured for some time, one of the exposure treatments discussed earlier are required.

DRUG AND PHYSICAL TREATMENTS FOR ANXIETY

Drugs

Sedative drugs

Sedative drugs are widely used as a palliative for tension; that is, they damp down the anxiety as long as the drug is in the body, but the effect disappears when the drug is excreted. While the drug is acting, it can produce side effects such as drowsiness and can also affect one's judgment and concentration. Examples of sedatives are the *benzodiazepines* (see the table on pp. 236—237). The most commonly used benzodiazepine drugs are *diazepam (Valium)* and its relative *chlordiazepoxide (Librium)*. Other drugs of this class are *oxazepam (Serenid D), medazepam (Nobrium), lorazepam (Atavan),* and *nitrazepam (Mogadon)*. Addiction to these drugs can occur occasionally. Among drugs of a different kind used to reduce anxiety are *oxypertine (Integrin)* and *benzoctamine (Tacitin)*.

Until 1960 the drugs most commonly used to reduce anxiety were barbiturates like *phenobarbitone* and *amylobarbitone*. Unfortunately these drugs cause quite frequent side effects and are also highly liable to produce addiction. Furthermore, when people have taken these drugs for a long time and stop them suddenly, they are liable to have convulsions. Moreover, overdoses of these drugs cause death much more easily than overdoses of benzodiazepines. For these reasons barbiturates are less used today in the treatment of anxiety.

The drugs described are given to most people by mouth. Only rarely do doctors give some of these compounds intravenously.

The most common drug of all is freely available in liquor stores. Alcohol has, since time immemorial, been used to relieve fear and tension. It is of great value socially as it loosens the tongue and helps people to mix better in potentially awkward situations. Many people with mild phobias find that some alcohol is useful, but, as with the sedative drugs, the value of alcohol is not long-lasting. A few people go on to drink so much that they become addicted and alcoholic. When phobics or obsessives get addicted to alcohol or sedative drugs, as sometimes happens, they can be treated successfully by being weaned off their drugs or drink while in a sheltered environment and then have exposure treatment for their fears.

Diazepam and similar drugs can be taken in small doses before people go out to face their frightening situation. However, if they do not remain in the situation until the effect of the drug has worn off, the fear might simply return. There is little point in taking diazepam (Valium) just before going for one's bus ride and then escaping once more as the drug effect wears off several hours later. One needs to remain on that bus for up to several hours while the effect of the drug is wearing off. It might be useful to take the drug three to four hours before one goes out and then to go for one's three-hour bus journey when its effect is just beginning to diminish. The journey will then end while one is relatively free of the drug effect. Improvement should then persist.

Although antidepressant drugs play a major role in the relief of depression, the role of sedatives for anxiety is more modest. It is probably true to say that though tens of millions of sedative tablets and gallons of alcohol are swallowed every year, there is little evidence that they do *lasting* good for anxiety or phobias. They help us *temporarily* over times of tribulation and are not to be scorned for such purposes, but they do not help us get over phobic difficulties more easily next time. Exposure approaches have a more lasting effect for these.

Antidepressant drugs

Phobias and rituals commonly get worse during spells of depression, and often treatment of the depression produces good results in the anxiety as well. Appropriate antidepressant drugs can quickly help many patients after a few weeks, and the anxiety goes as the depression subsides. After depressed patients have improved, they may need to continue taking their drugs for several months or, rarely, even years to prevent relapse. Whether the drugs are still needed can be decided by slowly withdrawing the tablets over several months. If the depression shows signs of returning, the previous dosage needs to be restored.

The most effective antidepressant drugs to date are of a class of compounds known as *tricyclics* because three benzene rings are part of their chemical structure (see the table on page pp. 236–237). Among the more common medicines of this range are *imipramine, trimipramine, amitriptyline, nortriptyline, protriptyline, prothiaden,* and *doxepin.* A newer relative, a tetracyclic drug, is *maprotiline.* These drugs usually take up to three or four

DRUGS COMMONLY USED IN ANXIETY

Generic Name	Trade Name	Daily Dose (in mgs)	
		Low	High
Benzodiazepines			
Sedatives (high doses undesirable during exposure treatment)			
chlordiazepoxide	Librium, Tropium	30	60
diazepam	Valium	5	15
flurazepam	Dalmane	15	45
lorazepam	Ativan	1	3
medazepam	Nobrium	15	30
nitrazepam	Mogadon	5	15
oxazepam	Serenid D or forte	15	60
oxypertin	Integrin	10	30
potassium clorazepate	Tranxene	—	15
Butyrophenones			
haloperidol	Haldol, Serenace	1	20
Other			
benzoctamine	Tacitin	10	20
meprobamate	Equanil, Mepavlon, Milonorm, Miltown	400	1200
Beta blockers			
oxpranolol	Trasicor	60	160
propanolol	Inderal	30	160
Antidepressants (do not interfere with exposure treatment)			
Tricyclics			
amitryptyline	Domical, Elavil, Lentizol, Saroten, Tryptizol	50	150
butriptyline	Evadyne	50	200

clomipramine	*Anafranil*	50	200
desipramine	*Pertofran*	75	200
dothiepin	*Prothiaden*	75	150
doxepin	*Sinequan*	30	300
imipramine	*Berkomine, Cocaps, Dimipressin, Norpramine, Tofranil*	50	200
iprindole	*Prondol*	45	180
nortriptyline	*Allegron, Aventyl*	50	100
protriptyline	*Concordin*	10	30
trimipramine	*Surmontil*	50	200
Tetracyclics			
maprotiline	*Ludiomil*	75	150
mianserin	*Bolvidon*	10	60
Bicyclics			
viloxazine	*Vivalan*	50	150

Monoamine oxidase inhibitors (require special diet)

iproniazid	*Marsilid*	50	150
isocarboxazid	*Marplan*	10	30
nialamide	*Niamid*	75	150
phenelzine	*Nardil*	15	45
tranylcypromine	*Parnate*	10	30

Mixed preparations

Amargyl (chlorpromazine 25 mg, amylobarbitone 50 mg)
Limbitrol (each tab = amitriptyline 25 mg, chlordiazepoxide 10 mg)
Motipress, Motival (each tab = nortriptyline 30 or 10 mg, fluphenazine 1.5 or 0.5 mg)
Parstelin (each tab = tranylcypromine 10 mg, trifluoperazine 1 mg)
Triptafen (each tab = amitriptyline 25 or 10 mg, perphenazine 2 or 4 mg)

weeks before they exert their beneficial effects, though the side effects can start immediately. Unpleasant side effects which may occur include dryness of the mouth and slight blurring of vision as well as tiredness. Serious side effects of tricyclic drugs, however, are very rare and no special diet is needed while one is taking these drugs. As patients recover from their depression, the anxiety usually goes too.

Another class of antidepressant drugs consists of *monoamine oxidase inhibitors,* so named because they retard action of the brain enzyme monoamineoxidase. Examples include *phenelzine, iproniazid,* and *tranylcypromine.* These compounds also may take weeks to help depression and are less effective than tricyclics, though sometimes they help patients in whom tricyclics have failed. The disadvantage of monoamine oxidase inhibitors is that people taking these drugs have to be on a special diet which avoids foods which contain much tyramine such as cheese, yeast, and meat extracts. The problem is that tyramine sometimes reacts on the drugs to produce high blood pressure, which can reach such dangerous levels that a brain hemorrhage might occur. This danger is greatly reduced if patients on the drugs stick to their diet, which is not always easy.

Electroshock therapy (EST)

Electroshock therapy (EST) is also called electroconvulsive therapy (ECT). This treatment, which sounds much more awful than it actually is, is useful for those few people with agitated depression who fail to get better with antidepressant drugs. This procedure is not unpleasant despite the adverse publicity it is given. In some states in the United States such obstacles have been placed in the path of doctors wanting to use it that EST is very rarely given. While this situation may curb the excessive use of EST in patients who do not need it, a less fortunate result is the denial to some patients of an effective treatment for their particular kind of depression.

Electroshock therapy is a potent treatment for serious agitated depression, although it tends to be used only where antidepressant drugs have failed to help the patient or where the risk of suicide is severe. In this treatment the patient is given an intravenous injection of two drugs together, one to put him to sleep and another to relax his muscles. While he is asleep and relaxed, a small electric current is passed through his brain via electrodes placed briefly on his temples. The electric current lasts for less than a second, and the patient does not have a fully fledged physical convulsion because the relaxing drug given intravenously just before the treatment prevents the muscles from moving. The convulsion consists of a special discharge of current by the brain cells. The patient wakes up within a few minutes of the convulsion and has no recollection of the treatment. He tends to be confused for a few minutes after waking up but after that can generally perform his normal activities. The main drawback to electric treatment of this kind is that patients have transient difficulty in remembering recent events for a short time after the treatment. This memory disturbance clears up quite quickly. It occurs even less often and to a smaller degree with recent modifications in which the current is passed through only one side of the brain instead of both.

Electroshock therapy in fact revolutionized the treatment of depression thirty years ago. At that time mental hospitals were full of chronically agitated and depressed melancholic patients for whom there were no drugs. Now that we also have efficient antidepressive drugs, electric treatment is used much less often, but it is still a very useful procedure. Useful as it is, we know nothing about the way ECT actually relieves depression. All that is know is that the benefit comes only if the treatment actually induces the current of an electrical convulsion in the brain. Subconvulsive currents do not help.

Psychosurgery

Surgical treatments for anxiety used to include *lobotomy,* as it was called in the United States, or *leucotomy,* as it was called in

Britain. This consisted of destruction of a small part of the white matter of the brain in the frontal lobes which reduces anxiety. The early operation that was done in the 1940s often caused undesirable personality changes, which gave the operation a very bad name. Subsequently, however, the operation was modified so that much less brain tissue is destroyed, with fewer undesirable side effects. Current scares about psychosurgery fail to recognize this improvement. During modern operations little radioactive pellets of yttrium can be implanted in a special portion of the frontal lobe so that a very small area of the lobe is irradiated. Recently other areas of the brain have been operated on, leading to different names for the operation, for example, *cingulectomy*. These later modified operations in fact cause very little change to the personality of patients and can be helpful in a few severely disabled patients with long-standing chronic anxiety in whom all other methods have failed. Only a very few operations are performed of this kind because most patients with fears are improved with the new forms of behavioral treatment. It is doubtful whether even 100 patients a year have such operations in Britain at the moment.

SUMMING UP

Anxiety is normal and can be helpful. Don't try to abolish it. Instead, try to put anxiety into perspective and recruit it as a spur to necessary action. Discussion of your troubles with other people can help to put them in a new light and suggest possible solutions. Where this approach alone does not help, behavioral treatments are needed.

The behavioral approach is now the treatment of choice for persistent phobias and obsessions, and it can be effective within a few days or weeks. It does not rake around for unconscious dirt but instead tries to eliminate phobias or obsessions directly by teaching the sufferer how to face those situations which trigger his discomfort so that he can eventually come to tolerate them. This approach works in most cases, even when the problems have been present for many years.

The principle involved is exposure of yourself to that which frightens you until you get used to it. Once you confront your fear determinedly, it will diminish. Longer exposure lasting several hours is better than shorter exposure for a few minutes at a time. The more rapidly you tackle your worst fears, the more quickly you will recover. Usually you will feel anxious during exposure treatment, but anxiousness is not generally harmful and soon dies down. After accidents, to prevent phobias developing, the golden rule is to nip them in the bud—avoid escape and encourage the facing of fear by reentering the traumatic situation immediately after the original accident.

Established phobias need structured exposure lasting several hours until the anxiety subsides. Enough time in the session should be allowed for this to be achieved, and determination and patience are essential to accomplish your goal. Failure is likely if you feel that treatment is unnecessary and embark on it in a half-hearted way.

There are many forms of exposure treatment ranging from very slow, gradual methods called desensitization to the more rapid approaches of flooding. The phobic situation to which you are exposed can be purely in your mind's eye (in fantasy), on slides or pictures, or in real life. Real-life exposure helps phobias reduce more quickly. The commonest approach is to enter the phobic situation in real life and stay there up to several hours until one feels better. Exposure treatment can be carried out with groups of phobics at a time. Nightmares, too, can be treated like phobias; reliving them in a deliberate, masterful fashion can lead to their disappearance.

Stress immunization involves preparing for difficulties, learning what these will be, what can be done to overcome or reduce them, and rehearsing possible solutions. This can help when the real time of trouble arrives. In this way people have dealt better with stressful situations such as surgical operations.

You can carry out your own exposure treatment without the intervention of experts like doctors, psychologists, or nurses, and there are many examples of self-exposure carried out without the help of a therapist. For self-help to be successful, it needs to be seriously structured and completed along the lines described in the next chapter.

Although behavioral treatments are the approach of choice for phobias and obsessions, under certain circumstances some drugs can be helpful, especially antidepressants for depressive illnesses which can complicate anxiety. The most proved compounds are the tricyclics. Sedative drugs are widely used to palliate anxiety temporarily, but are not of lasting benefit. Alcohol is an oft-used crutch.

Electroshock therapy is valuable for a few people, but it is especially helpful for those patients with severe depression. Modern psychosurgical techniques are less destructive than earlier operations, but are very rarely needed, though they might help chronic sufferers in whom all other approaches have failed.

12

Self-Help
for
Your Fears and Anxiety

We all know that exercise is healthy, but few of us take enough exercise. Yet if a dog needs to be taken for regular walks, we might walk the soles off our shoes for its sake. Many people are terribly lonely only yards away from others longing for their company but can't push themselves to make the first approach. Yet provide their apartment house with a communal room with washing machines and they will meet and gradually develop friendships. We know we should go for walks or arrange social contacts, but we often don't act on common sense until a suitable framework is provided.

Much behavioral treatment is a framework for applying common sense to behavioral problems. You can overcome your anxiety more effectively within such a framework than by a simple command to "pull yourself together" or "use your will-power," which we have heard all too often. Behavioral treatment can do for your conquest of fear what the dog does for exercise and the communal laundry does for socializing. Before you read the steps in behavioral treatment, first determine whether it is likely to be helpful for your problem.

"WILL IT BENEFIT ME?" TEN TESTS

Behavioral self-management is worth considering when your problem is not severe, professional therapists are not readily available, or you want to see what you can do by yourself anyway. Not all problems are suitable for behavioral treatment, and, even where they are, certain conditions are necessary to increase the chances of success. Before you put yourself to trouble which might not be worthwhile in the end, work through the next ten tests. These are questions therapists might ask you to decide whether you could benefit from behavioral treatment.

First, two conditions often found with anxiety indicate you should see a doctor rather than treat yourself.

TEST 1: *Are you so depressed that you're seriously thinking of suicide?*

If yes: Consult a doctor for help. Severe depression will probably prevent you from completing a self-management program, and serious suicidal intent requires prompt medical treatment, which can be very effective. *Do not proceed to Test 2.*

If no: Proceed to Test 2.

TEST 2: *Are you often drinking alcohol to the point of being drunk and/or taking sedative drugs in the higher range of dose in the Table on page 236–237?*

If yes: Either come down to less than three drinks a day and take less than the high range of sedatives in Table 1, or consult a doctor. Self-management is likely to fail if you are drunk with alcohol or sedated by drugs during your exercises. *Do not proceed to Test 3.*

If no: Proceed to Test 3.

You may need medical advice about disease before carrying out self-management.

TEST 3: *Do you have confirmed physical disease such as heart trouble, asthma, peptic ulcer, or colitis?*

If yes or unsure: Ask your physician whether severe panic can complicate your condition.
    If he does not think it will, *proceed to Test 4.*
    If he thinks it is safe for you to tolerate moderate anxiety, you can carry out exposure treatment *slowly.* Remember this when you do your exposure exercises (pages 256 to 263). *Proceed to Test 4.*

If he thinks any anxiety at all might be harmful, *exposure treatment is not indicated.*

If no: Proceed to Test 4.

Your anxiety needs to be of a certain kind for your program to succeed.

TEST 4: *Is your anxiety triggered by specific situations, people, or objects?*

Answer *Yes* if your fears are set off by particular events, for example, cocktail parties, crowded stores, getting your hands dirty, going out alone, dogs, sexual intercourse, meeting someone in authority, etc. Anxiety related to specific situations can be treated behaviorally.

If yes: Proceed to Test 5.

Answer *No* if you cannot think of any events which repeatedly start off your anxiety.

If no: Exposure treatment is not indicated. If you wish to try a more general approach to anxiety *proceed to relaxation* (page 231–232) *or to coping tactics* (step 5, page 257).

TEST 5: *Can you define your problems in precise, observable terms?*

Yes, my problems in order of importance are (write in pencil so you can amend them later if necessary):

1. _____

2. _____

3. _____

Compare your answers with the following:

Examples of *precise* definitions of problems you can treat behaviorally:

Problem 1: I panic whenever I go out of doors alone, and so I stay indoors unless I have an escort.

   2: I cannot bear people looking at me, and so I avoid friends, parties, and social receptions.

   3: I am terrified of airplanes and always avoid air travel.

   4: I worry about dirt and germs so that I wash my hands all day and cannot work.

   5: I tense up as soon as my husband requests intercourse and find it painful.

Examples of *general* statements which don't lend themselves to a behavioral approach

   I want to be cured, to get better.

   I'm a bundle of nerves.

   I just feel miserable all day.

I want to know what sort of person I am.

I want to have a purpose and meaning in life.

Although general statements are meaningful, they do not allow you to work out the steps by which such problems can be solved, and behavioral management cannot help until you can describe what you want clearly in observable terms.

If you wish, amend the problem definitions you wrote down earlier to make them more precise.

If you can now say, "*Yes,* my problems are precise and observable," *proceed to Test 6.*

If your answer is "*No,* my problems are too general to be defined," *exposure self-management is not indicated. You can try relaxation* (pages 231–232) *or coping tactics* (Step 5, page 257).

TEST 6: *For each precise problem you wrote down in Test 4, can you name a specific goal you wish to achieve in treatment?*

Before doing so, read examples of more and of less useful goals for Problems 1 to 5 above.

	Well-defined goal	*Less preferable goal*
Problem 1:	I want to spend two hours a week shopping alone in the nearest shops or mall.	I want to get out and about by myself.
2:	At least once a week I want to visit friends or go to a party or reception and stay to the end.	I want to become more sociable.

3:	I want to fly from New York to Los Angeles and back.	I want to lose my fear of air travel.
4:	I want to be able to touch the floor, my shoes and the garbage can every day without washing my hands afterwards.	I want to get over my hangup about dirt.
5:	I want to have sexual relations with my spouse twice a week with satisfactory orgasm.	I want my sex life to improve.

Can you now write down tangible goals for your particular problems?

Yes, the goals for my problems are:

Problem 1: _____

2: _____

3: _____

Proceed to Test 7.

If your answer is "*No, I'm not sure what I want to achieve in treatment,*" until you have clarified what you desire in tangible terms, *behavioral management is unlikely to help.*

TEST 7: *Will it really make a difference to your life if you overcome these problems?*

Before listing what you, your family, or friends might gain if you lose your worry, read the examples below:

Self-help for Your Fears and Anxiety

Agoraphobia: We will be able to go on vacation together for the first time in five years.
I will be able to take a job again.

School phobia: My child will resume attending school.
There won't be arguments every morning at breakfast time.

Compulsive rituals: I will be able to hug my children again without worrying that I'm infecting them with germs.
I will be able to help with the running of the house and spend time with my family.

Sex dysfunction: My spouse and I will have regular sexual relations.
We won't talk endlessly about divorce.

If overcoming your problem really will make a difference, write your gains below:

Yes, the gains from losing my worry will be:

1. _____

2. _____

3. _____

Proceed to Test 8.

If your answer is "*No, I can't think of any way in which my life or my family's life would benefit if treatment were successful*," *then it may not be worth your while going to the trouble of a self-management program.*

TEST 8: *Will you invest the time and effort necessary to overcome your worry?*

Will you set aside a regular time to practice your homework, promise not to run away when you feel fear, record what you have done, and map out what you need to do next time to overcome even more of your anxiety? Daily practice is preferable, and if your timetable is already overcrowded you may have to give up some other activity in order to concentrate on dealing with your problem.

If your answer is "*Yes*, I promise to follow my program diligently," *proceed to Test 9.*

If your answer is "*No*, I don't really have the time or inclination," *your self-management program is less likely to work well, but you may improve a bit with only limited practice if you are lucky.* If you fail to improve, don't be disappointed, just wait until you really have the time and energy to carry out your program fully, and the chances are that you will then achieve the goals you wrote down in Test 4.

TEST 9: *Would your self-management program need relatives or friends involved as your co-therapist(s)?*

The answer is probably *Yes*:

- If you hate keeping appointments even with yourself, and dislike recording your activities and planning ahead. A friend or relative can be your co-therapist and help you devise the framework of your treatment and stick to the detailed work necessary to get over your difficulties. Your co-therapist could regularly sign the diaries you keep, praise you for progress you have made, and help you plan each step in turn.

- If you are so frightened of going out that your family or friends must accompany you everywhere.

- If you have compulsive rituals in which you persuade your family to wash or check things for you or take over your role in the home, or to give you repeated reassurance about whether you are clean, safe, healthy, etc. Whoever you involve in your rituals needs to help as your co-therapist, whether spouse, parent, child, or other relative or friend.

- If you as a parent are trying to help your child over a phobia. Your spouse would be useful as co-therapist. It is easier, though not essential, if *both* parents cooperate in working out and implementing the child's program. This prevents parents from working at cross-purposes with each other, and prevents the child from divisively playing one parent off against the other.

If you have a problem in sexual activity. Your sexual partner should be involved in the treatment program.

Question: What if my partner isn't interested?

Answer: Treatment is unlikely to help until your partner can be persuaded to join in.

Question: What if I don't have a partner?

Answer: You need to get one.

Question: What if I'm too shy to get one?

Answer: You need to restructure your self-treatment program with the goal of overcoming your social fears and establishing a friendship with somebody who could become a sexual partner.

If your answer is "*Yes,* I need a co-therapist," *proceed to Test 10.*

The answer to Test 9 is probably *No:*

- If your problem concerns only your own life-style, does not interfere with anybody else's activities, and you don't mind working out and monitoring your own treatment program, for example:
- If your checking or washing rituals keep only you awake at night.

- If your phobia of travel restricts only your movements, not other people's.

- If your dread of dogs inconveniences only you, not your friends or relatives.

If *No: Proceed to "strategy for treatment" below.*

TEST 10: *Can you enlist the help of a co-therapist where this is needed?*

If Yes: Proceed to "strategy for treatment" below.

If *No:* Absence of a co-therapist will make your self-treatment less likely to succeed, but it might be worth a try. *Proceed to "strategy for treatment" below.*

STRATEGY FOR TREATMENT: FIVE STEPS

STEP 1: *Work out exactly what you fear; don't waste time treating the wrong thing.*

In your self-management program you will systematically allow yourself to face all those things which upset you, and to stay with them until you feel better about them. Your treatment plan needs to be tailored to your own needs. If you hate going alone into public places, is it because you're afraid you'll look foolish, or because you're scared you'll have a heart attack, or because you get dizzy in crowds? If you are upset by dirt, is it just ordinary dirt from the floor or trash can, or is it that you might catch or transmit certain diseases, and if so which ones? If an attractive person makes you go weak at the knees, is it because he or she might look down on you or find you ugly or smelly, or that you feel sexual attraction with which you can't cope?

It is easy to overlook worries in planning your treatment, so it is worth completing the following *fear* questionnaire to see what you might have missed. If you have obsessive-compulsive problems, you might also complete the *obsessive* questionnaire.

Date:_____

FEAR QUESTIONNAIRE

Choose a number from the scale below to show how much you avoid each of the situations listed, because of fear or other unpleasant feelings. Then write the number you chose in the box opposite each situation.

0	1	2	3	4	5	6	7	8

| Would not avoid it | | Slightly avoid it | | Definitely avoid it | | Markedly avoid it | | Always avoid it |

1. Traveling alone by bus or coach ☐
2. Walking alone in busy streets ☐
3. Going into crowded shops ☐
4. Going alone far from home ☐
5. Large open spaces ☐
6. Injections or minor surgery ☐
7. Hospitals ☐
8. Sight of blood ☐
9. Thought of injury or illness ☐
10. Going to the dentist ☐
11. Eating or drinking with other people ☐
12. Being watched or stared at ☐
13. Talking to people in authority ☐
14. Being criticized ☐
15. Speaking or acting to an audience ☐
16. Other situations (describe, e.g., animals, thunder) ☐

GRAND TOTAL ☐

Below describe in your own words the *main* phobia you want treated (e.g., "shopping alone in a busy supermarket" or "fluttering birds"):

Rate how bad it is in this box. ☐

Date:_____

OBSESSIVE-COMPULSIVE CHECKLIST

People with your kind of problem occasionally have difficulty with some of the following activities. Answer each question by writing the appropriate number in the box next to it.

0   No problem with activity—takes me same time as average person. I do not need to repeat or avoid it.

1   Activity takes me twice as long as most people, or I have to repeat it twice, or I tend to avoid it.

2   Activity takes me three times as long as most people, or I have to repeat it three or more times, or I usually avoid it.

Score	Activity	Score	Activity
	Having a bath or shower		Visiting a hospital
	Washing hands and face		Turning lights and taps on or off
	Care of hair (e.g., washing, combing, brushing)		Locking or closing doors or windows
	Brushing teeth		Using electrical apparatus (e.g., heaters)
	Dressing and undressing		Doing arithmetic or accounts
	Using toilet to urinate		Getting to work
	Using toilet to defecate		Doing own work
	Touching people or being touched		Writing
	Handling waste or waste bins		Form filling
	Washing clothing		Posting letters
	Washing dishes		Reading
	Handling or cooking food		Walking down the street
	Cleaning the house		Traveling by bus, train or car
	Keeping things tidy		Looking after children
	Bed making		Eating in restaurants
	Cleaning shoes		Going to cinemas or theaters
	Touching door handles		Going to public places
	Touching own genitals, petting or sexual intercourse		Keeping appointments
			Looking at and talking to people
	Throwing things away		Buying things in shops

Subtotal 1   +   Subtotal 2   =   Total

If your anxieties are about sex, which of the following describe your problem?

SEX QUESTIONNAIRE

Circle those sexual problems which apply to you and your partner:

Women: 1. My vagina gets so tight that the penis cannot be inserted.
2. I have pain during intercourse.
3. I don't have orgasm as often as desired.

Men: 4. I don't get an erection.
5. I can't maintain an erection long enough during intercourse to achieve orgasm.
6. I maintain my erection but don't ejaculate.
7. I ejaculate sooner than desired.

Either sex: 8. Heterosexual intercourse appeals less to me than other sexual activities (describe): _____

_____

(If this is the case, *ask for professional help* as self-management is not indicated.)

Proceed to Step 2.

STEP 2: *Write down the specific problems and goals you definitely want to work with now:*

You did this earlier on pages 246 and 248, but may wish to amend what you wrote now that you have completed Step 1 and the questionnaire(s):

My problems and goals, in order of priority, are:

Problem 1: ——————— Goal 1: ———————————

——————————————— ———————————————

Problem 2: ———————

——————————————— Goal 2: ———————————

——————————————— ———————————————

Problem 3: ——————— Goal 3: ———————————

STEP 3: *Prepare your timetable for exposure to the things which trouble you, and record what happened immediately after each session (see the accompanying table). Revise your plans each week in the light of your progress.*

How many practice sessions a week can you promise yourself? When will they be, and for how long? Remember that one 2-hour session of exposure yields more improvement than four ½ hour sessions. Allow enough time to complete your session properly. Immediately after your session, rate the maximum anxiety you felt on a scale where 0 is complete calm and 100 is absolute panic, and 25, 50, and 75 represent mild, moderate and severe anxiety respectively. Write down your plans for the coming week and record what you did on your diary record of exposure tasks (see page 258).

It might be helpful to discuss your program with a friend or relative who can act as co-therapist, monitor your progress, sign your records, praise your progress, and advise on the next step.

Proceed to Step 4.

STEP 4: *What sensations do you have when you're frightened?*

Underline those of the following sensations which you experience most:

I want to scream or run away.	My heart pounds and beats fast.
I freeze in my tracks.	I feel dizzy, faint, lightheaded, about to fall.
I tremble and shake.	I can't breathe properly.
I feel nauseous.	I break into a cold sweat.
My stomach gets churned up or tight.	I feel I'm going crazy.

Other sensations (write down): _____

_____

Read what you've just underlined, and whenever you're facing the situation you hate, remember to use these sensations as signals to employ the coping devices you will now decide on.

Proceed to Step 5.

STEP 5: *From the following list of tactics, choose three you might find useful to do or say to cope with your anxiety while carrying out your exposure tasks.* Circle those you would prefer to use. Remember to *adopt those tactics as soon as you are aware of the fear sensations* you just identified in Step 4, because that is when the tactics are easiest to bring into play. Write your chosen tactics on small cards which you keep in your pocket. Take them out and read them aloud to yourself the moment anxiety strikes.

(*a*) I must breathe slowly and steadily in, and out, in, and out, and gradually learn to deal with this situation. I feel terrible at the moment, but it will pass.

(*b*) I feel horribly tense. I must tense all my muscles as much as I possibly can, then relax them, then tense them again, then relax them, until slowly I feel easier in myself.

(*c*) I'm thinking of the worst possible things which might happen to me. Let's see if they are so bad after all. Let me imagine myself actually going crazy and being carted off to a mental

STEP 3: DIARY RECORD OF EXPOSURE TASKS

Day	Session Date	Began	Ended	The exposure task I performed was:	(0 = complete calm, 100 = absolute panic) My anxiety during the task was:	Comments, including coping tactics I used:	Name of co-therapist if any: _____ (Co-therapist's signature that task was completed)
Sunday							
Monday							
Tuesday							
				Example from an agoraphobic			
Wednesday		2:30 p.m.	4:30 p.m.	Walked to local supermarket and surrounding shops, bought food and presents for family, had coffee at drug store	75	Felt worse when shops were crowded, practiced deep-breathing exercises	J. Smith (husband)

258

| Thursday | 10 a.m. | 11:30 a.m. | Walked to local park, sat there for 1/2 hour till I felt better, then caught a bus downtown and back home | 70 | Felt giddy and faint, practiced imagining myself dropping dead | J. Smith |
| Friday | 2 p.m. | 4 p.m. | Rode a bus downtown and back 3 times till I felt better about it | 60 | Worst when bus was crowded—did deep-breathing exercises | J. Smith |

Plan for next week: Repeat exposure exercises in bus, park and shops every day until my anxiety is no higher than 30. Thereafter start visits to my hairdresser, and short surface train journeys.

Saturday						
Sunday						
Monday						

hospital, or fainting on the sidewalk, or just plain dropping dead. How vividly can I paint those scenes to myself? Let me start with the ambulance taking me away while I froth at the mouth and spectators laugh at me in the street . . . or (make up your own scene of horror) _____

_____

(*d*) What can I do? I have to stay here until I can tolerate this panic, even if it takes an hour. Meanwhile let me experience the fear as deliberately and fully as possible.

(*e*) I have to get away, but I know I must remain here.

(*f*) I feel awful. I could feel better if I imagined something pleasant. For me that would be lying in the warm sun, listening to the sound of the waves or (make up your own pleasant scene) _____

_____

(*g*) These sensations are ghastly, but maybe I can transform their meaning. This pounding of my heart, it could be because I've just been running a race and that's also why I'm breathing so heavily now. This dizziness in my head, that's because I got up suddenly a moment ago or (make up your own transformation) _____

_____

(*h*) I am so terrified but I will get over this in time.

(*i*) I will never get over this, I think, but that's just the way I feel, and in time I will feel better.

(*j*) I am so embarrassed, but it's something I'll have to get used to.

Decide now which three tactics you will use during your exercises, and the order in which you'll bring them into play.

"My coping tactics will be *a b c d e f g h i j*" (Circle the appropriate letter and indicate 1, 2, 3 underneath to show which you'll try first, which second, and which third.) Now for three minutes timed on your watch, imagine yourself in your most terrifying situation, and use one of your chosen tactics to deal with the fear. Repeat this at least three times so that you can employ these tactics *immediately* when you feel anxious during exposure exercises.

Ready? Now start your exposure tasks and record what happened. Remember, you will feel anxious and miserable at least some of the time during your exercises. Don't be put off by this, but press on until you've beaten your worry. If you have physical disease which limits how much anxiety your doctor thinks you can safely experience, remember to proceed slowly, pacing your tasks to the amount of fear you are allowed to tolerate.

Good luck. It's hard but worthwhile.

During exposure remember the rules

Rules for your sessions

1. Before starting each session plan exactly which goals you are going to achieve this time to overcome your fear.

2. Leave enough time—up to several hours if need be—to reach these goals properly by the end of the session.

3. During the session use your fear sensations as reminders to practice the coping tactics you chose. Make sure they are written on cards in your pockets; be ready to take them out and read them at any time.

4. At the end of the session, record what you achieved each time, work out the next session's program, and write down the date and time you plan to carry it out.

The Treatment of Anxiety

And the golden rules at all times

- Anxiety is unpleasant but rarely harmful.
- Avoid escape.
- Encourage the facing of fear.
- The longer you face it the better.
- The more rapidly you confront the worst, the quicker your fear will fade.

Repeat and repeat your appointment with fear

Take your first steps at a moderate but steady pace. Carry on relentlessly, confronting your fears, until you find that those things that used to strike terror in you are now a bit of a bore, and you have forgotten what you used to feel. Though you will have setbacks, these are part of the game, and constant repetition will make them less and less frequent. With repetition your coping tactics will become second nature and enable you to overcome your fear increasingly easily.

Helpful tips from a former agoraphobic:

1. Arrange the expected phobic situations into groups according to the amount of distress which *you* anticipate in *your* particular case. An example may be:

(*a*) Going into a quiet street—fairly easy

(*b*) Going into a busy street—hard

(*c*) Taking a ride on a bus—very hard

(*d*) Shopping in a busy town center—almost impossible.

2. Choose an easy situation, enter it, *and force yourself to remain there for as long as possible up to an hour or so.* It is most important not to run away from the phobic situation too soon.

3. Repeat exposure to the easy situation—the phobic reaction should not be less unpleasant.

4. Select a more difficult situation and repeat the procedure outlined in 2 and 3.

5. Carry on this process with progressively more difficult situations. This should result in generalization of the improvement so that work, etc., can be resumed. This approach to regaining mobility is very unpleasant and involves a lot of personal distress, but it seems to be the most rapid treatment in existence where the patient can help himself. I have found it well worth the effort.

If real life exposure is not possible, confront your fear in fantasy

Some phobic situations are not readily available for sufferers when they want to enter them. God does not provide thunderstorms on schedule for thunderstorm phobics. Those who are phobic of flying find it expensive to fly repeatedly. Instead you can try to rehearse your contact with your fear in fantasy, allowing plenty of time for your anxiety to fade. Do this at least twenty times, recording your practice in a log book, and when the real event actually happens, remember how you coped in your imagination.

Don't let setbacks set you back

Expect setbacks and be prepared to deal with them. You are bound to feel fresh panic and depression at some stage of your treatment. Just when you think you have conquered crossing a wide street in an agoraphobia program, your next step fails. You stand at the curb frightened and disappointed. Setbacks can last a minute or weeks. When they occur, you may feel dejected for days: "I thought I had conquered that phobia, that particular street, yet there were those feelings again, preventing me from crossing." Realize that setbacks are part of the whole learning process connected with phobias. Don't dwell on why you can eat in a restaurant one day and not the next. Accept your bad days and rejoice in the good days. Setbacks are especially likely to happen if for any reason you are unable to practice your exposure tasks for a while. If you have to be in bed for a few days because of flu or some other illness, it will be more difficult to get started again, but perseverance will get you over the hump. Setbacks are the signals for you to try again until you have conquered the situation where it occurred. Setbacks gradually fade once you no longer avoid the fact that they occurred and tackle them instead: "Next week I'll cross that wide street—the one that I couldn't cross this week. I'll have coffee in that shop on the other side."

Though setbacks are inevitable, you can learn to cope with them. Don't be bluffed by any strange new nervous feelings. What will be will be. It is no use being confident on Saturday and to be put out on Sunday when panic strikes out of the blue. You have to be ready for it and deal with it, to try, try, and try again until you have reached the stage described by one phobic after treatment: "Yes, I still get the panics from time to time now, but it's different, you know—now I don't have to run away from them. I can just experience them and let them pass while I carry on with whatever I happen to be doing at the time." Recovery lies in meeting precisely those situations you fear; those are the ones you have to master.

As soon as you feel fear, use your coping tactics

It is important to deal with your discomfort *early* in its development, before it becomes a runaway reaction. This principle holds not only for fear but for other problems as well. Maybe we can learn from Rex, a large German shepherd dog who belonged to a psychologist.[1] He used to roam all over the town, which he decided belonged to him. Invariably when Rex was taken for a walk, he would get into fights with other dogs. While walking at heel, Rex would see another dog approaching at a great distance. Without barking or giving any other sign, Rex would suddenly bolt for the other dog, paying no attention to his owner's shouts of "down," "come," "heel," and much worse. Under other circumstances, Rex was very obedient and would immediately respond to any of the above commands. Through trial and error, the owner found that if he spotted the other dog first, he could abort the runaway reaction by saying No firmly, as soon as he detected an incipient approach response in Rex. In this way he was able to lead Rex completely calmly without incident right in front of other dogs. The impulse to attack that could not be inhibited when it was full-blown could easily be inhibited when it was an incipient tendency.

Just as Rex's aggression could be inhibited early, before it really got intense, so your panic can be aborted by bringing in your preferred coping tactics as early as you possibly can—as soon as you feel that premonition of dizziness, or a faint flutter in your chest, or just a hint of goose pimples on your skin.

Learn to live with fear and it will subside

You will obviously be frightened when you enter your phobic situations. Expect it. Try to experience your fear as fully as possible when it comes. Seize the opportunity for you to overcome it. Don't shut it out or run away. Remember, your sensations are normal bodily reactions. When fear appears, wait; concentrate on remaining where you are until it dies down. This it will do, though waiting for this to happen can seem like an eternity. If you look at your watch you will see that the fear usually starts to lessen within 20 to 30 minutes, and exceptionally within an hour, provided you remain in the situation and concentrate on feeling the fear instead of running away from it. If you do run away physically or mentally, your fear might actually increase. While you are waiting for the fear to pass, focus on where you happen to be. Just stay right where you are until you have calmed down. Learn to recognize and label your fear by rating your level of anxiety on a 0 to 100 scale. Watch your fear slowly come down as time passes. Plan what to do next.

Take out those coping cards from your pocket, read them out to yourself and do what they say. Keep the level of your fear manageable, by very slow deep breathing, or tensing and relaxing your muscles, or doing mental arithmetic, solving crossword puzzles, counting the beads on a rosary, or whatever else you find useful. Gradually you will learn to reduce your anxiety to a reasonable level, though you will not eliminate it completely for a long time. Learn to carry on your normal activities even when you are a little frightened.

We cannot abolish fear. What we can do is learn to live with it as we do with any other emotion. We can face it, accept it, float with the fear, and let time pass until it becomes manageable. We have to go along with the feelings without resistance. There is no need to be frightened of our heart beating loudly or of our crying. After all, our heart beats and we cry when we are very happy as well as when we are anxious, and few of us run away from the tears and heartbeats of great joy. Bodily sensations do not need to be feared. Flashes of intense panic are bound to come, but they will go away in time if our attitude is "let it pass" and if we do not run away. We need to go with the tide, to tread water until the worst is over. The flash experiences of fright will eventually expend themselves.

Welcome the worst and the present will feel better

Many people get relief by learning to envisage the most horrible consequences without flinching. If you have visions of going mad in the street, then deliberately imagine yourself screaming, frothing at the mouth, soiling yourself, running amok, until you can do this in a matter-of-fact way. Eventually these ideas will bore you utterly. If you are at the edge of a cliff and fear throwing yourself off, sit down at a safe distance from the edge and rehearse doing it in your mind's eye, time and time again until the idea loses its power over you. If you are in an automobile in a traffic jam, feeling hemmed in, pull over to the side, continue sitting in the vehicle, and see yourself all crowded in and suffocating. Resume your journey only when you can laugh at the whole idea.

Self-help for Your Fears and Anxiety

I myself find this device useful on bumpy airplane rides while plummeting through airpockets. I imagine the plane crashing and killing all of its passengers, myself included, see our corpses, and think resignedly, "Well, there's nothing more to be done, let's just get through this episode as best we can." This exercise stills my anxiety about the journey.

The dramatic relief of anxiety through mental resignation was vividly brought home to me one night when I was on a train nearing the end of its long nonstop journey. Standing near the door was a man from a commercial aircrew, waiting to rush off to join his flight as soon as the train entered the station. To his mortification, the train stopped for ten minutes 300 yards before the station, and he could not jump out on the electrified line. For the first five minutes he was intensely agitated, puffing furiously at his cigarette, fuming and fretting, swearing and looking repeatedly at his watch. Then suddenly he said, "It's too late now, I've missed my plane, it's no use." And with that all his anxiety ceased, and he relaxed completely. This transformation appeared as he abandoned hope of achieving his target, but it was the calm of resignation, not of despair.[2] This attitude can be very therapeutic in tense situations.

SPECIAL TACTICS FOR SPECIFIC PROBLEMS

Worry about sleeplessness

Maybe you have that common plague of lying awake at night worrying about all the beauty sleep you are missing; this builds up more tension and ensures that you don't fall asleep. One solution is to try and do the opposite. Try to stay awake as long as possible, repeatedly going over what you did during the day, or doing mental calculations, or reading boring books. Eventually, your body's natural controls will take over, your eyes will droop, and sleep will take over no matter how hard you struggle to keep awake.

As an alternative, close your eyes and imagine a pitch black window shade slowly unrolling downward. On it you see in large letters the word SLEEP. Concentrate on seeing this word on the shade as it gradually winds down. Feel yourself sinking steadily into sleep as the shade comes down.

Breathing difficulties from anxiety

If you feel that you can't catch your breath or breathe deeply, try this. Take a deep breath and hold it as long as you possibly can until you feel you are absolutely bursting. Don't cheat by taking little breaths. Time yourself. You will find that in about sixty seconds you simply can't keep from breathing any longer. Your body's reflexes will force you to take a deep breath. Repeat this exercise each time you feel you can't breathe properly.

Maybe your breathing problem is the opposite one—taking too many deep breaths. This washes out the carbon dioxide in one's blood and can lead to tingling in the fingers and painful contractions of the hands and feet. The remedy is simple. Continue breathing deeply but simply hold a paper bag over your mouth so that you inhale back the carbon dioxide you have just breathed out. The overbreathing is also then likely to stop. Keep a paper bag in your pocket ready for use every time you catch yourself overbreathing.

Anxiety about swallowing

Perhaps your tension makes it hard for you to swallow solid food. Try to chew a dry biscuit. The idea is to chew it, not to swallow. Chew on and on until the biscuit is very soft and moist. Eventually after you chew for long enough you will swallow the moist biscuit automatically without noticing. You need only chew; the swallowing will look after itself.

Excessive tidiness

Ensure that you untidy something in the house everyday if your problem is excessive tidiness. Start by leaving a carpet askew on the floor in the living room. Tomorrow put a vase deliberately in the wrong place. The next day leave something unwashed in the kitchen sink. Expose yourself to increasing untidiness until you have reached the degree of untidiness you want to live with. My colleague, Dr. Leonard Cammer, asked a tidy, clean woman to empty a full ashtray in the center of her living room rug and to leave it there for forty-eight hours. At intervals she would return to glare at it, but gradually she felt less and less sore about it. Eventually whenever she spotted something dirty or untidy she would shrug and say, "Oh well, it can wait for another forty-eight hours if need be."[3]

Hoarding

If you are a hoarder, notice how the clutter in your house prevents you and others from moving about. Think what you can do with all the space that will become available to you when you throw away all your excess rubbish. Ask a spouse or friend to help you cart away your papers, tins, or whatever. A charity or thrift shop may be interested in buying some of your hoard. Do not buy back. Make sure you throw away things when you have finished with them or you will rekindle the hoarding habit. At first you will feel anxious when you have got rid of surplus possessions, but after some days you will be relieved at the extra space you've cleared. Make a resolution to throw away something every day that previously you might have started to hoard.

List making

If making lists is your addiction, count the number of items you have on your list. Cross out two of these today, three tomorrow, four the next day, and so on until finally you have no more items on your list. You will worry about what you have missed out for some days. Accept that you may in fact forget things and realize that this won't be crucial, that the world won't come to an end. If you want to be quick about it, tear up every list you have even if it convulses you and resolve never to make any others.

Reread relevant earlier descriptions of treatment

Earlier in this book you encountered descriptions of successful treatments. Where the treated problems resemble yours, reread those sections to see what helpful tips you can apply to your own treatment:

EXAMPLES OF SELF-HELP

At this stage you may find it instructive to follow the progress of two people who largely carried out their own treatment.

Overcoming agoraphobia

Molly, aged forty, had had classic agoraphobia since her pregnancy five years earlier.[4] Fears of going out of the house made her give up her job as a physiotherapist. She had hardly been on a bus or train alone for the previous four years and was able to take the dog out for a walk only around the corner. If accompanied she could do more. She was attending an outpatient department every day. She was married to a doctor, and until five years previously she had led a busy social life and loved her work. She thought her parents had overprotected her as a child.

I saw Molly and her husband only once for an hour. I explained that panic could never kill Molly. With prolonged exposure the panic does not go completely but gradually lessens as one learns to tackle it without running. One has to go out and meet the panic. She could overcome her phobia if she systematically exposed herself to those situations she feared, and I showed her how to keep a diary of the exposure tasks she completed. Setbacks would come, but she must then go out again. As she lived 200 miles from London, no further appointments were arranged, further contact being by letter.

The next week she wrote:

> Since you saw my husband and me last week I have spent three days in the center of Bristol traveling alone by bus. Today I walked around Bristol for three hours. I am amazed how, faced with an open-ended cut off from home or escape—I coped. I have achieved more in 4 days than during the last four years, and only feel afraid that I shall wake up and find it's a dream. I would never have thought it possible and it was only your reassurances, that fear will never kill you, that enabled me to take the first bus ride. I still do not really understand quite why the panics are diminished with the prospects of long exposure away from home, but they certainly are. It's incredible.[5]

With her letter, Molly Smith enclosed a diary detailing the frightening situations she had been in over those four days (see pages 258–259).

Two months later Molly wrote again.

I have enclosed my schedule and I hope that you will be as pleased with my progress as we are. . . . I still run away from anxiety, especially in social situations, e.g., coffee mornings, dinners, and on the bus, where I feel panicking with its "sweat, shake, and tears" routine would be hard to explain away. However, as you can see local shopping, walking with the dog, even going to the Zoo, are everyday events now and practically cause no trouble. This is wonderful to me—as you can imagine. I rather clash with my phobic friends in hospital who are still undergoing gradual desensitization (in fantasy). My husband is very pleased too with the way things are going.

After four more months Molly sent her up-to-date schedule showing that she had been traveling freely everywhere and had increased her improvement. A year later she was still better.

Last Friday I travelled on my own to London on an express train to meet my husband and stay with friends for the weekend. You can imagine how thrilled we all are that my progress has allowed me to travel alone again.

Everyone says I am better than I have been for years and I have to agree. My whole life style has changed since my visit to you. I lead quite a busy life now and rarely stay at home. I only visit the day hospital occasionally now but I do appreciate their help if I hit a bad patch, e.g., after flu, etc., as you warned. I still feel very uncomfortable at times but panics do not depress me like they used to. I can soon bounce back and have another go. I now belong to a badminton group, I have music lessons, take friends for music and movement, love taking the dog for walks, and go to parties with very little problem, quite a difference.

I know we have a little way before I completely disregard panics but I do feel well on the way. I enclose a copy of my diary, which I still like to keep up. Sometimes I think that I have taken the easy way out again but I hope you will agree that my horizons have widened.

I saw Molly and her husband only once, and yet she grasped the principles of self-help so well that without further ado, she carried out her necessary exercises and steadily overcame her fears, not by magic, but by systematically facing each one in turn. Molly did not get cured overnight. It was not easy. She had setbacks which were to be expected, and dealt with them with renewed efforts at self-exposure. Her reward was freedom from the bonds of fear that had tied her for five years.

Overcoming obsessions and rituals about dirt

Now we turn to Sue, who had been terrified of dirt for nine years.[6] Although a nurse-therapist helped her for a few days to get started, Sue did much of the treatment herself. Her program can give you an idea how to set about overcoming obsessive difficulties. The description is long in order to show how much you need to attend to detail. If obsessions aren't your problem, you may prefer to skip this section and go to page 278.

First let's get an overview, and then look at her own description of what she did. Notice the principles of treatment. *Face up to precisely what you fear. Never avoid discomfort. Practice, practice, and practice doing what you are frightened of over and over again until it is second nature.* In Sue's case the situations she had to practice were those she thought were connected with dirt, bacteria, or poison.

The problem

Sue, now thirty-seven, had been crippled for nine years with severe obsessive phobias. They began nine years earlier after she read of a local death from Weil's disease (transmitted by rats) and saw a dead rat in the road. Over the next few months there was rapid progressive development of ruminations, rituals, and avoidance concerning imagined dirt, bacteria, and poison, and she washed her hands fifty times a day. She was constantly preoccupied with "germs" and what she might have touched ("Have I caught anything?" "Have I passed it on?"), particularly those germs which might be connected with the rats. She repeatedly threw away "contaminated" articles, including a washing machine. Her husband and two teenage sons cooperated in carrying out rituals, giving reassurance, and doing things she avoided because of her fears, for example, cooking, washing, and other household tasks. This led to many family quarrels. She managed to hold down a full-time unskilled job, as her fears were less marked outside than at home. Over the previous five years she obtained little benefit from treatment, including admission to a hospital, antidepressant drugs, ECT, tranquilizers, and supportive psychotherapy. With brief behavioral treatment that did not involve her family she made some improvement but relapsed each time she stopped contact with her therapist.

The therapist's description

Treatment began with five days in the hospital, during which time she was encouraged to "contaminate" herself with "germs" and refrain from washing her hands for increasingly long periods of time. Despite initial anxiety she persevered with the program and quickly obtained relief. She managed to transfer her improvement to her home, where she began to perform all household duties she had previously avoided, and her hand-washing was reduced to eight times per day. The family became co-therapists, each having specific roles to play; for example, the children had to touch their mother when entering the house and the husband had to stop doing the cooking and housework. Improvement continued to follow-up at one year.

From this summary you wouldn't guess the hard work on so many details that Sue had to complete to get over her problem.

Sue's description of her treatment

When I came into the hospital for 5 days my nurse-therapist wrote out a detailed program of treatment which was signed and stuck to my mirror above the washbasin.
Day 1. Here is the program for *Monday, February 23.*

1. Two handwashes allowed per day.

2. No soap allowed in bedroom except one dry bar, which is to remain unused.

3. Bedroom to be dirtied and not cleaned until further notice.

4. Prepare coffee and tea for several people after previously "contaminating" cups.

5. "Contaminate" knives, forks, spoons by dropping them on the floor, picking them up and eating a meal with them.

6. Towel in room not to be changed.

7. Not allowed to wash clothes.

8. "Contaminate" hands at 9 *a.m.* and not wash for at least 5 hours.

9. Bath allowed in the late evening, but only if I keep to the program. (This is an incentive to be diligent.)

10. All visits to the toilet to be supervised. *No washes.*

I agree to keep to this program. Signed _____

Sue

We then carried out instructions on the program. Soap and my towels were taken to the staff room. I was allowed one clean and one "dirty" hospital towel ["dirty" here means simply used once by somebody else]. The "dirty" towel was placed at the bottom of the bed and I had to sit on it. Then we took the wastepaper basket and went outside collecting muck from around a drain cover in the road and long grass from under nearby huts. We went back to my room and threw the muck all round it. I threw my washing on the floor, and my therapist and I both wiped our hands on the clean towel to dirty it. Without washing my hands I opened my suitcase, handled all my clean clothes and put them on coat hangers and in drawers. I went to the canteen and made tea, putting my hands in all the cups and the milk jug, rubbed the spoons in my hands, and then served tea which we all drank. All the people knew what had happened and that I had not washed my hands. At supper time I rubbed my cutlery on the floor, touched my shoes and licked my fingers at every possible moment. I had not washed since 9 *a.m.* Before going to sleep I had a bath for 10 minutes.

The Treatment of Anxiety

Tuesday February 24   I washed, dressed and made up my face, and made tea for the patients and staff, "contaminating" the cups first. Using "dirty" cloths, dustpan and broom I cleaned the cabins I had dirtied the previous day with rubbish, grass and leaves. At 4 *p.m.* I went and touched toilet seats and then asked 4 people if I could clean their shoes for them. After cleaning their shoes I made 4 people some toast, found two people who wanted their beds made and tidied them. I touched a little girl I was afraid of, wrote a letter to my husband and children, telling them the letter was full of germs, and posted it. I went shopping after touching the toilet seats and bought grapes which I served at supper to unsuspecting patients. I bought a chemical toilet cleaner which I handled and sat with on my lap—I was terrified this would harm me. Before going to bed I had to put my arm round 6 people. I went to sleep with a "contaminated" towel on my bedclothes, and wore someone else's nightdress.

Wednesday February 25 After breakfast I went through my "contaminating" exercises—going down corridors touching lightswitches, handles, phones, pictures, rubbish bins, soiled linen, urinal bottles, bedpans, basins containing unknown liquids, irons, ironing board, brooms, dusters, vacuum cleaner, mops, bleach bottles. As I was afraid of diseases which might be transmitted by rats I went to see rats in a cage and touched them, after which I made toast for the staff and touched a lady and her child. In the patients' toilets I touched the seats, made tea, served cakes and touched the cups. A nurse usually came with me to make sure I did everything and even woke me as I was sitting in a chair to remind me that I had forgotten to make the toast for patients. This I did. I had to read a magazine used by other patients and put on clothes I had worn the previous day and practice touching other people's hair. I washed dirty underclothes in the bath before I could bathe in it. I resolved that I would let a rat run over me, and risk getting its disease.

Thursday February 26 Completed the "contaminating" exercises involving other people and myself. Bought a book to send my son, and on the walk back to the hospital touched several trash cans and every car stationary at the side of the road. Arrived back at the hospital really filthy and without washing I then made tea for the patients.

Day 5 Friday February 27   Completed my exposure routine, cleaned my bedroom, packed my clothes, mixing dirty with clean and avoided using plastic bags. Contaminated myself again before my husband arrived. Managed to pick up the little girl on the ward for a few moments and then went home with my husband.

Self-management at home—general principle

Touch whatever I am scared of without washing afterwards. Instructions for my exposure exercises are on cards around the house and done every day.

1. "Contaminate" my hands by touching garbage can, toilet seat and brush, wheelbarrow with rubbish in it, bird aviary, bird droppings, raw meat. Touch laundry basket and clothes whenever I pass them. Hug my three sons regularly (previously avoided this completely). Fill the dog's waterbowl then touch taps in kitchen with unwashed hands.

2. "Contaminate" worksurfaces, plates, cutlery, pots and all food before eating.

3. With unwashed hands lie on couch, answer phone and touch switches and door handles, television and curtains.

4. After touching the garbage cans tidy beds, lie on them and handle items on the dressing table.

5. Touch the toilet seat and thereafter towels, switches, medicine cabinet, my own hair.

Program I devised for March 5   Got up and dressed, put on unwashed clothes which I had worn yesterday, washed my hands and then contaminated myself and had breakfast after contaminating all the food. Completed my exposure routine, then cleaned the bathroom and the toilet seat using a cloth usually reserved for the bath. Cleaned the bathroom cabinet with the cloth usually reserved for the bath, thereafter handled all medicines. Poured old medicines down the sink. Polished the floor using dirty cloth in bucket usually reserved for the kitchen, and made sure I trapped germs under the polish. Cleaned the toilet brush and holder using the floor cloth and poured dirty water down the bath. Picked up the ironing board and iron, rubbed them against the dirty clothes and with them ironed a "clean" dress. Touched all my clean clothes. Went into town with dirty hands, tried on bras, bought one, walked home without checking where I was walking, and opened the door with the key (which previously I could not do). Without washing my hands then prepared lunch, hugged my sons, and went to the hairdresser with dirty hands. Had manicure with nailpolish, came home and had a bath without cleaning the bath first. Used a "dirty" towel for drying, placed the used towel where the family could use it and put on the dress I had previously ironed and ironed my husband's shirt. Then touched the rubbish bin and toilet. Went to the dance, shook hands with everybody. I came home, put the dress in the wardrobe next to all the other clothing rather than in the washbasket. Washed my hands and went to bed.[7]

DOES EXPOSURE TREATMENT WORK? THE SCIENTIFIC EVIDENCE

You may be getting impatient at the testimonials from patients. "That's all very well," you might think, and not without justice, "but we all know about miracle cures which can't be repeated. Will it work for me? What's the scientific evidence that exposure treatments work reliably for most people with my kind of trouble?"

In many controlled studies, behavioral exposure treatments were found to be significantly more effective than other treatments in improving phobias, obsessions, and sexual problems. They worked better than contrasting methods such as relaxation or analytic types of insight psychotherapy. Moreover, the improvement doesn't disappear after a few weeks. Patients who improved tended to stay that way over the two to four years they were followed up after discharge. Improvement in their anxiety freed them and their families from the restrictions which formerly hemmed them in.

One thing is *not* changed by exposure treatments. Before treatment many sufferers from phobias and obsessions have a tendency to get depressive spells. Even after they lose their specific anxieties, this tendency to depressive spells does not change. If and when it happens to you, it can usually be dealt with adequately by antidepressant medication from your doctor.

The detailed scientific evidence for the value of exposure treatments would be out of place in a book like this, but if you want to read more about the research, you will find references to the literature on page 281.

SELF-HELP CLUBS

Sufferers of many different kinds find it helpful to join lay groups of people who have problems similar to their own, so that they can share common experiences, learn helpful tips about how to cope, and have an additional social outlet. People with anxiety are no exception. In Britain a national correspondence club called The Open Door at one time had about 3,000 members. Similar organizations exist in the United States, Canada (Vancouver), Australia, and Holland. Agoraphobics can club together for outings, help run children to and from school, arrange programs to retrain themselves out of their phobias, and organize many other activities. A few people are reluctant to join because they are afraid that listening to other people's troubles will make their own worse. In general this does not happen.

The important point is not to make the club a grouse group just out to swap complaints, but a mutual aid society devoted to overcoming problems. This has been done in many ways. People with phobias about eating in restaurants went to lunch together, supporting and encouraging one another as they ventured out together. Others with flying phobias banded together in an organization called Air Fraidy Cats, chartered an airplane, and after preliminary instruction went for a group flight together. Club members can help one another even if their phobias are not the same. A driving phobic and a walking phobic worked closely together, together driving on various highways and walking in several stores, thus helping both themselves and each other.

Organizations and newsletters for agoraphobics in 1978 include:

United States:

New York: Manhattan Dealing-with-Fear Discussion Group, Inc., 160 W. 96 Street, New York, N.Y. 10025, which publishes a newsletter called "Dealing with Fear"

P.M. News, from the Phobia Clinic, White Plains Hospital, 41 East Post Road, White Plains, N.Y. 10601. Telephone (914) 949-4500, Ext. 2017

California: Terrap (the name is derived from "territorial apprehensiveness") Arthur B. Hardy, M.D., 1010 Doyle Street, Menlo Park, Calif. 94025

Britain:

London: The Open Door, 2 Manor Brook, London, SE3

Manchester: The Phobics Society: Mrs. Katharine Fisher, Cheltenham Road, Chorley-cum-Hardy, Manchester, M21 1QN. Telephone (061) 881-1937

Northumberland: Mrs. Pauline Ayre, "Horizon", 8 Tynedale Gardens, Stocksfield, Northumberland

Belfast: Northern Ireland Phobics Society, Lance MacManaway, 25 Pennington Park, Belfast BT8 4GJ, Northern Ireland

Eire:

Out and About: Morny Murrihy, St. Gabriel's Day Centre, St. Gabriel's Road, Clontarf, Dublin 3, Eire

SUGGESTIONS FOR FURTHER READING

For scientific evidence on the value of exposure treatments, there are three chapters that I have written:

1. "Behavioral Psychotherapy of Adult Neurosis," chapter in A. E. Bergin and S. Garfield (eds.), *Handbook of Psychotherapy and Behavior Change,* John Wiley & Sons, Inc., New York, 1978.
2. "Exposure Treatments," two chapters in W. S. Agras, (ed.), *Behavior Modification in Clinical Psychiatry,* 2d ed., Little, Brown and Company, Boston, 1978.

For information and self-help on sexual matters you might consider two books.

1. Alex Comfort, *The Joy of Sex,* Simon & Schuster, 1974. This manual has many illustrations and descriptions of normal sex.
2. D. J. Kass and F. F. Stauss, *Sex Therapy at Home,* Simon & Schuster, New York, 1975. This is a step-by-step approach designed to overcome sexual problems.

For information on children's phobias, refer to the chapter with that title in my book entitled *Fears and Phobias,* Academic Press, Inc., New York, 1969.

Further references

Bond, D. D.: *The Love and Fear of Flying,* International Universities Press, Inc., New York, 1952. Excellent description of fear in aircrew during World War II.
Cammer, L.: *Freedom from Compulsion,* Simon & Schuster, Inc., New York, 1976. Good description of obsessive-compulsive phenomena.
Hinton, J.: *Dying,* Pelican Books, London, 1967. No. A866. Compassionate coverage of the neglected area of death as it affects us all.
Kubler-Ross, Elizabeth: *On Death and Dying,* Macmillan, Inc., New York, 1975. Useful book for medical staff and families of the terminally ill.

Lader, M. H. and I. M. Marks: *Clinical Anxiety,* Heinemann Medical, London, 1971. Detailed account of anxiety phenomena.

Landis, C.: in F. A. Mettler (ed.), *Varieties of Psychopathological Experience,* Holt, Rinehart and Winston, Inc., New York, 1964. Collection of autobiographical descriptions of abnormal mental states.

Marks, I. M.: *Fears and Phobias,* Academic Press, London, 1969. Detailed account of phobic phenomena.

Marks, I. M., et al.: *Nursing in Behavioural Psychotherapy,* Research Series of Royal College of Nursing, Henrietta Street, London, W.C.1. 1977, £ 2.40. Detailed descriptions of treatment of phobias and obsessions.

Rachman, S.: *The Meaning of Fear,* Penquin Books, Inc., Baltimore, 1974. Describes different aspects of fear.

I hope that these books and this volume are of some help to you. Remember that treating yourself is bound to be hard work. The anxiety you will experience while treating yourself is not harmful, and your efforts will be well rewarded once you confront your fears systematically. Good luck with your program!

FEEDBACK FORM

Though the treatments described in this book have helped many sufferers, they don't work for everybody. There is always room for refining our methods. If you wish to aid this ongoing process by writing of your experiences, you may fill in the next page and tear it out (or make a facsimile) and mail it to me:

Dr. Isaac Marks
c/o Professional and Reference Books Division
−35th Fl.
McGraw-Hill Book Company
1221 Avenue of the Americas
New York, N.Y. 10020

1. What I didn't like about your book or treatment methods: —

_____

_____

2. Your treatment suggestions that I personally found most helpful: _____

_____

_____

3. Changes I think you might make in the light of my experience:

_____

_____

4. Other comments: _____

_____

_____

Yours sincerely,

Optional: Name: _____

Address: _____

_____

Notes

Chapter 1

1. J. Leff, lecture to Royal College of Psychiatrists, London, 1974.
2. C. Darwin, *On the Expression of Emotions in Man and Animals,* John Murray, London, 1872.
3. Ibid.
4. For the three examples mentioned here, see M. H. Lader and I. M. Marks, *Clinical Anxiety,* Heinemann Medical, London, 1971.
5. Report of author's experience, 1966.
6. The two examples are contained in D. D. Bond, *The Love and Fear of Flying,* International Universities Press, New York, 1952.
7. Patient's report to author.
8. Ibid.
9. Ibid.
10. Ibid.
11. F. Kraupl Taylor, *Psychopathology, Its Causes and Symptoms,* Butterworths, London, 1966, pp. 156—159.
12. J. Price and J. Kasriel, lecture to the Indian Psychiatric Society Silver Jubilee meeting, Chandigarh, India, June 1973.

13. Ibid.
14. Ibid.
15. Ibid.
16. Ibid.
17. Ibid.
18. Ibid.
19. Ibid.
20. Ibid.
21. Ibid.
22. Ibid.
23. Ibid.
24. R. Burton, *The Anatomy of Melancholy,* 11th ed., London, 1813; first published in 1621.
25. Ibid.
26. A. Le Camus, *Medicine de l'Esprit,* rev. ed., vol. 1, pp. 259–265, Paris, 1769.
27. I. MacAlpine, "Syphilophobia," *Brit. J. Venereal Disease,* vol. 33, 1957, pp. 92–99.

Chapter 2

1. Cited by I. M. Marks, *Fears and Phobias,* Heinemann Medical, London, 1969.
2. C. W. Valentine, "The Innate Bases of Fear," *J. Genet. Psychol.,* vol. 37, 1930, pp. 394–419.
3. *The Observer,* London, Feb. 18, 1968, p. 21.
4. Ibid.

Chapter 3

1. Cited by J. Hinton, *Dying,* Pelican Books, London, 1967.
2. Ibid.
3. C. Parkes, "The First Year of Grief," *Psychiatry,* vol. 33, 1970, pp. 444–467.
4. Ibid.
5. Ibid.
6. Ibid.

7. Ibid.
8. Ibid.
9. Ibid.
10. Ibid.
11. E. Lindemann, "The Symptomatology and Management of Acute Grief," *Amer. J. Psychiat.*, vol. 101, 1944, pp. 141–148.
12. Parkes, op. cit.
13. Ibid.
14. Ibid.
15. Ibid.
16. Ibid.
17. Ibid.
18. Ibid.
19. Ibid.
20. Ibid.
21. Ibid.
22. Ibid.
23. Ibid.
24. Ibid.
25. Ibid.
26. Ibid.
27. This and the above two paragraphs come from Bond, *The Love and Fear of Flying*, International Universities Press, New York, 1952.
28. L. Eitinger, "Anxiety in Concentration Camp Survivors," *Australia and New Zealand Journal of Psychiatry*, vol. 3, 1969, pp. 348–351.

Chapter 4

1. *Bethlem-Maudsley Gazette*, 1970.
2. I. M. Marks, *Fears and Phobias*, Heinemann Medical, London, 1969.
3. Ibid.
4. Ibid.

5. Cited by M. H. Lader and I. M. Marks, *Clinical Anxiety,* Heinemann Medical, London, 1971.
6. Ibid.
7. P. W. Ngui, "The Koro Epidemic in Singapore," *Australia and New Zealand Journal of Psychiatry,* vol. 3, 1969, pp. 263–266.
8. Ibid.

Chapter 5

1. Cited by I. M. Marks, *Fears and Phobias,* Heinemann Medical, London, 1969.
2. Ibid.
3. Ibid.
4. Ibid.
5. Ibid.
6. *Lancet,* "Disabilities," Section "Anxiety Neurosis," pp. 79–83, 1952.
7. C. Westphal, "Die Agoraphobie," *Archiv. fur Psychiatrie und Nervenkrankheiten,* vol. 3, 1871, pp. 138–171, 219–221.
8. F. Kraupl Taylor, *Psychopathology, Its Causes and Symptoms,* Butterworths, London, 1966.
9. *Lancet,* op. cit.
10. I. M. Marks et al., *Nursing in Behavioral Psychotherapy,* Royal College of Nursing, London, 1977, Appendix, patient 6.
11. Ibid. patient 3.

Chapter 6

1. I. M. Marks, *Fears and Phobias,* Heinemann Medical, London, 1969.
2. Patient's report to author.
3. Ibid.
4. Ibid.
5. Phone call to B.B.C. radio program "Phone In," 1974.

6. R. Burton, *The Anatomy of Melancholy,* 11th ed., London, 1813, p. 272; first published in 1621.
7. Patient's report in author's unit.
8. Ibid.
9. Ibid.
10. Mary McArdle, "Treatment of a Phobia," *Nursing Times,* 1974, pp. 637–639. This case was treated in the author's unit.

Chapter 7

1. Patients' reports to author.
2. S. Freud, *Totem and Taboo,* Hogarth, London, 1913, p. 127.
3. Phone calls to B.B.C. radio program "Phone In," 1974.
4. Ibid.
5. Patient's report to author.
6. Ibid.
7. Phone calls to B.B.C. radio program "Phone In," 1974.
8. Ibid.
9. I. M. Marks et al., *Nursing in Behavioral Psychotherapy,* Royal College of Nursing, London, 1977, Appendix, patient 1.
10. Patient's report to author.
11. Phone call to B.B.C. radio program, "Phone In," 1974.
12. Patient's report to author.
13. Ibid.
14. Ibid.
15. Ibid.
16. Ibid.
17. Ibid.
18. Patient seen in author's unit.
19. Bond, op. cit.
20. Patient's report to author.
21. Ibid.
22. Ibid.

23. Ibid.
24. I. M. Marks et al., *Nursing in Behavioral Psychotherapy,* op. cit., Appendix, patient 2.
25. Y. Lamontagne and I. M. Marks, "Psychogenic Urinary Retention Treatment by Prolonged Exposure," *Behavior Therapy,* vol. 4, p. 581, 1973.
26. Patient's letter to author.
27. E. B. Blanchard, "Brief Flooding Treatment for a Debilitating Revulsion," *Behavior Research and Therapy,* vol. 13, 1975, p. 193.

Chapter 8

1. A. A. Milne, *When We Were Very Young,* Methuen Paperbacks, London, 1975, pp. 12–13; first published 1924.
2. Patient's report to author.
3. Ibid.
4. Ibid.
5. K. Stewart, "Dream Theory in Malaya," in C. Tart (ed.), *Altered States of Consciousness,* Wiley, New York, 1969, chap. 9.
6. Ibid.

Chapter 9

1. E. Fenwick, *World Medicine,* 1972.
2. I. M. Marks, *Patterns of Meaning in Psychiatric Patients,* Oxford University Press, London, 1965. pp. 1–2.
3. Patients treated in author's unit.
4. Cited by C. Landis, in F. A. Mettler, *Varieties of Psychopathological Experience,* Holt, New York, 1964.
5. Ibid.
6. Patients' reports to author.
7. Ibid.
8. Ibid.
9. Ibid.

10. Ibid.
11. Ibid.
12. L. Cammer, *Freedom from Compulsion,* Simon & Schuster, New York, 1976.
13. Ibid.
14. I. M. Marks et al., *Nursing in Behavioral Psychotherapy,* Royal College of Nursing, London, 1977, Appendix, patient 5.
15. Patient seen by author.
16. Patient treated by author.
17. Ibid.
18. Ibid.
19. Ibid.

Chapter 10

1. Patient's report to author.
2. Ibid.
3. Ibid.
4. Ibid.
5. Couple treated by author.
6. Ibid.
7. J. Lopiccolo, "Direct Treatment of Sexual Dysfunction," in J. Money and H. Musaph (eds.), *Handbook of Sexology,* A. S. P. Biological and Medical Press, B. V., Amsterdam, 1975.

Chapter 11

1. V. Frankl, personal communication.
2. *Lancet,* "Disabilities," Section "Anxiety Neurosis," 1952.
3. Letter from patient to author.
4. Ibid.
5. Ibid.
6. N. Malleson, "Panic and Phobia: Possible Methods of Treatment," *Lancet,* vol. 1, 1959, p. 225.
7. V. Frankl, "Paradoxical Intention," *Amer. J. Psychother.,* vol. 14, 1960, pp. 520–535.

8. Report of patient in author's unit.
9. J. P. Watson, R. Gaind, and I. M. Marks, "Prolonged Exposure: A Rapid Treatment for Phobias," *British Medical Journal,* vol. 1, 1971, p. 13.
10. Patient treated by author.
11. I. Hand, Y. Lamontagne, and I. M. Marks, "Group Exposure (flooding) in vivo for Agoraphobics," *British Journal of Psychiatry,* vol. 125, 1974, pp. 588–602.
12. Ibid.
13. I. Silverman and J. H. Geer, "The Elimination of Recurrent Nightmare by Desensitisation of a Related Phobia," *Behavior Research and Therapy,* vol. 6, 1968, pp. 109–112.
14. R. Surwit. Unpublished Ph.D. dissertation, McGill University, 1974.
15. R. S. Lazarus, *Psychological Stress and the Coping Process,* McGraw-Hill, New York, 1966.
16. Cited by D. Meichenbaum, *Cognitive Behavior Modification,* Plenum, New York, 1977.
17. Ibid.
18. Ibid.
19. Ibid.
20. Ibid.
21. Ibid.
22. C. Weekes, *Peace from Nervous Suffering,* Angus & Robertson, Sydney, 1962.
23. Meichenbaum, op. cit.
24. I. M. Marks, *Fears and Phobias,* Heinemann Medical, London, 1969.
25. Patient seen in author's unit.
26. *Lancet,* "Disabilities," Section "Anxiety Neurosis," 1952.
27. Marks, op. cit.

Chapter 12

1. D. Meichenbaum, *Cognitive Behavior Modification,* Plenum, New York, 1977.

2. Observation made by author.
3. L. Cammer, *Freedom from Compulsion,* Simon & Schuster, New York, 1976.
4. Patient seen by author.
5. Letter from patient to author.
6. Patient treated in author's unit.
7. Letter from patient to author.

Index

'Living with Fear', Marks, I.M., McGraw-Hill

Suggested insert about Triumph Over Phobia (TOP U.K.)

Triumph Over Phobia (TOP U.K.) was started in 1987 under the auspices of Professor Isaac Marks by Celia Bonham Christie, who had recovered from a 100% fear of flying by using the program in 'Living with Fear'. TOP U.K.'s mission is to help phobics to become ex-phobics by using this book as a self-help manual in a self-treatment group. The groups are run by lay people (ex-phobics) and the measurable outcomes are a 46% recovery rate over an average recovery time of five months.

For more information, time and place of meetings contact

Head Office
Triumph Over Phobia (TOP U.K.)
4 Marlborough Buildings
Bath
BA1 2LX
U.K.   Telephone: 0225 314129

Local groups (1993) in:

U.K.   *Channel Islands*

Bath   Jersey
Birmingham
Bristol
Kidderminster
Liverpool
York

About the Author

ISAAC M. MARKS, M.D., a clinical psychiatrist and internationally recognized authority on the nature and treatment of fear and anxiety, is now at the world-famous Institute of Psychiatry, Bethlem-Maudsley Hospital, London, as a Reader in Experimental Psychopathology. He is the author of numerous books and scientific articles on topics of anxiety and its management.

Catalog

If you are interested in a list of fine Paperback
books, covering a wide range of subjects
and interests, send your name and address,
requesting your free catalog, to:

McGraw-Hill Paperbacks
11 West 19th Street
New York, N.Y. 10011